中国石油大学（华东）“211工程”建设
重点资助系列学术专著

New Explorations of **Semantics**

语义学新探

戴瑞亮　编著

中国石油大学出版社
CHINA UNIVERSITY OF PETROLEUM PRESS

图书在版编目(CIP)数据

语义学新探 / 戴瑞亮编著 . —东营:中国石油大学出版社,2016. 10

ISBN 978-7-5636-5364-5

Ⅰ. ①语…　Ⅱ. ①戴…　Ⅲ. ①语义学—研究　Ⅳ. ①H030

中国版本图书馆 CIP 数据核字(2016)第 257731 号

书　　名:语义学新探
作　　者:戴瑞亮

责任编辑:隋　芳(电话 0532—86983568)
封面设计:王凌波

出 版 者:中国石油大学出版社
(地址:山东省青岛市黄岛区长江西路 66 号　邮编:266580)
网　　址:http://www.uppbook.com.cn
电子邮箱:shiyoujiaoyu@126.com
排 版 者:青岛友一广告传媒有限公司
印 刷 者:山东省东营市新华印刷厂
发 行 者:中国石油大学出版社(电话 0532—86981531,86983437)
开　　本:165 mm × 235 mm
印　　张:21
字　　数:374 千
版 印 次:2016 年 12 月第 1 版　2016 年 12 月第 1 次印刷
书　　号:ISBN 978-7-5636-5364-5
印　　数:1—1 000 册
定　　价:72.00 元

PREFACE

总　序

“211工程”于1995年经国务院批准正式启动，是新中国成立以来由国家立项的高等教育领域规模最大、层次最高的工程，是国家面对世纪之交的国内国际形势而做出的高等教育发展的重大决策。“211工程”抓住学科建设、师资队伍建设等决定高校水平提升的核心内容，通过重点突破，带动高校整体发展，探索了一条高水平大学建设的成功之路。经过17年的实施建设，“211工程”取得了显著成效，带动了我国高等教育整体教育质量、科学研究、管理水平和办学效益的提高，初步奠定了我国建设若干所具有世界先进水平的一流大学的基础。

1997年，中国石油大学跻身“211工程”重点建设高校行列，学校建设高水平大学面临着重大历史机遇。在“九五”“十五”“十一五”三期“211工程”的建设过程中，学校始终围绕提升学校水平这个核心，以面向石油石化工业重大需求为使命，以实现国家油气资源创新平台重点突破为目标，以提升重点学科水平，打造学术领军人物和学术带头人，培养国际化、创新型人才为根本，坚持有所为、有所不为，以优势带整体，以特色促水平，学校核心竞争力显著增强，办学水平和综合实力明显提高，为建设石油学科国际一流的高水平研究型大学打下良好的基础。经过“211工程”建设，学校石油石化特色更加鲜明，学科优势更加突出，“优势学科创新平台”建设顺利，5个国家重点学科、2个国家重点（培育）学科处于国内领先、国际先进水平。根据ESI 2012年3月更新的数据，我校工程学和化学2个学科领域首次进入ESI世界排名，体现了学校石油石化主干学科实力和水平的明显提升。高水平师资队伍建设取得实质性进展，培养汇聚了两院院士、长江学者特聘教授、国家杰出青年基金获得者、国家“千人计划”、“百千万人才工程”入选者等一批高层次人才队伍，为学校未来发展提供了人才保证。科技创新能力大幅提升，高层次项目、高水平成果不断涌现，年到位科研经费突破4亿元，初步建立起石油特色鲜明的科技创新体系，成为国家科技创新体系的重要组成部分。创新人才培养能力不断提高，开展“卓越工程师教育培养计划”和拔尖创新人才培育特区，积极探索国际化人才的培养，深化研究生培养机制改革，初步构建了与创新人才培养相适应的创新人才培养模式和研究生培养机制。公共服务支撑体系建设不断完善，建成了先进、高效、快捷的公共服务体系，学校办学的软硬件条件显著改善，有力保障了教学、科研以及管理水平的提升。

17年来的“211工程”建设轨迹成为学校发展的重要线索和标志。“211工程”建设所取得的经验成为学校办学的宝贵财富。一是必须要坚持有所为、有所不为，通过强化特色、突出优势，率先从某几个学科领域突破，努力实现石油学科国际一流的发展目标。二是必须坚持滚动发展、整体提高，通过以重点带动整体，进一步扩大优势，协同发展，不断提高整体竞争力。三是必须坚持健全机制、搭建平台，通过完善“联合、开放、共享、竞争、流动”的学科运行机制和以项目为平台的各项建设机制，加强统筹规划、集中资源力量、整合人才队伍，优化各项建设环节和工作制度，保证各项工作的高效有序开展。四是必须坚持凝聚人才、形成合力，通过推进“211工程”建设任务和学校各项事业发展，培养和凝聚大批优秀人才，锻炼形成一支甘于奉献、勇于创新的队伍，各学院、学科和各有关部门协调一致、团结合作，在全校形成强大合力，切实保证各项建设任务的顺利实施。这些经验是在学校“211工程”建设的长期实践中形成的，今后必须要更好地继承和发扬，进一步推动高水平研究型大学的建设和发展。

为更好地总结“211工程”建设的成功经验，充分展示“211工程”建设的丰富成果，学校自2008年开始设立专项资金，资助出版与“211工程”建设有关的系列学术专著，专款资助石大优秀学者以科研成果为基础的优秀学术专著的出版，分门别类地介绍和展示学科建设、科技创新和人才培养等方面的成果和经验。相信这套丛书能够从不同的侧面、从多个角度和方向，进一步传承先进的科学研究成果和学术思想，展示我校“211工程”建设的巨大成绩和发展思路，从而对扩大我校在社会上的影响，提高学校学术声誉，推进我校今后的“211 工程”建设有着重要而独特的贡献和作用。

最后，感谢广大学者为学校“211 工程”建设付出的辛勤劳动和巨大努力，感谢专著作者孜孜不倦地整理总结各项研究成果，为学术事业、为学校和师生留下宝贵的创新成果和学术精神。

中国石油大学（华东）校长

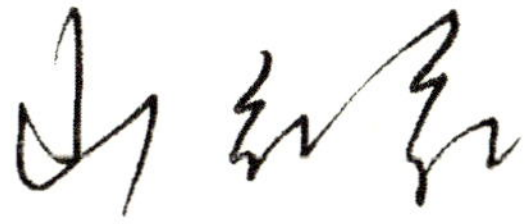

2012 年 9 月

FOREWORD

前　言

2002年至今，笔者一直为中国石油大学（华东）文学院英语专业研究生讲授语义学课程。10多年来，笔者阅读了许多国内外与语义研究相关的文献，记录整理了大量的一手资料，对语义学的众多理论、流派及最新的研究成果有了全面系统的把握。在此基础上，笔者利用近些年来在认知心理学和认知语义学领域中出现的新理论对一些重要的语义问题进行了新的思考和探索，在一些方面提出了新见解和新观点。为了把自己在语义学教学过程中所搜集整理的国内外最新语义理论以及在语义学研究中所取得的成果呈现给读者，笔者撰写了这本《语义学新探》。

全书共分10章。

第1章介绍了语义学的定义、语义学与符号学及语义学与语用学之间的区别与联系。本章还介绍了一些语义学核心术语的内涵以及它们之间的关系并概述了几个重要的理论。

第2章介绍了语言、思维与现实之间的关系。内容涉及语言相对论、认知语言学对语言相对论的看法、思维语、客观论、心智建构论和经验现实主义。

第3章是关于词汇意义的研究，主要探讨了词的定义、词汇歧义、词义模糊以及词汇之间的各种语义关系，如同义关系、反义关系、上下义关系、多义关系、部分－整体关系等。

第4章介绍了句子之间的语义关系以及“真值”这一概念在句子意义描写中的运用。内容包括逻辑学与真值、真值的分类、蕴涵关系和预设关系。

第5章从情景类型、情态、证据性等方面论述了相关语义范畴在句子意义分析中的作用。

第6章从构成情景的实体出发探讨句子意义，前5节依次讨论了题元角色、题元角色的识别、题元角色与语法关系之间的关系、题元角色分析中存在的问题、识别题元角色的原因，第6节讨论了语态如何反映题元角色和语法关系之间的联系。

第7章从语用学的角度研究意义，研究围绕着语境和推断两个方面展开，着重讨论了几个与语义理解密切相关的概念——指示语、语境、信息结构、推断以及会话隐义。

第8章利用言语行为理论进一步研究了语言的语用意义。重点介绍了奥斯丁的言语行为理论及其中所涉及的施为句和叙事句的区分以及言语行为三分说、希尔的言语行为理论、间接言语行为和礼貌表达。

第9章介绍了语义成分理论，涉及语义成分分析法、凯茨的语义理论以及语义成分组合方式。本章最后对英汉移动动词语义成分组合方式进行了对比研究。

第10章论述了认知语义学的语言观、语义观以及认知语义学的一些重要研究成果，这些研究成果主要体现为以下一些理论：概念隐喻、概念转喻、意象图式、原型论、理想化认知模型、象似性、语法化、心理空间、概念整合理论。这些理论是当前语义学研究的最新成果。

本书的独特之处在于除了论述传统语义学的主要内容之外，还引入了语言哲学、体验哲学、认知心理学、认知语言学的最新理论，并用这些理论对以往语义学研究中的一些根本性问题重新进行了梳理和思考，做出了尝试性的阐释和论证，可供其他语义研究者参考。

在撰写本书的过程中，笔者参考了大量的国内外相关论文和论著，这些论文和论著都列在书后的参考文献内。引用较多的文献有：Brown and Yule（1983），Fauconnier（1985），Lakoff and Johnson（1980），Lakoff（1987），Lakoff and Johnson（1999），Radden and Kövecses（1999），Saeed（1997），Ungerer and Schmid（2001），Evans and Melaine（2006），胡壮麟（2006），戴炜栋和何兆熊（2002），刘润清和文旭（2006），李雪（2011）。在此，谨向有关作者表示衷心的感谢。

本书的读者对象包括高等院校英语教师、英语语言文学专业研究生和本科生,以及其他语义学研究爱好者。

本书作为中国石油大学(华东)“211工程”建设重点资助系列学术专著之一,在撰写过程中得到了中国石油大学(华东)学科建设处以及文学院的大力支持,在此一并致谢。

由于笔者水平有限,书中难免存在纰漏和不妥之处,诚望读者批评指正。

戴瑞亮

2016年9月

目　录

Chapter 1 *Semantics in linguistics*

1.1 Definition of semantics

Semantics is the branch of linguistics which studies meaning in language. This definition is simple and straightforward. Semantics, however, is probably the most controversial branch of linguistics. This is not surprising if we look at it more closely. For one thing, there are several aspects of meaning in language. We can study the meanings of individual words, that is, lexical meaning. We can also study the meaning of sentences, that is, structural meaning. We may also want to examine the meaning resulting from uttering certain words and sentences in certain sequences. This will involve us with logic. In addition, it is reasonable to ask generally about the nature of meaning in relation both to our minds and to the outside world. This will involve us with philosophy. As a result of these differing aspects of meaning, there have been many approaches to semantics. They have involved not only logic and philosophy but also sociology, psychology and cognitive science. So those who are intended to do semantics should at least have a nodding acquaintance with these branches of study.

1.2 Semantics and semiotics

Semiotics investigates the types of relationship that hold between a sign (linguistic or non-linguistic) and the object it represents, or in Ferdinand de Saussure's terminology between a **signifier** and its **signified**. Semantics only studies the relationship that holds between a verbal or linguistic sign and the object it represents. In other words, semantics only studies the meaning of linguistic signs. Thus we may say that semantics is a sub-discipline of semantics. C. S. Peirce divides the non-linguistic signs into three kinds: **icon**, **index**, and **symbol**. An icon is where there is a similarity between a sign and what it represents, as for example between a portrait and its real subject, or a diagram of an engine and the real engine. An index is where the sign is closely associated with its signified, often in a casual relationship; thus smoke is an index of fire. Finally, a symbol is where there is only a conventional link between the sign and its signified, as in the use of insignia to denote military ranks, or perhaps the way that mourning is symbolized by the wearing of black clothes in some cultures, and white clothes in others.

1.3 Semantics and pragmatics

Both semantics and pragmatics are linguistic studies of meaning, but each of them studies different aspects of meaning. Semantics studies the meaning that is context-free, while pragmatics studies the meaning that is context-dependent. This distinction is based on the assumption that what essentially distinguishes semantics and pragmatics is whether in the study of meaning the context of use is considered: if it is not considered, the study is confined to the area of traditional semantics; if it is considered, the study is being carried out in the area of pragmatics. But this is not a successful assumption for differentiating between the two. We know from our own experience of language use that semantics also has to make use of contextual clues and enrich the information provided by words and grammatical constructions. Hence both semantics and pragmatics make use of context to a smaller or greater degree: the two fields are not disjoint. That is why some topics specially studied in pragmatics are also discussed in this book (See chapter 7 and 8).

1.4 Some important assumptions

In this section, we will introduce some basic ideas that are assumed in many semantic theories. These basic ideas will be mentioned frequently in the following chapters. So it is quite necessary for readers to have a first acquaintance with them if they want to be fully prepared for a thorough understanding of what is to come.

1.4.1 Reference and sense

One important point made by the linguist Ferdinand de Saussure (1974), whose ideas have been so influential in the development of modern linguistics, is that the meaning of linguistic expressions derives from two sources: the language they are part of and the world they describe. Words stand in a relation to the world, or our mental classification of it, so do larger linguistic units such as phrases and sentences. Words allow us to identify parts of the world, and make statements about them. Thus if a speaker says *He saw Paul* or *She bought a dog*, the underlined nominals identify, pick out, or **refer** to specific entities in the world. However words also derive their value from their position within the language system. The relationship by which language hooks onto the world is usually called **reference**. The semantic links between elements within the vocabulary system is an aspect of their **sense**.

The German philosopher, Gottlob Frege, proposes that the meaning of an expression be called "sense", and if the expression refers to something, it has "reference". Frege's (1892) classic example, which is frequently used in discussions of sense and reference, is the sentence below:

1) The Morning Star is the Evening Star.

As Frege points out, the two expressions "the Morning Star" and "the Evening Star" have the same reference, since both of them refer to the same planet. But they could not be said to have the same sense. For, if they did, sentence 1) would be tautologous, or analytic, as in sentence 2) below:

2) The Morning Star is the Morning Star.

But sentence 1), unlike sentence 2), is potentially informative: it can make the hearer aware of some fact of which he or she is not previously aware and which he or she could not derive simply from his or her understanding of the meaning of the sentence.

Noun phrases normally have sense and can be used to refer. Let us look at the noun phrases in the following:

3) a. the man who married my sister

b. the man who is my bother-in-law

The phrase in 3)a refers to a certain individual and has a certain sense or meaning that is different from that of the phrase in 3)b, though both expressions may have the same referent.

The meaning of linguistic expressions involves two aspects: sense and reference. Some words or phrases have both sense and reference, while others may have only sense but no reference, as the following sentences show.

4) The present queen of America is arrogant.

5) By the year 3000, our descendants will have left the Earth.

6) Whoever tries to kill the president is insane.

Speakers of English can understand these sentences, even though America has no queen, our descendants of a millennium from now do not exist and the possible killer is unidentified.

To conclude, the relationship by which language hooks onto the world is usually called reference and the semantic links between elements within the vocabulary system is an aspect of their sense. To put this more explicitly, sense is concerned with the inherent meaning of the linguistic form. It is the collection of all the features of the linguistic form; it is abstract and decontextualized. It is the aspect of meaning that dictionary compilers are interested in. Reference is related to what a linguistic form refers to in the real, physical world; it deals with the relationship between the linguistic element and the non-linguistic world of experience. In talking of sense we deal with relationships inside the language; in talking of reference we deal with the relationships between language and the world.

1.4.2 Utterances, sentences and propositions

These three terms are used to describe different levels of language. The most concrete is utterance: an utterance is created by speaking a piece of language in specific situations. If you say *I'm listening to my teacher talking semantics*, this is one utterance. If another person in the same room also says *I'm listening to my teacher talking semantics*, then we would be dealing with two utterances.

Sentences, on the other hand, are abstract grammatical elements obtained from utterances. Sentences are abstract because if a third and fourth person in the room also say *I'm listening to my teacher talking semantics*, with the same intonation, we will want to say that we have met four utterances of the same sentence. In other words, sentences are abstracted, or generalized, from actual language use. Sentences are obtained from utterances by filtering out certain types of information: the difference in pitch levels between men, women and children; perhaps some accent differences due to regional or social variation; and certainly those phonetic details which identify individual speakers.

One further step we come to propositions. Propositions are descriptions of states of affairs and are regarded as a basic element of sentence meaning. Logicians have discovered that certain elements of grammatical information in sentences (e.g. voice, information structure, intonation, etc.) are irrelevant, and the grammatical differences between them will never be significant in a chain of reasoning and thus can be ignored. For instance:

7) a. The boy kicked the ball.
   b. The ball was kicked by the boy.

7)a and b are different in voice: one is active in voice and the other is passive in voice. From a logician's perspective, these sentences share the same proposition for whenever 7)a is true, so is 7)b. Let us consider another example.

8) a. John broke the window.
   b. The window was broken by John.
   c. It was John who broke the window.
   d. It was the window that John broke.
   e. The one who broke the window was John.
   f. What was broken by John was the window.
   g. John did break the window.

Despite all the grammatical differences, the sentences seem to share a description of the same state of affairs. That is, if one is true all are true, and if one is false then all are false. Once again, all the sentences share the same proposition.

In semantic analysis, every proposition contains one predicate and one, two, or more arguments (sometimes a proposition only has predicate, but no argument, for example, the proposition expressed by the sentence "It is raining"). In logic, a proposition is represented in various ways to avoid confusion with the different sentences which represent it, e.g. by using capitals:

9) THE BOY KICKED THE BALL.

Logicians commonly use formulae for proposition in which the verb is viewed as a function, and its subject and any objects as arguments of the function. Such formulae often delete verb endings, articles and other grammatical elements, so that corresponding to 7) and 8) we would get 10) and 11) below:

10) kick (boy, ball)

11) break (john, window)

This notion of proposition and the use of logical formulae have been widely applied to the field of linguistics, especially semantics. They are employed to identify a description of an event or situation which might be a shared element in different sentences. So, for example, the statement *John closed the window*, the question *Did John close the window?*, and the command *John, close the window!* might be seen to share a propositional element: JOHN CLOSE THE WINDOW. In this view, these different sentences allow the speaker to do different things with the same proposition: to assert it as a past event; to question it; or to request someone to bring it about. Therefore, propositions can be a way of capturing part of the meaning of sentences. They are more abstract than sentences.

To sum up: **utterances** are real pieces of speech. By filtering out certain types of (especially phonetic) information we can get to abstract grammatical elements, **sentences**. By going on to filter out certain types of grammatical information, we can get to **propositions**, which are descriptions of states of affairs and which are seen as a basic element of sentence meaning. In other words, utterances are different realizations of the same sentence, and sentences are different realizations of the same proposition.

1.4.3 Sentence meaning and utterance meaning

As has been shown in 1.4.2, a sentence is a grammatical concept, and the meaning of a sentence is often studied as the abstract, intrinsic property of the sentence itself in terms of predication. But if we think of a sentence as what people actually utter in the course of communication, it becomes an utterance, and it should be considered in the situation in which it is actually uttered (or used). So it is impossible to tell if "The dog is barking" is a sentence or an utterance. It can be either. It all depends on how we look at it and how we are going to analyze it. If we take it as a grammatical unit and consider it as a self-contained unit in isolation from context, then we are treating it as a sentence. If we take it as something a speaker utters in a certain situation with a certain purpose, then we are treating it as an utterance.

While the meaning of a sentence is abstract, and decontextualized, that of an utterance is concrete, and context-dependent. The meaning of an utterance is based on sentence meaning; it is the realization of the abstract meaning of a sentence in a real situation of communication, or simply in a context. Now, take the sentence "My bag is heavy" as an example. Semantic analysis of the meaning of the sentence results in the one-place predication BAG (BE HEAVY). Then a pragmatic analysis of the utterance will reveal what the speaker intends to do with it. The utterance meaning of the sentence varies with the context in which it is uttered. For example, it could be uttered by a speaker as a straightforward statement, telling the hearer that his bag is heavy. It could also be intended by the speaker as an indirect, polite request, asking the hearer to help him carry the bag. Another possibility is that the speaker is declining someone's request for help. All these are possible interpretations of the same utterance "My bag is heavy". How it is to be understood depends on the context in which it is uttered and the purpose for which the speaker utters it.

1.4.4 Literal and non-literal meaning

The basic distinction between literal and non-literal meaning seems to be a common-sense one: distinguishing between instances where the speaker speaks in a neutral, factually accurate way, and instances where the speaker deliberately describes something in untrue or impossible terms in order to achieve special effects. Thus if one afternoon you are feeling the effects of missing lunch, you might speak literally as in 12), or non-literally as in 13)-15):

12) I'm hungry.

13) I'm starving.

14) I could eat a horse.

15) My stomach thinks my throat's cut.

Non-literal uses of language are traditionally called **figurative** and are described by a host of rhetorical terms including **metaphor**, **irony**, **metonymy**, **synecdoche**, **hyperbole**, **litotes**, etc. On close examination, however, it proves difficult to draw a firm line between literal and non-literal uses of language. Some literal words used to be non-literal, such as *junk bonds*, *toy boy*, *mouse* (for the computer board extension), *glass ceiling*, and the like. They become fossilized as time goes on and their metaphorical quality is no longer apparent to speakers. It is doubtful, for example, whether anyone taking advantage of the commuter air service between London and Brussels or between New York and Washington thinks of looms or sewing machines when they talk of catching a *shuttle*. The vocabulary of a language is littered with such words. As a language changes over time, this continuing process makes it difficult to decide the point at which the use of a word is literal rather than non-literal. Facts such as these have led some linguists to claim that there is no principled distinction between literal and metaphorical or non-literal uses of language as the literal and non-literal meanings are so closely related that they cannot qualify as disjunctive. Many scholars see metaphor as an integral part of human categorization: a basic way of organizing our thoughts about the world. Lakoff and Johnson identify clusters of metaphoric uses, giving them labels such as "Time is money" to explain clusters such as 16) (Lakoff and Johnson, 1980: 7):

16) You're **wasting** my time.
This gadget will **save** you hours.
I don't have the time to **give** you.
How do you **spend** your time these days?
That flat tire **cost** me an hour.
I've **invested** a lot of time in her.

Their claim is that while semantic fields are systematically organized around central metaphors such as these, and their use is not just an isolated stylistic effect: that we think, culturally, of time as a commodity. Clearly, if sentences like *How do you spend your time these days?* are identified as metaphorical, then it will prove difficult to find any uses of language that are literal. Many linguists, however, would deny that this use of *spend* is metaphorical. They argue that this is an example of a faded or dead metaphor. The idea is that metaphors fade over time, and become part of normal literal language, much as we described for *shuttle* above. This is called the **literal language theory**. In this approach, there is a valid distinction between literal and non-literal language. Metaphors and other non-literal uses of language require a different processing strategy than literal language. One view is that hearers recognize non-literal uses as semantically odd, i.e. factually nonsensical, but then are motivated to give them some interpretation by an assumption that speakers generally are trying to make sense. The hearer then makes inferences with various kinds of contextual knowledge in order to make sense out of a non-literal utterance.

In chapter 10, we will discuss arguments from writers in cognitive semantics, like Lakoff (1987), that the literal language theory is mistaken in viewing metaphor as something extra to, and different from, ordinary literal language.

1.4.5 Refer and denote

According to some linguists, like John Lyons (1977: 396-409), **denote** is used for the relationship between a linguistic expression and the world, while **refer** is used for the action of a speaker in picking out entities in the world. For instance, if someone says *A sparrow flew into the room*, he is using the two noun phrases *a sparrow* and *the room* to **refer** to things in the world, while the nouns *sparrow* and *room* **denote** certain classes of items. In other words, referring is what speakers do, while denoting is a property of words. Another difference which follows from these definitions is that denotation is a stable relationship in a language which is not dependent on any one use of a word. Reference, on the other hand, is a moment by moment relationship: what entity somebody refers to by using the word *sparrow* depends on the context.

1.4.6 Referents and extensions

The term **referent** of an expression is used for the thing picked out by uttering the expression in a particular context; so the referent of *the capital of the People's Republic of China* would be, since 1949, the city of Beijing. Similarly, the referent of a toad in *I've just stepped on a toad* would be the unfortunate animal on the bottom of my shoe. The term extension of an expression is the set of things which could possibly be the referent of that expression. So the extension of the word *toad* is the set of all toads. In the terminology of John Lyons (1977), the relationship between an expression and its extension is called **denotation**.

1.4.7 Conceptual meaning and associative meaning

Conceptual meaning covers those basic, essential components of meaning which are conveyed by the literal use of a word. Some of the basic components of a word like *needle* in English might include "thin, sharp, steel, instrument". These components would be part of the conceptual meaning of *needle*. However, you may have "associations", or "connotations", attached to a word like *needle* which lead you to think of "painful" whenever you encounter the word. This "association" is not treated as part of the conceptual meaning of *needle*. In a similar way, you may associate the expression *low-calorie*, when used to describe a product, with "good for you", but we would not want to include this association within the basic conceptual meaning of the expression. Poets and advertisers are, of course, very interested in using terms in such a way that their associative meanings are evoked, and some linguists do investigate this aspect of language use.

Associative meaning is influenced or conditioned by factors such as culture, experience, etc. It follows that the same word may evoke similar or different associative meaning among language users depending on whether or not they have similar experiences or cultural background. Take the word *dog* for example. The associative meaning it stirs up in us Chinese people in some aspects different from the one it elicits in people of the western countries because of the different cultural attitudes towards dogs. Therefore it can be said associative meaning is subjective: it is apt to vary from individual to individual, from period to period, or from community to community, while conceptual meaning does not have this property, that is, it is objective and keeps constant in all contexts and with all people.

In some literature of semantics conceptual meaning and associative meaning are also called respectively **denotative** meaning and **connotative** meaning.

1.5 Meanings of meaning

Semantics is defined as the study of meaning communicated through language. But what is meaning? Philosophers have debated the question, with particular reference to language, for well over 2 000 years. No one has yet produced a satisfactory answer to it. Meaning has meant many different things to different linguists. And it is this very word that baffles them very much with various theories and interpretations. The following are some of these theories and interpretations.

1.5.1 The referential theory: meaning as naming

This theory is also called the **naming theory**, according to which the form is a word in a language and the meaning is the object in the world that it "stands for" "refers to" or "denotes". Words are "names" for things. In other words, the semantic relationship holding between "words" and "things" is the relationship of *naming*. This view was held for a long time, but there are many difficulties associated with it. One of the difficulties with this view is that it is not always immediately obvious what is being named. For instance, what do conjunctions like *and* and *but* refer to? What do prepositions like *to* and *for* stand for? Even with nouns, the theory of naming will still face some difficulties. What do nouns like *fairy*, *ghost*, *heaven*, *dragon*, *unicorn*, which relate to creatures or things that do not exist, stand for? Or what do abstract nouns like *love*, *hate*, *nonsense*, *happiness*, which do not refer to physical objects at all, denote? What is more, many expressions that can be correctly used to denote a single object do not mean the same thing, as the case with *the morning star* and *the evening star* discussed in 1.4.1.

1.5.2 Conceptualism: meaning as concept

This view argues that meanings are *ideas* or *concepts*, which can be transferred from the mind of the speaker to the mind of the hearer by embodying them in the forms of one language or another. At its simplest, this view suggests that any particular sound image is psychologically associated with a particular concept. Therefore, when the word *bird* is spoken, the concept of *bird* is called up in the mind of the hearer. Even if there is no real flying horse for *Pegasus* to denote, there is surely such an *idea*, and this idea is the meaning of *Pegasus*. One best known example to illustrate this view is the **semantic triangle** or **triangle of significance** suggested by Ogden and Richards in their *The Meaning of Meaning* (1923), as shown in Fig. 1-1.

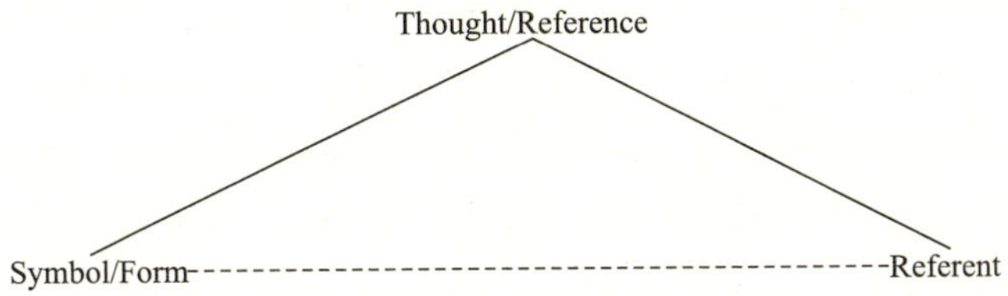

Fig. 1-1

In this diagram, the *symbol* or *form* refers to the linguistic elements (words, phrases), the *referent* refers to the object in the world of experience, and *thought* or *reference* refers to concept. According to this theory there is no direct relation between *symbol* and *referent* (between words and the things they stand for) as is indicated by the dotted line — the relation is via *thought* or *reference*, the concepts of our minds; and the concept looked at from this point of view is the meaning of the word.

This theory avoids many of the problems that the naming theory has encountered, but it also raises some new problems of its own.

First, for a linguistic study of meaning, the semantic triangle offers both too little and too much. Too much because the referent, the non-linguistic feature or event as such, clearly lies outside the linguist's province. An object may remain unchanged and yet the meaning of its name may change for us if there is any alteration in our awareness of it, our knowledge about it, or our feelings toward it. For example, the atom is the same as it was many years ago, but since it has been split we know that it is not the smallest constituent of matter, as its etymology suggests (from Greek *atomos* "that cannot be cut, indivisible"); moreover, it has been enriched with new connotations, some fascinating, others terrifying, since the advent of the atomic age — and the atomic bomb. The linguist will therefore be well advised to confine his attention to the left-hand side of the triangle, the connection between "symbol" and "thought or reference".

Second, if we say the meaning of a word is the concept it expresses the question that comes next is: what is concept? One traditional approach defines concept as something composed of a set of characteristics or attributes. For example, the attributes that the concept ZEBRA has include: being an animal; having four legs; being striped; being a herbivore. These attributes can be seen as conditions: if something must have them to be a zebra, then they can be called necessary conditions; if we can find the right set, so that just that set is enough to define a zebra, then they can be called sufficient conditions. This can be formulated as: X is a zebra if and only if L, where L is a list of attributes. If we understand concept this way, an animal that is cognitively regarded as a zebra (e.g. a three-legged zebra) will be excluded from the category of zebra as it does not satisfy the necessary and sufficient conditions of the concept ZEBRA. So it is no easy task to decide which conditions of a concept are necessary and how many conditions are sufficient. Some semanticists point out that concepts might be too specific and experience-based in that various speakers' concepts of X might include information that is specific to the way they developed the concept but are not a part of the related word. There is psychological evidence that our system of cognitive classification is structured in terms of *prototypes*, in that some instances of a concept are more typical (closer to the prototype) than others; robins are more typical birds than penguins, chairs are more typical examples of furniture than ashtrays, and so on. Yet these are not features of the meaning of *bird* and *furniture*.

Another approach to defining concept is to take concept as mental image. Though this might work for words like *Pegasus*, it is not obvious how it would work for nouns like *dog* and *triangle*, or a verb like *kick*. For instance, if one really does form an image of a dog or a triangle, more than likely the dog will be of some particular species and will not comprise both a shepherd dog and a Saint Bernard; the triangle will be isosceles or equilateral but will not comprise all triangles. Similar problems arise with *kick*. If one really forms an image of X kicking Y, then that image probably will have properties not essential to kicking, such as the sex of the kicker, which leg was used, the kind of thing being kicked, and so forth. In general, mental images are just not abstract enough to be the meanings of even common nouns and verbs.

Third, even if concepts work as meanings for some words, such as common nouns, adjectives, and maybe verbs, there are still many other kinds of words that do not have clear conceptual content, such as *only*, *not* and *hello*. Furthermore, it is not clear what concept would be assigned to a sentence, though sentences are clearly meaningful. Sentences usually denote situations and events rather than concepts.

1.5.3 Contextualism: meaning as context

The contextualist view of meaning is based on the assumption that one can derive meaning from, or reduce it to, the observable context, that is, meaning can only be found in the context within which a particular expression is used. Two kinds of context are recognized: the situational context and the linguistic context.

Every utterance occurs in a particular spatiotemporal situation, the main components of which include: the time and place of the utterance, the speaker and the hearer, the actions they are performing at the time, and the various objects and events existent in the situation. The interpretation of each utterance is limited by various factors of the situational context.

The linguistic context, sometimes known as context, is concerned with the probability of one word's co-occurrence or collocation with another word, which forms part of the "meaning" of the word, and also with the part of text that precedes and follows a particular utterance.

For example, the meaning of the word *black* differs in the three collocations of *black hair*, *black tea* and *black coffee*, and in "*There was a car on the road. The* ***vehicle*** *was running too fast*", the referent of *the vehicle* can only be determined by referring to the phrase *a car* in the first sentence. Similarly, the meaning of the word *seal* in the sentence "*The seal could not be found*" cannot be made clear unless the context in which the sentence occurs is restored.

Another example often used to illustrate this point is as follows:

17) a. I don't like her. She's tall and thin and moves like a crane.
    b. I do like her. She's tall and thin and moves like a crane.

The second parts of the above two sentences are identical but in 17)a we have the impression of awkwardness whereas in 17)b we have the impression of elegance. They have assumed different meanings as a result of the different contexts supplied by the first sentence in each case.

1.5.4 Behaviorism: meaning as behavior

The contextualist view of meaning was further strengthened by Bloomfield, who drew on behaviorist psychology when trying to define the meaning of linguistic forms. Behaviorists attempted to define the meaning of a language form as "the situation in which the speaker utters it, and the response which it calls forth in the hearer" (Bloomfield, 1933). This theory is somewhat close to contextualism but linked with the psychological interest. Bloomfield illustrated this view of meaning with the well-known story about *Jack* and *Jill*. "*Jill is hungry. She sees an apple and gets Jack to fetch it for her by speaking to him.*" He interpreted this sequence of events as a chain of *stimulus* and *response* as shown in Fig. 1-2.

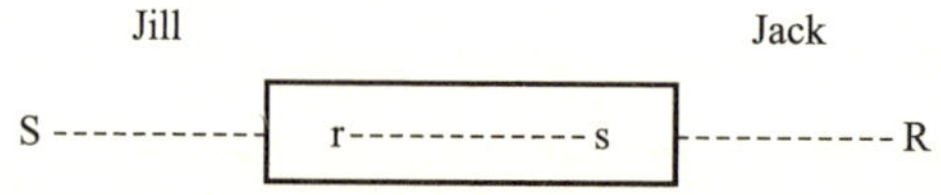

Fig. 1-2

Jill's hunger is the initial stimulus (S) and what she says to Jack is her response (r) to her hunger. The sound waves reaching Jack act as a linguistic stimulus (s) to him and his fetching the apple is his response (R) to the linguistic stimulus. Bloomfield argued that meaning exists in the relation between Jill's speaking and Jack's hearing (which is shown by [r ----------- s]) and the practical events (which is shown by S and R) that precede and follow the linguistic events. One difficulty with this view is that the practical stimulus is not always obvious although behaviorists attempt to account for such situation in terms of displaced behavior or disposition to respond. Another difficulty is that it is not always clear what we are actually being asked to observe since a disposition is not more observable than a concept.

1.6 Summary

In this chapter we first gave a brief definition of semantics, then we analyzed some different but related concepts that are much discussed in the literature of semantics: reference and sense; utterances, sentences and propositions; sentence meaning and utterance meaning; literal and non-literal meaning; refer and denote; referents and extensions; conceptual meaning and associative meaning; semantics and semiotics; semantics and pragmatics, and so on. Finally, we introduced four theories of meaning: meaning as naming, meaning as concept, meaning as context, and meaning as behavior. Some of these concepts and theories of meaning will be picked up again in the following chapters of this book.

Chapter 2 Language, thought and reality

2.1 Language and thought

From the moment that children begin to utter their first words, language and thought appear to go hand in hand. That this should be so is not surprising, given that one of the functions of language is to express thought. But the exact nature of the relationship between language and thought is far from straightforward. It has haunted the philosophers ever since the time of ancient Greeks and has long been a subject of discussion. Classical theorists like Plato and Aristotle argued that the categories of thought determine the categories of language. To them, language can be regarded as the dress of thought. An opposing view was expressed by the behaviorist J. B. Watson. According to him, thought is language. He believed that thought is sub-vocal speech, like a very quiet whisper to oneself. A less radical position is that language determines thought. According to this view, the categories of thought are determined by linguistic categories. At the risk of oversimplification, we can say that there are mainly two groups: those who believe that language determines thought and those who think that thought determines language.

2.1.1 Language determines thought

In the study of the world's cultures, it has become clear that different tribes not only have different languages, they have different world views which are reflected in their languages. For example, the Aztecs not only did not have a figure in their culture like Santa Claus, they also did not have a word for this figure either. If two languages appear to have very different ways of describing the way the world is, then it may be that, as you learn one of those languages, the way your language is organized will determine how you perceive the world being organized. That is, your language will give you a ready-made system of categorizing what you perceive and, as a consequence, you will be led to perceive the world around you only in those categories. Stated in this way, you have a theory of language which has been called **Linguistic determinism** and which, in its strongest version, holds that "language determines thought". In short, you can only think in the categories which your language allows you to think in.

A much quoted example used to support this view is the number of words the Eskimos have for what, in English, is described as snow. When you, as an English speaker, look at wintry scenes, you may see a single white entity called snow. The Eskimos, viewing similar scenes, may see a large number of different entities and have as many as seven different words for snow to distinguish among different types of snow (falling snow, snow on the ground, fluffy snow, wet snow, and so forth), because their language allows them to categorize what they see differently from the English speakers. On the contrary, certain African cultures in the equatorial forests of Zaire have no word at all for snow. Similarly, French speakers often note that English has more words for sounds (*crash*, *splash*, *roar*) than French has. The question then arises: Do these differences between languages mean that people from different cultures think differently or perceive the world differently?

2.1.1.1 Linguistic relativity

The notion of linguistic relativity is associated with the three great American scholars — Franz Boas (known as the "father of American anthropology"), Edward Sapir, and Benjamin Whorf in the first part of the 20th century. Boas suggests that different languages, reflecting their speakers' cultural practices, might embody different conceptual classifications of the world:

> *As an example of the manner in which terms that we express by independent words are grouped together under one concept, the Dakota language may be selected. The terms naxta' ka* TO KICK, *paxta' ka* TO BIND IN BUNDLES, *yaxta' ka* TO BITE, *ic' a' xtaka* TO BE NEAR TO, *boxta' ka* TO POUND, *are all derived from the common element xtaka*

> *TO GRIP, which holds them together, while we use distinct words for expressing the various ideas.*
>
> *It seems fairly evident that the selection of such simple terms must to a certain extent depend upon the chief interests of a people; and where it is necessary to distinguish a certain phenomenon in many aspects, which in the life of the people play each an entirely independent role, many independent words may develop, while in other cases modifications of a single term may suffice.*
>
> *Thus it happens that each language, from the point of view of another language, may be arbitrary in its classification; that what appears as a single simple idea in one language may be characterized by a series of distinct phonetic groups in another.* (Boas, 1966: 22)

Boas observed that the effect of this was largely unconscious because the use of language is largely an automatic process which we do not normally pause to reflect on.

Boas's most famous student, the anthropologist and linguist Edward Sapir, proposes the view that the particular language we speak conditions our conceptualization of the world:

> *Language is a guide to "social reality"... Human beings do not live in the objective world alone, nor alone in the world of social activity as ordinarily understood, but are very much at the mercy of the particular language which has become the medium of expression for their society ... the "real world" is to a large extent unconsciously built up on the language habits of the group. No two languages are ever sufficiently similar to be considered as representing the same social reality. The worlds in which different societies live are distinct worlds, not merely the same world with different labels attached ...*
>
> *We see and hear and otherwise experience very largely as we do because the language habits of our community predispose certain choices of interpretation ... From this standpoint we may think of language as the* ***symbolic guide*** *to culture.* (Sapir, 1949: 162)

It seems fair to say that Sapir had a stronger view of the determining role of language than Boas. Stronger still are the views of Benjamin Lee Whorf, a linguist well-known for his work on native American languages, especially the Uto-Aztecan languages of the south west United States and Mexico. Whorf strengthened this idea of the link between language and thought into the notion he called linguistic relativity. Its basic premise is that the way we think about the world is determined by our cultural and linguistic background:

> *It was found that the background linguistic system (in other words, the grammar) of each language is not merely a reproducing instrument for voicing ideas but rather is itself the shaper of ideas, the program and guide for the individual's mental activity, for his analysis of impressions, for his synthesis of his mental stock in trade. Formulation of ideas is not an independent process, strictly rational in the old sense, but is part of a particular grammar and differs, from slightly to greatly, as between different grammars. We dissect nature along lines laid down by our native languages. The categories and types that we isolate from the world of phenomena we do not find there because they stare every observer in the face; on the contrary, the world is presented in a kaleidoscopic flux of impressions which has to be organized by our minds — and this means largely by the linguistic systems in our minds. We cut nature up, organize it into concepts, and ascribe significances as we do, largely because we are parties to an agreement to organize it in this way — an agreement that holds through our speech community and is codified in the patterns of our language. The agreement is, of course, an implicit and unstated one,* BUT ITS TERMS ARE ABSOLUTELY OBLIGATORY; *we cannot talk at all except by subscribing to the organization and classification of data which the agreement decrees.* (*Whorf, 1956: 213–214*)

This passage means that the way people think is determined by the structure of their native language and people do not perceive the world freely but rather they do so through language, a filtering structure which will distort the reality and thus influence and control their thought.

Whorf's observation is not restricted to word meaning; indeed, he believed that meanings derived from grammatical systems (e.g. notions of number and space in nouns, or aspect and tense in verbs) were even stronger determinants of thought. The idea is that speakers can reflect on word meanings but grammatical systems are largely unavailable to conscious reflection.

While this view is attractive, there are some problems with it. First of all, if thought were determined by language, it would be difficult to imagine how people from different cultural backgrounds could communicate at all. Second, many people in the world are bilingual or multilingual from a very early age. Would we want to say that these people have different "thought compartments" in their brains, each one associated with a different language? Obviously not. Third, the fact that a particular category does not exist in a language does not mean that native speakers of the language cannot understand (and hence, think about) the category: the grammatical system marking the source of information in the Hopi language (language of American Indians of Arizona) can be explained in English even though it does not exist in English grammar. Finally, the lexicons and grammars of all languages share many universal patterns, even though at first glance the languages of the world differ so strikingly from one another. This view overestimated the variability in the structure of languages.

Today, many linguists take the position that language may have some influence on thought but thought may also influence the structure of language. So the interaction between thought and language is a two-way street rather than an absolute cause-and-effect relationship. Language and thought do appear to be closely connected in various ways.

2.1.1.2 Linguistic relativity and cognitive linguistics

The idea held by Edward Sapir and Benjamin Lee Whorf on the nature of the relationship between language and thought is commonly referred to as Sapir-Whorf hypothesis. The hypothesis consists of two parts: **linguistic determinism** (the idea that language determines non-linguistic thought) and **linguistic relativity** (the idea that speakers of different languages will therefore think differently). There are two versions of the hypothesis: the strong version and the weak version. The former holds that language entirely determines thought: a speaker of language X will understand the world in a fundamentally different way from a speaker of language Y, particularly if those two languages have significantly different grammatical systems. In other words, a speaker will only have access to cognitive categories that correspond to the linguistic categories of his or her language. The latter, on the other hand, holds that the structure of a language may influence (rather than determine) how the speaker performs certain cognitive processes, because the structure of different languages influences how information is "packaged".

Since the rise of the generative model in the 1960s, proponents of formal linguistics have tended to reject the Sapir-Whorf hypothesis altogether, given its incompatibility with the hypothesis that there might exist a universal set of pre-linguistic conceptual primitives, and therefore a universal "mentalese" or "language of thought".

While most modern linguists would probably agree that the strong version of the Sapir-Whorf hypothesis is untenable, some interesting findings have emerged in cognitive linguistics and related fields, particularly in linguistic anthropology, cognitive psychology and language acquisition research, which suggest that language can and does influence thought and action. Therefore, a cognitive linguistic approach to the relationship between language, thought and experience, together with the facts of cross-linguistic diversity, is compatible with a weaker form of the linguistic relativity thesis.

Setting aside the theoretical objections to the Sapir-Whorf hypothesis put forth by proponents of the generative approach, there is independent empirical evidence against the strong version of the hypothesis. This evidence originally came from work on color categorization. It may surprise readers who are only familiar with English to learn that some languages have an extremely small set of **basic color terms**. These are terms that are morphologically simple (for example, *bluish* is excluded) and are not subsumed under another color term (for example, *crimson* and *scarlet* are not basic color terms because they fall within the category denoted by *red*). For instance, the Dani, a tribe from New Guinea, only have two basic color terms in their vocabulary. The expression *mola*, which means "light", refers to white and warm colors like red, orange, yellow, pink and purple. The expression *mili*, which means "dark", refers to black and cool colors like blue and green. Yet, in color experiments where Dani subjects were shown different kinds of **focal colors** (these are colors that are perceptually salient to the human visual system) they had little difficulty remembering the range of colors they were exposed to (Heider, 1972; Rosch, 1975). These experiments involved presenting subjects with a large set of colored chips, from which they were asked to select the best examples of each color; in later experiments, they were asked to recall what colors they had selected previously. If language entirely determines thought, then the Dani should not have been able to categorize and remember a complex set of distinct focal colors because they only have two basic color terms in their language. In another experiment, Rosch taught the Dani subjects sixteen color names based on words from their own language (clan names). She found that the names for the focal colors were learnt faster than names for non-focal colors. These findings illustrate that humans have common perceptual and conceptualizing capacities. Due to shared constraints, including environment, experience, embodiment and perceptual apparatus, we can, and often do, conceptualize in fundamentally similar ways, regardless of language. However, this does not entail that variation across languages has no influence on non-linguistic thought.

If there is empirical evidence against the hypothesis that language *determines* thought (the strong version of the Sapir-Whorf hypothesis), then the question that naturally arises is whether language can *influence* or *shape* thought in any way. It is this weak version of the Sapir-Whorf hypothesis that underlies much recent research into the nature of the relationship between language and thought, and some of the findings suggest that the answer to this question might be “yes”. There are two lines of evidence that support a weak version of the Sapir-Whorf hypothesis. These are considered below.

• *Language facilitates conceptualization*

The first line of evidence relates to linguistic determinism and the idea that language facilitates our conceptualizing capacity. The assumption in cognitive linguistics is that language reflects patterns of thought, and can be seen as a means of encoding and externalizing thought. It follows from this view that patterns of meaning in language represent a **conventional** means (an accepted norm in a given linguistic community) of encoding conceptual structure and organization for purposes of communication. This is known as the **symbolic function** of language. It also follows from this view that different ways of expressing or encoding ideas in language represent different patterns of thought, so that encountering different linguistic “options” for encoding ideas can influence the way we reason.

A clear example of the influence of language upon thought is the experiment described by Gentner and Gentner (1982) in which they trained different English-speaking subjects in **analogical models** of electricity. An analogical model relies upon a relatively well known scenario or system for understanding a less well known system, where the parts and relations of the well known system stand in a similar relation to those in the less well known system, here electricity. Through **analogy** (comparison based on perceived similarity) subjects can reason about electricity using the well known model. One group was taught that electricity can be represented as a teeming crowd of people, while another group was taught that electricity can be represented as water flowing through a pipe, as in a hydraulic system. The mappings between these two analogical models and an electrical circuit are summarized in Tables 2-1 and 2-2.

Table 2-1 Hydraulic system model (based on Gentner and Gentner, 1982: 110)

Hydraulic system	Electric circuit
Pipe	Wire
Pump	Battery
Narrow pipe	Resistor
Water pressure	Voltage
Narrowness of pipe	Resistance
Flow rate of water	Current

Table 2-2 Moving crowd model (based on Gentner and Gentner, 1982: 120)

Moving crowd	Electric circuit
Course/passageway	Wire
Crowd	Battery
People	Resistor
Pushing of people	Voltage
Gates	Resistance
Passage rate of people	Current

Importantly, each analogical model correctly predicted different aspects of the behavior of an electrical circuit. For example, a circuit with batteries connected serially will produce more current than a circuit with batteries in parallel. This is predicted by the analogy based on the hydraulic system, where serial pumps one after the other will produce a greater flow rate of water. In the moving crowd model, where the battery corresponds simply to the crowd, it is difficult to think of a meaningful contrast between a serial and a parallel connection.

Serial resistors in an electrical circuit reduce current, while parallel resistors increase it. The moving crowd model is better at predicting this aspect of the behavior of electricity, where resistance is modeled in terms of gates. Parallel gates allow more people through, while serial gates allow fewer people through. Gentner and Gentner hypothesized that if subjects used different analogical models to reason about the circuit, then each group should produce dramatically divergent results, which is exactly what they found. Subjects who were trained in the hydraulic system model were better at correctly predicting the effect of serial versus parallel batteries on current, while subjects who were familiar with the moving crowd model were better at predicting the effect of serial versus parallel resistors on current. This study reveals that different "choices" of language for representing concepts can indeed affect non-linguistic thought such as reasoning and problem-solving.

• *Cross-linguistic differences and their effect on non-linguistic thought and action*

The second thread of evidence in support of a weak version of the Sapir-Whorf hypothesis relates to linguistic relativity: how cross-linguistic differences influence non-linguistic thought and action. We consider a study that investigated the influence of the language of time on non-linguistic thought and action. This study was carried out by cognitive psychologist Lera Boroditsky (2001). Boroditsky was interested in investigating whether the different lexical concepts for TIME in English and Mandarin would produce a noticeable effect on reaction time in linguistic experiments. We have observed through study that a common way of elaborating the concepts EARLIER and LATER in Chinese is by means of positions on the vertical axis: "upper" and "lower". In English, these concepts are elaborated primarily in terms of the horizontal axis: "before" and "after". Boroditsky exposed Mandarin and English speakers to primes like the ones in Fig. 2-1, which represented either the vertical or the horizontal axis. A prime is a particular stimulus manipulated by researchers in psycholinguistic experiments. Boroditsky then asked the subjects to answer a series of "true or false" questions employing the temporal concepts EARLIER or LATER (for example, *March comes earlier than April: true or false?*). Boroditsky found that Mandarin speakers were faster in responding to questions involving the terms earlier and later when the prime related to the vertical axis. In contrast, English speakers were faster when the prime related to the horizontal axis. This remained the case even when both sets of subjects were carrying out the task in English. As Boroditsky puts it, "it appears that habits in language encourage habits in thought. Since Mandarin speakers showed vertical bias even when thinking for English, it appears that language-encouraged habits in thought can operate regardless of the language that one is currently thinking for" (Boroditsky, 2001:12).

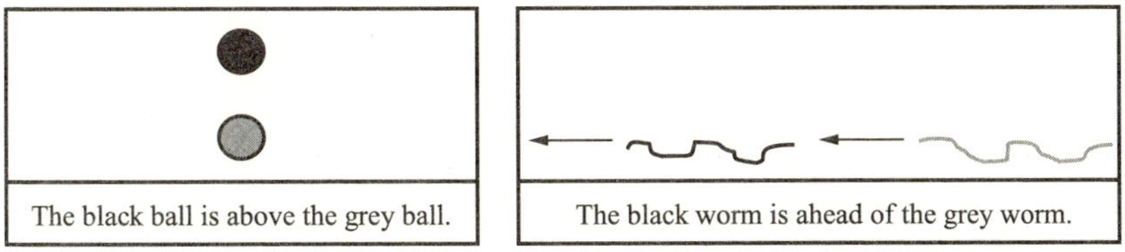

Fig. 2-1 Spatial primes (adapted from Boroditsky, 2001)

In sum, the position adopted in cognitive linguistics is that there are commonalities in the ways humans experience and perceive the world and in the ways human think and use language. This means that all humans share a common conceptualizing capacity. However, these commonalities are no more than constraints, delimiting a range of possibilities. As we have seen, there is striking diversity in the two domains we have surveyed, which shows that the way English speakers think and speak about space and time by no means represents the only way of thinking and speaking about space and time. According to cognitive linguists, language not only *reflects* conceptual structure, but can also *give rise to* conceptualization. It appears that the ways in which different languages "cut up" and "label" the world can differentially influence non-linguistic thought and action. It follows that the basic commitments of cognitive linguistics are consonant with a weak version of the Sapir-Whorf hypothesis, a position that some linguists argue is gathering increasing empirical support.

2.1.2 Thought determines language

Those who believe that thought determines language would say that cognitive development comes earlier in the life of children and that cognitive categories they develop determine the linguistic categories that they will acquire. They argue that if the strong version of the Whorfian hypothesis is accepted, that language totally determines thought, there will be no thought without language.

Furthermore, if the Whorfian hypothesis is true, then we are helplessly trapped by the language we speak. We could not escape from it and even if we could, we would fall into the framework of another language which would determine what we think, what we perceive and what we say. What is more, if language determines thought, people speaking diverse languages would never understand each other. The fact is that people of the world have been communicated over the centuries and that there have been radical changes of world-views within languages.

2.1.3 The language of thought hypothesis

The idea of linguistic relativity is rejected by many linguists and researchers in **cognitive science**, the interdisciplinary study of intelligence which draws on cognitive psychology, computer science and linguistics. A typical response is to dismiss as a fallacy such a strict identification of thought and language. We can identify two main types of argument used to support this view. The first is that there is evidence of thinking without language; and the second is that linguistic analysis has shown us that language underspecifies meaning. We can look briefly at these two types of argument. A succinct presentation of the first type of argument is given by Pinker (1994), who presents various kinds of evidence that thinking and language are not the same thing. He gives examples of evidence of thought processes, such as remembering and reasoning, which have been identified in psychological studies of human babies and of primates, both providing examples of creatures without language. He also recounts the various reports of artists and scientists who claim that their creativity sometimes derives from ideas which are non-linguistic images. There is also evidence from psychological experiments of visual thinking: subjects seem able to manipulate images mentally, rotating them, scanning them, zooming in and out, etc., exhibiting a variety of mental processes which do not seem to involve language. Finally Pinker casts doubt on the various attempts in psychological experiments to suggest that people from different linguistic communities perform reasoning or other cognitive tasks in any very different ways.

Such evidence for mental processes not involving language is often used to argue that cognitive processes do not employ a spoken language like English or Arabic but make use of a separate computational system in the mind: a **language**

of thought. Stillings et al. (1995) provide a range of evidence from psychological experiments to support the same view. The basic idea is that memory and processes such as reasoning seem to make use of a kind of propositional representation that does not have the surface syntax of a spoken language like English.

Turning to the second type of argument — that language underspecifies meaning — some indirect support for this position emerges from the characteristic view of the communication of meaning that has emerged from research in semantics and pragmatics. It has become clear that meaning is richer than language at both ends, so to speak, of the communication process. Speakers compress their thoughts, and often imply rather than state explicitly what they mean, while hearers fill out their own version of the intended meaning from the language presented to them. This idea, that language underspecifies meaning and has to be enriched by hearers, would seem to fit naturally with the idea that speakers are putting their thoughts into language, i.e. translating into the spoken language, rather than simply voicing their thoughts directly. This does not of course provide direct evidence for this view: we could equally imagine English speakers thinking in English and still compressing their thoughts when speaking, on some grounds of economy and social cooperation.

Nonetheless these different types of argument are often taken, especially in cognitive science, to support the view that we think in a language of thought, sometimes called mentalese. When we want to speak, we translate from **mentalese** into our spoken language, be it Chinese or Russian. One natural extension of this view is the proposal that everybody's mentalese is roughly the same, that is, that the language of thought is universal. Thus we arrive at a position diametrically opposed to linguistic relativity: human beings have essentially the same cognitive architecture and mental processes, even though they speak different languages.

2.2 Thought and reality

To have a thorough understanding of the meaning of language, we have to take into consideration questions concerning the relationship between thought and reality. One of the questions is "Do we believe that reality exists independently of the workings of the human minds?" If not, we are adherents of **idealism**. If we do believe in an independent reality, another question is "Can we perceive reality or the world as it really is?" One response is to say yes. We might assert that knowledge of reality is attainable and comes from correctly conceptualizing and categorizing the world. We could call this position **objectivism**. On the other hand we might believe that we can never perceive the world as it really is: that reality is only graspable through the conceptual filters derived from our biological and cultural evolution. We could explain the fact that we successfully interact with reality (run away from lions, shrink from fire, etc.) because of a notion of ecological viability. Crudely: that those with very inefficient conceptual systems (not afraid of lions or fire) died out and weren't our ancestors. We could call this position **mental constructivism**: we can't get to a God's eye view of reality because of the way we are made. Different theories of semantics often presuppose different answers to these very basic questions. The study of meaning based on objectivism is characteristic of **formal semantics** and the study of meaning based on mental constructivism is characteristic of **cognitive semantics**. These two approaches will be described respectively in chapters 4, 9 and 10.

2.3 Language and reality

A widely held view in formal semantics is that the role of language is to describe states of affairs in the world. This rests on the assumption that there is an objective world "out there", which language simply reflects. However, cognitive linguists argue that this **objectivist approach** misses the point that there cannot be an objective reality that language reflects directly, because reality is not objectively given. Instead, reality is in large part constructed by our cognition of the objective world which is in turn based on our bodily experience. This is not to say that cognitive linguists deny the existence of an objective physical world independent of human beings. After all, gravity exists, and there is a color spectrum (resulting from light striking surfaces of different kinds and densities), and some entities give off heat, including body heat, which can only be visually detected in the infrared range. However, the parts of this external reality to which we have access are largely constrained by the ecological niche we have adapted to and the nature of our bodily experience. In other words, language does not directly reflect the world. Rather, it reflects our unique human construal of the world: our "world view" as it appears to us through the lens of our embodied experience.

This view of reality has been termed **experientialism** or **experiential realism** by cognitive linguists George Lakoff and Mark Johnson. Experiential realism assumes that there is a reality "out there". Indeed, the very purpose of our perceptual and cognitive mechanisms is to provide a representation of this reality, and thus to facilitate our survival as a species. After all, if we were unable to navigate our way around the environment we inhabit and avoid dangerous locations like clifftops and dangerous animals like wild tigers, our cognitive mechanisms would be of little use to us. However, by virtue of being adapted to a particular ecological niche and having a particular form and configuration, our bodies and brains necessarily provide one particular perspective among many possible and equally viable perspectives. Hence, experiential realism acknowledges that there is an external reality that is reflected by concepts and by language. However, this reality is mediated by our uniquely human experience which constrains the nature of this reality "for us".

In sum, from the perspective of cognitive linguistics, language does not reflect the physical world directly but through the mediation of human cognition. In other words, language expressions are neither objective reflection of the outside world nor external to human beings. They do not reflect the objective events and situations directly, as what the truth-conditional semantics holds, but rather through human's cognitive construction and construal. Cognitive linguistics rejects the traditional objectivist view on the relationship between language and reality which assumes a direct correspondence between real world entities and language expressions.

2.4 Summary

In this chapter we discussed the relationship between language, thought and reality. There are mainly two opposing views on the relationship between language and thought: one holds that language determines thought and the other insists that thought determines language. We gave a detailed introduction of the first view by probing into the quite controversial notion of **linguistic relativity** and the reactions to this notion from cognitive linguistics and cognitive science. About the relationship between thought and reality, we mentioned two positions:

objectivism and **mental constructivism**. The former asserts that knowledge of reality is attainable and comes from correctly conceptualizing and categorizing the world; the latter believes that we can never perceive the world as it really is: that reality is only graspable through the conceptual filters derived from our biological and cultural evolution. These two positions are related respectively to the study of meaning in formal semantics and cognitive semantics. Finally, we touched upon the relationship between language and reality. One view in formal semantics is that there is a direct relation between language and reality, and language simply mirrors reality. Another view in cognitive linguistics rejects this view. It holds that language does not directly reflect the world but our unique human construal of the world: our "world view" as it appears to us through the lens of our embodied experience. Now it has been widely acknowledged that the latter view is much more reasonable and convincing.

Chapter 3 *Word meaning*

In this chapter, we turn to the study of word meaning, or **lexical semantics**. We will mainly discuss three topics: the definition of the unit *word*; lexical ambiguity and vagueness; sense relations between words such as synonymy, antonymy, hyponymy, homonymy, meronymy, etc.

3.1 What is a *word*?

Although *word* is a unit of expression that native speakers can recognize by intuition, whether it is expressed in spoken or written form, it is no easy job to give *word* a scientific definition that can cover everything.

Traditionally, *word* is defined as a linguistic form that expresses a single concept — concrete or abstract or purely relational (as in *of* or *by* or *and*). But this is not a sound definition of word. As Edward Sapir (1949: 32) noted, it is no good simply basing the definition on meaning or concept, since across languages speakers package meaning into words in very different ways. For example, though a word can be defined as the symbolic, linguistic counterpart of a single concept, it sometimes expresses a complete thought (as in Latin *dico* "I say" or, with greater elaborateness of form, as in a Nootka verb form denoting "I have been accustomed to eat twenty round objects [e.g. apples] while engaged in [doing so and so]"). In the latter case the word becomes identical with the sentence.

The famous American linguist Leonard Bloomfield suggests a word be defined as a *minimum free form*, that is, the smallest unit which can constitute, by itself, a complete utterance. For example,

1) — Is Jane coming this evening?

— Possibly.

It is interesting to note that there is heated discussion in respect to this statement. The opponents argue that not all word-like units can satisfy this criterion, as the articles *a*, *an*, *the*, prepositions *at*, *or*, conjunctions *and*, *if* could not stand by themselves as complete sentences. But the advocators cite the following exceptions:

2) — What is missing in the sentence "Dog is barking"?

— A.

Correspondingly,

3) — What is missing in the sentence "Don't look me"?

— At.

But this is not a sound test to identify a word. Look at the following example,

4) — What is missing in the sentence "He walk into the room a moment ago"?

— -ed.

Obviously, *-ed* is not a word, but a bound morpheme though it constitutes a complete utterance by itself.

A better approach to defining words is to acknowledge that there is no one totally satisfactory definition, but that we can isolate five of the most frequently implied meanings of *word*: the phonological word, the orthographic word, the morphological word, the lexical word and the semantic word.

A phonological word may be seen as a cluster of sound segments between two pauses. For example, in /ɪt ɪz ˈwʌndəfl/, three phonological words are recognized.

An orthographic word is one which has space on either side of it. Thus in the sentence *It is wonderful*, we have three orthographic words.

The problem with phonological and orthographic word is that, in casual speech or writing, one tends to give expression to the same idea phonologically or orthographically as follows:

/ɪts ˈwʌndəfl/; It's wonderful.

In these examples, liaison and contracted form are used. Based on the definitions of phonological word and orthographic word, there should be two words in each case. This, of course, contradicts our common sense of the hierarchical structure of the two phonological and orthographic forms: in each there are three words rather than two words.

A morphological word is a unique form. It considers form only and not meaning. *Ball*, for example, is one morphological word, even though it can refer to both a bouncing object and a dance. *Ball* and *balls* would be two morphological words because they are not identical in form.

A lexical word comprehends the various forms of items which are closely related by meaning. Thus, *chair* and *chairs* are two morphological words, but one lexical word. Similarly, *take*, *takes*, *taking*, *taken* and *took* are five morphological words but only one lexical word. Often in linguistics, when capital letters are used for a word, for example TAKE, it implies that we are dealing with a lexical word and so TAKE comprehends all the various forms, that is, *take*, *takes*, *taking*, *taken* and *took*.

A semantic word involves distinguishing between items which may be morphologically identical but differ in meaning. We have seen above that *ball* can have two distinct meanings. This phenomenon of "polysemy" is common in English. Thus, *table* can refer to a piece of furniture or to a diagram. The diagram and the piece of furniture are the same morphological word but they are two semantic words because they are not closely related in meaning.

3.2 Lexical ambiguity and vagueness

Ambiguity refers to the phenomenon that the meaning of a phrase or sentence can be interpreted in two or more different ways. Depending on whether it results from different understandings of specific lexemes or from different understandings of certain syntactic structures, ambiguity can be divided into two types: lexical ambiguity and syntactic ambiguity. In the following sentences, 5), 6), 7), 8), 9), 10) are examples of lexical ambiguity, while 11), 12), 13), 14), 15), 16), 17) are examples of syntactic ambiguity.

5) He is a poor mechanic.

6) John is drawing a cart.

7) We saw her duck.

8) Is he really that kind?

9) They can fish here.

10) She cannot bear children.

11) The thing that bothered Bill was crouching under the table.

12) the love of God

13) my small child's cot (= my small cot for a child, my cot for a small child, or the cot of my small child)

14) I found him in the classroom.

15) Visiting relatives sometimes can be boring.

16) Distinguished students and teachers were invited to the conference.

17) Please stop hurrying people.

Vagueness means certain semantic features of a linguistic expression are left unspecified. For example, the word *person* is not specified with reference to the features [MALE] vs. [FEMALE], [OLD] vs. [YOUNG].

The basic difference between vagueness and ambiguity lies in that in examples of vagueness the context can add information that is not specified in the sense, but in examples of ambiguity the context will cause one of the senses to be selected. Kempson (1977) proposed a test to distinguish vagueness from ambiguity. This test relies on the use of abbreviatory forms like *do so*, *do so too*, *so do*, which are short forms used to avoid repeating a verb phrase, e.g.:

18) a. John hates cabbage and **so does** Mary.

b. He took a form and Smith **did too**.

Such expressions are understandable because there is a convention of **identity** between them and the preceding verb phrase: thus we know that in 18)a Mary hates cabbage and in 18)b Smith took a form. Kempson's test relies on this identity: if the preceding verb phrase has more than one sense, then whichever sense is selected in this first full verb phrase must be kept the same in the following do so clause. For example 19)a below has the two interpretations in 19) b and c:

19) a. Duffy discovered a mole.

b. Duffy discovered a small burrowing mammal.

c. Duffy discovered a long dormant spy.

This relies of course on the two meanings of *mole*, and is therefore a case of lexical ambiguity. If we add a *do so* clause as in 19)d:

d. Duffy discovered a mole, and so did Clark.

whichever sense is selected in the first clause has to be repeated in the second, i.e. it is not possible for the first clause to have the mammal interpretation and the second the *spy* interpretation, or vice versa. By contrast where a word is vague, the unspecified aspects of meaning are invisible to this *do so* identity. Basically, they are not part of the meaning and therefore are not available for the identity check. We can compare this with the word *publicist* which can be used to mean either a male or female, as 20) below shows:

20) a. He's our publicist.

b. She's our publicist.

Is *publicist* then ambiguous? In a sentence like 21) below:

21) They hired a publicist and so did we.

it is quite possible for the publicist in the first clause to be male and in the second, female. Thus this test seems to show that publicist is unspecified, or vague, for gender. We can see that vagueness allows different specifications in *do so* clauses, but the different senses of an ambiguous word cannot be chosen.

Ambiguity can be eliminated with the help of contextual or background information, e.g.:

22) They are requested not to overlook the ladies' bathing place.

This sentence is ambiguous, which is caused by a reader's two different interpretations of the verb *overlook*. As is shown below, once contextual information is added to the sentence, only one of the two interpretations can be selected:

23) They are requested not to overlook the ladies' bathing place. That is why they are working out a plan to improve the bathing conditions in the place.

24) They are requested not to overlook the ladies' bathing place because it is a hooligan behavior.

In their study of ambiguity, Kess and Hoppe (1985) also find the importance of background knowledge in helping listeners detect and resolve ambiguity. It is a well known fact about English sentence structure that adding a prepositional phrase to a verb phrase can cause ambiguity, as in 25) below:

25) a. John chased the dog.
    b. John chased the dog with a stick.

The ambiguity in 25)b is in whether John or the dog has the stick. Kess and Hoppe provide a list of similar ambiguous sentences to illustrate the role of background knowledge in removing ambiguity, as in 26):

26) John chased the dog with the stick.
John chased the dog with the bone.
John chased the dog with the broom.
John chased the dog with the trombone.
John chased the dog with the white tail.
John chased the dog with the pointed ears.
John chased the dog with the black spot.
John chased the dog with the wound.

They suggest that while, structurally, ambiguity should be present in all of these sentences, in fact background knowledge about dogs and people will mean that for most people there is no ambiguity in any but the first sentence in the list. Of course these sentences are given without a context: since background knowledge here is a prediction of how typically dogs and people behave, based on experience, the normal interpretation can be overruled in a particular context.

3.3 Sense relations

Words are in different sense relations with each other. For example, if you were asked to give the meaning of the word *conceal*, you might simply reply "it's the same as *hide*", or give the meaning of *shallow* as "the opposite of *deep*", or the meaning of *daffodil* as "it's a kind of *flower*". In doing so, you are characterizing the meaning of a word in terms of its relationship to other words. The following are some kinds of sense relations often discussed in the literature of semantics.

3.3.1 Synonymy

Synonymy refers to the sameness or close similarity of meaning. Words that are close in meaning are called **synonyms**. Examples of synonyms are the pairs *break/snap*, *hide/conceal*, *almost/nearly*, *big/large*, *liberty/freedom*, *answer/reply*.

It should be noted that true or exact synonyms are very rare. Synonyms often have different distributions along a number of parameters. They may belong to different dialects like the British English *autumn* and the American English *fall*. Or they may belong to different registers, those styles of language, colloquial, formal, literary, etc. that belong to different situations. Thus *wife* or *spouse* is more formal than *old lady* or *missus*, and in the context "Little Tom ______ a toy bear", *buy* is more appropriate than *purchase*. The synonyms may portray positive or negative attitudes of the speaker: for example, *naive* or *gullible* seem more critical than *ingenuous*, and *politician* more critical than *statesman*. Finally, synonyms may be collocationally restricted. For instance, whereas the word *answer* fits in this sentence: *John had only one answer correct on the test*, its near-synonym, *reply*, would sound odd, and even though *big* and *large* are synonyms, the phrases *my big sister* and *my large sister* certainly do not have the same meaning.

3.3.2 Antonymy

Antonymy is the general term applied to the sense relation involving oppositeness of meaning. Words that are opposite in meaning are **antonyms**. There are three types of antonyms, namely (1) gradable antonyms, (2) binary (or complementary) antonyms and (3) converse (or relational) antonyms.

(1) Gradable antonyms refer to pairs of items such as *big/small*, *good/bad*, *young/old*. In other words, *big*, *good* and *young* can only be interpreted in terms of *being bigger*, *better* or *younger* than something which is established as the norm for the comparison. Thus, when we say that one dog is bigger than another, we imply that *big* is to be understood in the context of dogs. This accounts for the apparent paradox of *a big dog* being smaller than *a small elephant* because *small* in the latter context means "small when compared with other elephants". Similarly, *a thick pencil* is likely to be thinner than *a thin girl*, and *a late dinosaur fossil* is earlier than *an early record of Michael Jackson*.

The semantic contrast in a pair of gradable antonyms is relative, that is, there are often intermediate terms between the two opposites. Take *hot/cold* for example. Not everything that can be *hot* or *cold* is, in fact, either *hot* or *cold*. A liquid may be neither *hot* nor *cold*; it can be in between, say, *warm* or *cool*.

In English, the larger item of the pair is the unmarked member. Thus we can ask *How big is it? How old is he?* and *How wide is the river?* without implying that the subject is either *big*, *old* or *wide*. On the other hand, to ask *How small is it?* does prejudge the matter, claiming that it is indeed small.

(2) Binary antonyms refer to the existence of such pairs as *male/female*, *dead/alive*, *married/single*, *present/absent*, *innocent/guilty*, *odd/even*, *pass/fail* (a test), *hit/miss* (a target). In binary antonyms the contrast between the two terms is absolute. That is, they are in such a relationship that "the denial of one implies the assertion of the other". For example, *John is not **single*** implies *John is **married***. Everything that can be *dead* or *alive* is, in fact, either *dead* or *alive*: there is no middle ground between the two. Notice the difference between gradable antonyms of the *good/bad* type and binary antonyms. To say *John is not **married*** implies *John is **single***. But to say *John is not **bad*** does not imply *John is **good***.

(3) Converse antonyms are pairs that describe a single relationship between two items from opposite perspectives. *Above* and *below* are examples of converse antonyms. If a picture, for example, is *above* a sofa, then the sofa is necessarily *below* the picture.

Other pairs of converse antonyms include *husband/wife*, *father/son*, *teacher/student*, *doctor/patient*, *host/guest*, *before/after*, *employer/employee*, and so on.

English also has a number of conversely related verbs. For example,

27) a. John ***lent*** the money to Peter.
    b. Peter ***borrowed*** the money from John.

Besides *lent/borrow*, pairs of verbs like *buy/sell*, *own/belong to*, *give/receive* are also examples of converse antonyms.

Occasionally, the same verb can be used in the conversely related pair of sentences as in:

28) a. John rented the house to Peter.
    b. Peter rented the house from John.

29) a. John married Mary.
    b. Mary married John.

The difference between gradable, binary and converse antonyms is represented in Fig. 3-1.

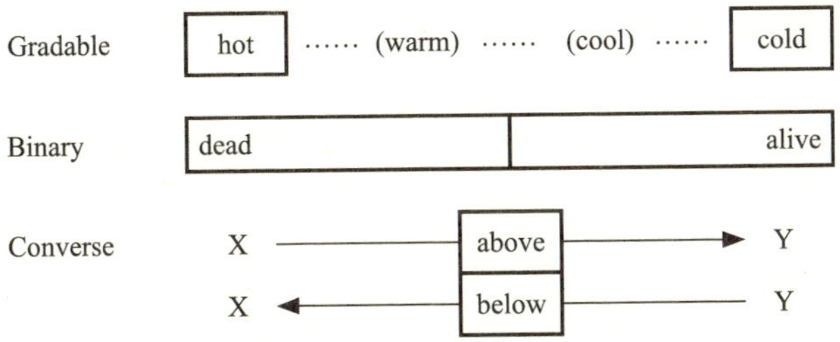

Fig. 3-1

It is not always easy to decide if a pair of antonyms is gradable, binary, or converse. There are, however, several useful tests. First, test the pair to see if they are converse antonyms. This can be done by putting them into the following form: *If X is ____ Y, then Y is ____ X*. For example, *If X is above Y, then Y is below X.* If the pair fits this form, they are converse antonyms. If they don't, then test them to see if they are binary antonyms. This can be done by putting the pair in the following form: *If X is not ____, then X must be ____*. For example, *If John is not dead, then he must be alive.* If the pair fits this form, they are binary antonyms. If they don't, then test them to see if they are gradable antonyms. This can be done by putting each member of the pair in the following form: *X is very ____*. For example, *This soup is very hot/cold.*

3.3.3 Hyponymy

Hyponymy refers to the relationship where the meaning of one word is included in the meaning of another. This can be exemplified by such typical pairs as *daffodil — flower*, *dog — animal*, *poodle — dog*, *carrot — vegetable*, *banyan — tree*. The concept of "inclusion" involved here is the idea that if any object is a *daffodil*, then it is necessarily a *flower*, so the meaning of *flower* is "included" in the meaning of *daffodil*. The "upper" term more general in meaning like *flower* is called the **superordinate** and the "lower" term more specific in meaning like *daffodil* is called the **hyponym**.

When we consider hyponymous relations, we are essentially looking at the meaning of words in some type of hierarchical relationship. We could, in fact, represent the relationships between a set of words such as *animal*, *ant*, *asp*, *banyan*, *carrot*, *cockroach*, *creature*, *daffodil*, *dog*, *flower*, *horse*, *insect*, *living things*, *pine*, *plant*, *snake*, *tree* and *vegetable* as a hierarchical diagram in the following way (Fig. 3-2).

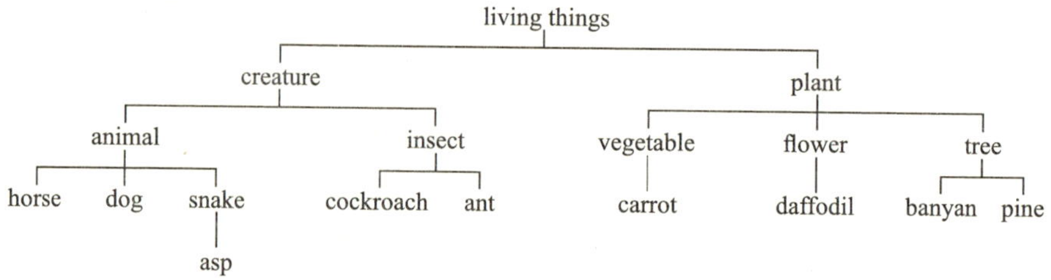

Fig. 3-2

In this diagram, *horse* is a hyponym of *animal* and *ant* is a hyponym of *insect*. Two or more terms which share the same superordinate term are **co-hyponyms**. So, *horse* and *dog* are co-hyponyms, and the superordinate term is *animal*.

The sense relation of hyponymy between words is transitive so that if *daffodil* is a hyponym of *flower* and *flower* is a hyponym of *plant*, *daffodil* is also a hyponym of *plant*.

The relation of hyponymy captures the idea of "is a kind of", as when you give the meaning of a word by saying "an *asp* is a kind of *snake*". It is often the case that the only thing some people know about the meaning of a word in their language is that it is a hyponym of another term. That is, you may know nothing more about the meaning of *asp* other than that it is a kind of *snake*.

One of the most useful features of the principle of hyponymy is that it allows us to be as general or as specific as a particular linguistic occasion warrants, as can be seen from Fig. 3-2. With each downward step we encounter terms of more specific meaning.

Hyponymy is a method of indicating the relationships that can exist between words. Occasionally, items have to be put into a context to see whether their relationships can best be illustrated by means of one classification rather than another. *Black* and *white* are co-hyponyms when considered as colors but they can be complementary in discussions about race, draughts and piano keys.

3.3.4 Homonymy

Homonymy refers to the phenomenon that words having different meanings have the same form, i.e. different words are identical in sound or spelling, or in both.

When two words are identical in spelling but different in pronunciation and meaning, they are described as **homographs**. Some examples are *tear* (a drop of salty liquid that flows from the eye) — *tear* (to pull apart), *lead* (to go before) — *lead* (metal), *close* (to shut) — *close* (near). When two words are identical in pronunciation but different in spelling and meaning, they are described as **homophones**. Some examples are *bare — bear, meat — meet, flour — flower.* When two words are identical in both pronunciation and spelling but different in meaning, they are described as **complete homonyms**. Examples of complete homonyms include *bank* (of a river) — *bank* (financial institution), *pupil* (at school) — *pupil* (in the eye) and *mole* (on skin) — *mole* (small animal). Each of them is regarded as a lexeme and the two are complete homonyms.

3.3.5 Polysemy

Relatedness of meaning accompanying identical form is technically known as **polysemy**, which can be defined as one form (written or spoken) having multiple meanings which are all related by metaphorical or metonymic extension. Examples are the word *head*, used to refer to the object on top of your body, on top of a glass of beer, on top of a company or department; or *foot* (of person, of bed, of mountain), or *run* (person does, water does, colors do) . Polysemy is a relation between the different senses of the same word, not a relation between different words.

The distinction between homonymy and polysemy is not always clear cut. However, one indication of the distinction can be found in the typical dictionary entry for words. If a word has multiple meanings (polysemic), then there will be a single entry, with a numbered list of the different meanings of the word. If two words are treated as homonyms, they will typically have two separate entries. Another way to distinguish polysemic words and complete homonyms is to see the etymology (i.e. the historical development) of the words in question. A polysemic word is the result of the evolution of the primary meaning of the word. The various meanings of the word are related to some degree, as we have seen in the cases of "head" and "foot" above. Complete homonyms are often brought into being by coincidence. For instance, "ball" meaning "a round object used in games" and "ball" meaning "a large formal social event at which people dance" are complete homonyms. The word "ball" bearing the first meaning is a native English word. It originally existed in the language. It so happened that in French there existed a word, spelt in the same way, bearing the second meaning. And this word somehow found its way into the English language. The result is that in English today we have the two complete homonyms "ball" and "ball".

One problem with the distinction between homonymy and polysemy is that sometimes speakers' intuitions of the distinction may contradict historical fact. For example, most English speakers seem to feel that the two words *sole* (bottom of the foot) and *sole* (flatfish) are unrelated, and should be given separate lexical entries as a case of homonymy. They are however historically derived via French from the same Latin word *solea* (sandal). So an argument could be made for polysemy. Since in this case, however, the relationship is really in Latin, and the words entered English from French at different times, dictionaries side with the speakers' intuitions and list them separately. A more recent example is the adjective *gay* with the two meanings "lively, lighted-hearted, bright" and "homosexual". Although the latter meaning was derived from the former in recent history, for many speakers the two senses are quite distinct, and they may like homonyms to some, especially younger, English speakers.

3.3.6 Meronymy

Meronymy is a term used to describe a part-whole relationship between lexical items. Thus *cover* and *page* are meronyms of *book*. We can identify this relationship by using sentence frames like *X is part of Y*, or *Y has X*, as in *A page is part of a book*, or *A book has pages*.

Meronymy differs from hyponymy in that the former reveals a "part of" relation while the latter a "kind of" relation. We can identify hyponymy by using the sentence frame *An X is a kind of Y* as in *A sparrow is a kind of bird*, or *A rose is a kind of flower*, *An ant is a kind of insect*, or *A poodle is a kind of dog*. Meronymy also differs from hyponymy in transitivity. Hyponymy is always transitive, but meronymy may or may not be. A transitive example is: *nail* as a meronym of *finger*, and *finger* of *hand*. We can say that *nail* is a meronym of *hand*, for we can say *A hand has nails*. A non-transitive example is: *handle* is a meronym of *door* (*A door has a handle*), and *door* of *house* (*A house has a door*); but *handle* is not a meronym of *house*, for we cannot say *A house has a handle* or

A handle is part of a house. Or *hole* is a meronym of *button*, and *button* of *shirt*, but we wouldn't want to say that *hole* is a meronym of *shirt* (*A shirt has holes*).

Meronymy reflects hierarchical classifications in the lexicon. This is shown in the following Fig. 3-3.

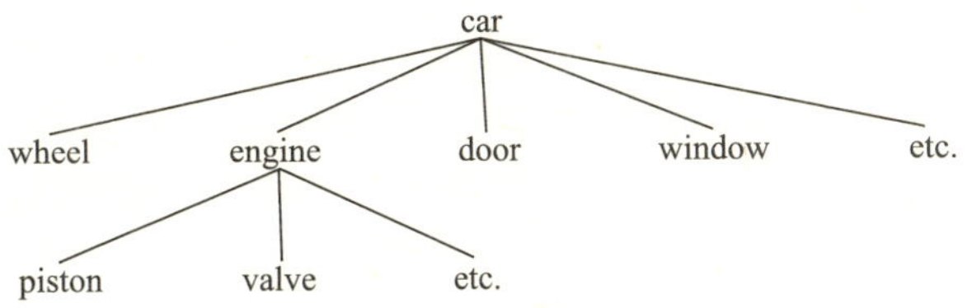

Fig. 3-3

There are a number of other lexical relations which seem similar to meronymy. The following are two of the most important.

3.3.7 Member—collection

This is a relationship between the word for a unit and the usual word for a collection of the units. Examples include:

30) ship	fleet
tree	forest
fish	shoal
book	library
bird	flock
sheep	flock
worshipper	congregation

3.3.8 Portion—mass

This is the relation between a mass noun and the usual unit of measurement or division. For example in 31) below the unit, a count noun, is added to the mass noun, making the resulting noun phrase into a count nominal.

31) drop	of	liquid
grain	of	salt/sand/wheat
sheet	of	paper
lump	of	coal
strand	of	hair

3.4 Summary

In this chapter we have looked at some important features of word meaning. In section one we discussed the difficulties linguists have had coming up with an airtight definition of the unit *word*. In section two we discussed lexical ambiguity and vagueness — the difference between them and the role of contextual information in eliminating ambiguity and vagueness. In section three we looked at some types of sense relations between words: synonymy, antonymy, hyponymy, homonymy, polysemy, meronymy, etc. These represent characteristic examples of the networking of the vocabulary that a semantic description must reflect.

Chapter 4 Sentence relations and truth

In the last chapter we looked at some of the semantic relations which hold between words and at the network effect that this gives to the lexicon. In this chapter we move on to semantic relations that may hold between sentences of a language. As we shall see, sometimes these relations are the result of particular words in the sentences, but in other cases the relations are the result of syntactic structure. As an example of an attempt to represent these relations, we will look at an approach to meaning based on the notion of **truth,** which has grown out of the study of logic. In particular we examine how successfully a truth-based approach is in characterizing the semantic relations of **entailment** and **presupposition**.

4.1 Logic and truth

The study of logic comes down to us from the Classical Greek world, most famously from Aristotle. The beginnings of logic lie in a research for the principles of valid argument and inference. A well-known example is Aristotle's **modus tollens**, a type of argument in three steps as shown in the following:

1) a. If Arnd is not in the bar, then he is in the lounge.
   b. Arnd is not in the bar.
   c. Arnd is in the lounge.

If steps a and b (called the premises) are true then step c (the conclusion) is also guaranteed to be true.

A part of this study is a concern for the truth of statements and whether truth is preserved or lost by putting sentences into different patterns. Truth here is taken to mean a correspondence with facts, or in other words, correct descriptions of states of affairs in the world. For the most part this truth is said to be **empirical** (or **contingent**), because we have to have some access to the facts of the world to know whether a statement is true or not. Thus the truth or otherwise of the sentence:

2) My father was the first man to visit Mars.

depends on the facts about the speaker's father's life: if her/his father did go to Mars and was the first man there, then the sentence is true; otherwise it is false. In the same way the empirical truth of 3) below:

3) The earth revolves around the sun.

depends upon the facts of the universe.

Semanticists call a sentence's being true or false its **truth value**, and call the facts that would have to obtain in reality to make a sentence true or false, its **truth conditions**. A simple example of a linguistic effect on truth value comes from negating a sentence. If we have a sentence like a below in English, adding *not* will reverse its truth value:

4) a. The man saw a wolf in the mountain yesterday.
   b. The man did not see a wolf in the mountain yesterday.

If 4)a is true then 4)b is false; also if 4)a is false then 4)b is true. To show that this relationship works for any statement, logicians use a schema called **logical form**, where a low case letter (p, q, r, etc.) stands for the statement and a special symbol for negation: ¬. So the logical form for 4)a is 5)a and for 4)b is 5)b:

5) a. p
   b. $\neg p$

The effect of negation on the truth value of a statement can be shown by a truth table, where **T** represents "true" and **F** "false", as below:

6)

p	$\neg p$
T	F
F	T

This is then a succinct way of describing the truth effect of negation.

The truth value of other linguistic elements is studied in logic in the same way. A number of connectives are especially important to logicians because they have a predictable effect on the truth conditions of compound statements. For example the truth value of a compound formed by using *and* to join two statements is predictable from the truth of the constituent statements. See, for example:

7) a. The house is on fire.
   b. The fire brigade are on the way.
   c. The house is on fire and the fire brigade are on the way.

If 7)a and b above are true, then the compound c is also true. If however either of a or b is false then the compound will be false. This can be shown by designing a truth table for *and*, and representing it by a special symbol ∧:

8)

p	q	$p \wedge q$
T	T	T
T	F	F
F	T	F
F	F	F

This table tells us that only when both statements connected by ∧ are true will the compound be true. So 7)c above will be false if the house is on fire but the fire brigade are not on the way, and also false if the fire brigade are on the way but to a false alarm: the house is not on fire. Most obviously of all, 7)c is false if there is no fire and no fire brigade on the way.

The study of the truth effects of connectives like ¬ and ∧ is called **propositional logic**①, and logicians have studied the truth effects of a number of other connectives, for example those corresponding to the English words *or* and *if... then.*

There are two logical connectives which can correspond to English *or*. The first is called **disjunction** (or alternatively **inclusive or**) and is symbolized as ∨, thus giving logical forms like $p \vee q$. The truth table for this connective is as follows:

---

① There is another kind of logic usually called predicate logic which studies the truth behavior of sentences with quantifiers like *all*, *every*, *each*, *some*, *one*, etc.

9)

p	q	$p \vee q$
T	T	T
T	F	T
F	T	T
F	F	F

Thus a compound created with $\vee$ is true if one or both of the constituent sentences is true. This connective corresponds to the use of English *or* in sentences like the following:

10) I'll see you today or tomorrow.

11) Students who do not arrive in time or have not completed all their assignments will be refused admission to the examination.

Sentences 10) and 11) are true if either p or q is true, or both. They are only false if both p and q are false.

The second connective which can correspond to English *or* is called **exclusive or**, which we can symbolized as $\vee_e$. This connective has the truth table in 12) below:

12)

p	q	$p \vee_e q$
T	T	F
T	F	T
F	T	T
F	F	F

From 12) we can see that $p \vee_e q$ is only true if just one of its disjuncts is true. This connective corresponds to the use of English *or* in sentences like 13) below:

13) You will pay the fine or you will go to the jail.

This exclusive or seems to have an implicit qualification of "but not both". Thus if a judge said sentence 13) to a defendant, it would seem very unfair if the defendant paid the fine and was still sent to jail, as would be consistent with inclusive or. 14) deserves a similar understanding:

14) For the main course you may have meat or fish.

The next connective we will look at here is the **material implication**, symbolized as $\rightarrow$. This connective has the truth table in 15).

15)

p	q	$p \rightarrow q$
T	T	T
T	F	F
F	T	T
F	F	T

As 15) shows, the expression $p \rightarrow q$ is only false when p (the **antecedent**) is true and q (the **consequent**) is false. This connective is something like our use of English *if...then* in the following example:

16) If it snows, then I'll stay at home.

The *if*-clause can be identified as the antecedent and the *then*-clause as the consequent. This conditional sentence can only be false if it snows and the speaker doesn't stay at home, namely, p=**T**, q=**F**. If it doesn't snow (p=**F**), the speaker's conditional claim cannot be invalidated by whatever the speaker does: whether he stays at home (p=**T**) or not (q=**F**). This relation can be described in this way: p is a **sufficient condition** for q (snow will cause the speaker to stay) but not a **necessary condition** (other things might make the speaker stay: it might rain).

This relation is a little confusing as speakers of English would intuitively try to match it with the ordinary use of conditional sentences. However conditionals in actual speaking usually have more to them than this truth-conditional connective shows. For example, there is often an assumption of a causal connection between the antecedent (the *if*-clause) and the consequent (the *then*-clause), as shown below:

17) If John goes shopping, then Mary will go too.

A natural implication of sentence 17) is that Mary is going **because** John is. This is partly like our connective → because if John goes shopping but Mary doesn't (p=**T**, q=**F**) then the conditional sentence 17) is false, as the truth table for → suggests. However because of the causal implication, speakers of English might feel that if John doesn't go (p=**F**) the conditional 17) implies that Mary won't go. Thus we might feel that if he does go (q=**T**), the claim is invalidated. The logical connective, however, doesn't work like this: as 17) shows, if the antecedent is false, the compound is true, whatever the truth value of the consequent.

The final related connective is **biconditional**, symbolized by ≡ (or alternatively ↔). This connective has the truth table in 18) below:

18)

p	q	$p \equiv q$
T	T	T
T	F	F
F	T	F
F	F	T

As 18) shows, a statement $p \equiv q$ is true when p and q have the same truth value. The name "biconditional" reflects the fact that the $p \equiv q$ is equivalent to the compound conditional expression $(p \rightarrow q) \wedge (q \rightarrow p)$, which can be paraphrased as "if *p* then *q* and if *q* then *p*". This connective corresponds to the English words *if and only if* as in 19):

19) We'll give up if and only if we are killed.

If we reverse the English clause order and identify the condition *if and only if we are killed* as p, and the consequent *we'll give up* as *q*, then we can say that *p* is a necessary condition for *q*, i.e. *p* is the only possible cause for *q*. In logic this relation "*q* if and only if *p*" is often abbreviated to "*q* iff *p*".

This has been just a brief look at logical connectives and their English counterparts. What we need to hold onto are these ideas from logic: that statements have a truth value; that this truth value depends upon a correspondence to facts, and that different ways of connecting statements have different effects on the truth value of the compounds produced. Words like the connectors *and*, *or*, *if... then*, the negative word *not*, and quantifiers like *all*, *every*, *each*, *some*, *one*, can influence the truth behavior of sentences. For this reason these words are sometimes called **logical words**. Because of the presence of these words the truth behavior of a sentence is predictable from its logical form.

4.2 Necessary truth, a priori truth and analyticity

As has been said, the notion of empirical truth depends on a correlation to states of affairs in reality. Philosophers and logicians have identified another type of truth which seems instead to be a function of linguistic structure. For example, we know that the tautology:

20) My father is my father.

is always true (in its literal meaning) without having to refer to the facts of the world, as in a sentence like:

21) Either he's still alive or he's dead.

We do not have to check a pulse to find out whether this sentence is true.

In the same way, contradictions are false simply by virtue of their own meaning, e.g.:

22) ?She was assassinated last week but fortunately she is still alive.

This second kind of truth has been the focus of much investigation. The question of how it is that we might know a statement to be true without checking the facts of the world has been discussed by many philosophers and various distinctions of truth have been made. For example, we started out by characterizing this type of truth in epistemological terms, i.e. in terms of what the speaker knows (or needs to know before making a judgement about truth). From this perspective, truth that known before or without experience has traditionally been called **a priori**. This *a priori* truth is contrasted with **a posteriori** truth: truth, as in our examples 2) and 3) earlier, can only be known on the basis of empirical testing.

Another related concept is the distinction between **necessary** truths, which cannot be denied without forcing a contradiction, for example the arithmetical statement *Two and two make four*, and **contingent** truths which can be contradicted, depending on the facts, for example the sentence *The dodo is extinct*. If someone unexpectedly found a dodo somewhere in the world, this latter sentence would become false. It is difficult, on other hand, to imagine circumstances in which *Two and two make four* would unexpectedly become false. This is similar to our *a priori/a posteriori* distinction but comes at truth from another viewpoint: not in terms of what the speaker knows but in terms of what the world is like. We can say that it is hard to think how our sentence about two and two making four could not be true without changing our view of the present facts of the world. From this perspective a sentence like 21) is also **necessarily true** and a contradiction like 22) is **necessarily false**.

In another, related terminology tautologies like 20) are **analytic** while a sentence like *My father is a sailor* is **synthetic**. Analytic statements are those where the truth follows from the meaning relations within the sentence, regardless of any relationship with the world, while a synthetically true statement is true because it accords with the facts of the world.

Thus we have three related distinctions of truth: between *a priori* and *a posteriori*, *necessary* and *contingent*, and *analytic* and *synthetic*. These notions are closely linked, yet not quite identical. Part of their difference comes from the concerns of the analyst: the *a priori/a posteriori* distinction is an epistemological one, it concerns what the speaker knows. The *necessary/contingent* distinction on the other hand is really a metaphysical one, where we are philosophically questioning the nature of reality. We can hypothesize that it is the nature of reality that ensures that a sentence like *Two and two make four* is a necessary truth. Finally, the *analytic/synthetic* distinction is semantic in orientation. The traditional claim has been that analytic sentences are true because of the meaning of the words within them.

We can see that the three notions are related because under the kind of definitions we have introduced so far, our example sentence *My father is my father* is an *a priori* truth, it is necessarily true and it is analytic. However, there are some problems with this classification of truth. One of them is that a statement might be a necessary truth but not an *a priori* truth. To parallel a standard example, a sentence of identity like *Mogadishu is Hamar* is necessarily true because these are two names for the same city, the capital of Somalia. Clearly, though, it is possible for a person not to know this and therefore for this person, the sentence is not an *a priori* truth. The person might have to ask people or look it up in a book, making the knowledge *a posteriori*.

Finally, we would like to draw readers' attention to the claim from cognitive linguistics: truth is not absolute; truth is a matter of degree; there is no clear-cut borderline between truth and falsity, that is, fuzzy areas exist between them. This can be illustrated with the following example:

23) a. A robin is a bird. (true)
    b. A chicken is a bird. (less true than a)
    c. A penguin is a bird. (less true than b)
    d. A bat is a bird. (false, at least very far from being true)
    e. A cow is a bird. (absolutely false)

4.3 Entailment

Some semanticists have claimed that by using the special meaning of "truth" discussed above they can define more rigorously the meaning relations between sentences. The claim is based on the finding that there are fixed **truth relations** between sentences which hold regardless of the empirical truth of the sentences. This claim can be examined by looking at the semantic relation of **entailment**. The following is an example of the relationship where 24)a is said to entail 24)b:

24) a. The anarchist assassinated the emperor.

b. The emperor died.

In this example, 24)a is termed as the entailing sentence, and 24)b the entailed sentence. There are a number of ways of informally describing this relationship. It could be said that if somebody tells us 24)a and we believe it, then we know 24)b without being told any more. Or it could be said that it is impossible for somebody to assert 24)a but deny 24)b. What such definitions have to try to capture is that entailment is not an inference in the normal sense: we do not have to reason to get from 24)a to 24)b, we just know it instantaneously because of our knowledge of English.

A truth-based definition of entailment might allow us to state the relationship more clearly and would be something like 25) below:

25) Entailment defined by truth:

A sentence *p* entails a sentence *q* when the truth of the first (*p*) guarantees the truth of the second (*q*), and the falsity of the second (*q*) guarantees the falsity of the first (*p*).

Let us come to see how this would work for 24):

Step 1 If *p* (The anarchist assassinated the emperor) is true, is *q* (The emperor died) automatically true? Yes.

Step 2 If *q* (The emperor died) is false, is *p* (The anarchist assassinated the emperor) also false? Yes.

Step 3 Then *p* entails *q*. Note if *p* is false then we can't say anything about *q*; it can be either true or false.

This relation can be shown in an accessible form in terms of the logician's truth tables. The symbols *p* and *q* are still used respectively for the entailing and the entailed sentence, and **T** and **F** for true and false, as in normal truth tables, but arrows (→ and ←) are added to show the direction of a relation "when… then". So the first line of 26) below is to be read "When *p* is true, *q* is true", and the last line is be read "When *q* is true, *p* can be either true or false". The truth relation of entailment can be shown in 26), a composite truth table:

26) Composite truth table for entailment

p		*q*
T	→	T
F	→	T or F
F	←	F
T or F	←	T

When this set of relations hold between *p* and *q*, *p* entails *q*. From this truth table we can see that only the truth of the entailing sentence or the falsity of the entailed sentence has consequences for the other sentence. When *p* is false, *q* can be either true or false: if all we were told was that the anarchist didn't assassinate the emperor, we wouldn't know whether the emperor was dead or alive. When *q* is true, *p* can be either true or false: if we just know that the emperor is dead, that doesn't tell us anything about whether the anarchist assassinated him or not.

The relation of entailment is known by means of linguistic knowledge alone: we do not have to check any fact in the world to deduce the entailed sentence from the entailing sentence.

There are two sources for entailment: one is related to lexical items, the other is related to syntactic forms. In our example above it is clearly lexical: the relationship of entailment between 24)a and b derives from the lexical relationship between *assassinate* and *die*. In some sense the meaning of *assassinate* contains the meaning of *die*. The following are some more examples of entailment produced by lexical items, in which sentence a entails sentence b:

27) a. John saw a *dog* in the street.
    b. John saw an *animal* in the street.

28) a. The boy broke a *flute* today.
    b. The boy broke an *instrument* today.

29) a. She put a bunch of *rose* into the basket.
    b. She put a bunch of *flower* into the basket.

It is quite obvious that the relationship of entailment holding between the two sentences in each example is produced by the sense relation between the two italicized words. In chapter 3 we called the sense relation between each pair of the italicized words **hyponymy**; and indeed hyponymy between lexical items is a regular source for entailment between sentences.

The other source for entailment is syntactic. One of the typical examples is the active and passive versions of the same sentence. Two versions entail each other. In the example below, sentence a entails sentence b, and vice versa:

30) a. The professor wrote the book.

b. The book was written by the professor.

In fact, such relationship of entailment allows us to define **paraphrase**. Paraphrases, like 30)a and b, are sentences which have the same set of entailments, or to put it another way, **mutually entail** each other. Such semantic relations can be characterized in terms of truth relations. Therefore, we have the following composite truth table for mutual entailment:

31) Composite truth table for mutual entailment

p		*q*
T	→	T
F	→	F
T	←	T
F	←	F

This truth table shows that *p* and *q* always have the same truth value, or to put it another way, the truth and falsity of one sentence have consequences for the other. When *p* is true, *q* is true; when *p* is false, *q* is false; and vice versa.

Sometimes, the truth of one sentence entails the falsity of another. This is the case with the following pair in 32).

32) a. Jones is a spinster.

b. Jones is married.

If it is true that Jones is a spinster, then it cannot be true that she is married. In other words, the two sentences cannot be true at the same time. The truth of one sentence entails the falsity of another sentence. This relationship is called **contradiction**. We can show such truth relations of entailment in 33).

33) Composite truth table for contradiction

p		*q*
T	→	F
F	→	T
T	←	F
F	←	T

The simplest examples of contradiction involve negation, as below:

34) a. Mr. Smith stole my car.
   b. Mr. Smith did not steal my car.

35) a. The house is red.
   b. The house is not red.

4.4 Presupposition

What is presupposition? Let us first put it in a simple way: sentence a presupposes sentence b if a implies b and further implies that b is somewhat already part of the background against which a is considered, that considering a at all involves taking b for granted. In the following examples sentence a presupposes sentence b in each pair:

36) a. John forgave Susan for her insult.
   b. Susan insulted John.

37) a. He's stopped beating his wife.
   b. He used to beat his wife.

38) a. Her son is very smart.
   b. She has a son.

39) a. I don't regret leaving London.
   b. I left London.

40) a. Tom started reading novels.
   b. Tom used not to read novels.

From these examples we can see the two main characteristics of presupposition: being backgrounded and being taken for granted.

Semanticists have identified two possible types of approach to presupposition: one is semantic, the other pragmatic. These two approaches have come from different ways of viewing language.

4.4.1 Two approaches to presupposition

In the first approach, rather in the philosophical tradition, sentences are viewed as external objects: we don't worry too much about the process of producing them, or the individuality of the speaker or writer and their audience. Meaning is seen as an attribute of sentences rather than something constructed by the participants. Semantics then consists of relating a sentence-object to other sentence-objects and to the world. When in the last section we characterized sentence relations in terms of truth relations we adopted this perspective. The second approach views sentences as the utterances of individuals engaged in a communication act. The aim here is about modeling the strategies that speakers and hearers use to communicate with one another. So we might look at communication from the speaker's viewpoint and talk about presupposition as part of the task packaging an utterance; or adopt the listener's viewpoint and see presupposition as one of a number of inferences that the listener might make on the basis of what the speaker has just said. The first approach is essentially semantic and the second pragmatic.

Let's use 41)a and its presupposition 41)b as examples to show these different views.

41) a. John's brother has just got back from New York.

b. John has a brother.

We can adopt the sentences-as-external-objects approach and try to identify a semantic relationship between these two sentences. One obvious way is to cast this as a truth relation, as we did for entailment. To do this we might reason as in 42), to set up the partial truth table in 43):

42) Presupposition as a truth relation

Step 1 If *p* (the presupposing sentence) is true, then *q* (the presupposed sentence) is true.

Step 2 If *p* is false, then *q* is still true.

Step 3 If *q* is true, *p* could be either true or false.

43) First composite truth table for presupposition

p		*q*
T	→	T
F	→	T
T or F	←	T

Viewing presupposition as a truth relation allows us to set up a truth table like 43), and allows us to capture an important difference between entailment and presupposition. If we negate an entailing sentence, then the entailment fails; but negating a presupposing sentence allows the presupposition to survive. Take for example the entailment pair in 44):

44) a. He met one of his classmates today.
    b. He met someone today.

If we negate 44)a, then it no longer entails 44)b, i.e. 44)b no longer automatically follows from 44)a: again it might be true, we just don't know. Compare this with the presupposition pair below:

45) a. The mayor of Liverpool is in town.
    b. There is a mayor of Liverpool.

If we negate 45)a the resulting sentence still has the presupposition 45)b. So negating the presupposing sentence does not affect the presupposition, whereas, negating an entailing sentence destroys the entailment. So it seems that viewing presupposition as a truth relation allows us to capture one interesting difference between the behavior of presupposition and entailment under negation.

By comparison, we can sketch an idea of how an alternative, interactional view of presupposition might work for our original example, *John's brother has just got back from New York*. This approach views presupposition as one aspect of a speaker's strategy of organizing information for maximum clarity for the listener. Let us say roughly that the speaker wants to inform the listener that a particular individual has returned from New York. The way he does this will depend on what he estimates about his listener's knowledge. If he thinks his listener knows John but not John's brother, we can see in his use of 41) an ordering of the assertions in 46) and 47):

46) John has a brother X.

47) X has come back from New York.

In our example 41) the first assertion is downgraded or backgrounded by being placed in a noun phrase [*John's brother*] while the second assertion is highlighted or foregrounded by being given the main verb. Why foreground one assertion rather than another? The answer must depend on the speaker's intentions and his guesses about the knowledge held by the participants. For example the speaker might judge that the listener knows 46) but that 47) is new information, therefore need to be foregrounded. Here we could speculate that the speaker decides to include the old information 46) to help the listener to identify the individual that the new information is about. Note too that a speaker can use 41) even if the listener does not know John has a brother. Her both assertions are new but the speaker has decided to rank them in a particular order.

4.4.2 Presupposition failure

One phenomenon which has traditionally caused problems for a truth relations approach but may be less problematic in an interactional approach is **presupposition failure**. It has been observed that using a name or a definite description to refer presupposes the existence of the named or described entity: so the sentences a below presuppose the sentences b:

48) a. David is a philosopher.

b. David exists.

49) a. The King of France is bald.

b. There is a King of France.

A problem arises when there exists no referent for the nominal. If there's no David or King of France, i.e. if the sentences b above are false, what is the status of the sentences a? Are they false, or are they in a grey area, neither true nor false? In a truth-based approach we need to add a line to our truth table, but what does the line look like?

50) A second truth table for presupposition

p		*q*
T	→	T
F	→	T
T∨F	←	T
?(T∨F)	←	F

What this table tries to show is that if *q* is false, the status of *p* is dubious, possibly neither true nor false. This is a problem for truth-based theories, known as a **truth value gap**. If a statement can be neither true nor false, it opens a nasty can of worms. Linguists, logicians and philosophers have generated a number of solutions to this problem, but none is convincing enough to be accepted by all scholars. Thus a good deal of the attractive simplicity of the truth-based approach seems in danger of being lost.

For an interactional approach, there is less of a problem with the so-called presupposition. Such an approach would claim that a speaker's use of definite NPs like names and definite descriptions to refer is governed by conventions about the accessibility of the referents to the listener. In some obvious way, the speaker has made a communication error if he says to you:

51) Heronymous died last month.

if you don't know any person called Heronymous. Your most likely response would be to ask "Who's Heronymous?", signaling a presupposition failure. So we can hypothesize that there is an interactional condition on referring: a speaker's use of a name or definite description to refer usually carries a guarantee that the listener can identify the referent.

So in an interactional approach the issue of presuppositional failure shifts attention from the narrow question of the truth value of statements about non-existent entities to the more general question of what conventions license a speaker's referring use of definite nominals.

4.4.3 Presupposition triggers

We have seen that the use of a name or definite description gives rise to a presupposition of existence. Other types of presupposition are produced by particular words or constructions, which together are sometimes called **presupposition triggers**.

Many presuppositions are produced by the presence of certain words. Many of these **lexical triggers** are verbs. The commonly used verbal lexical triggers include factive verbs, verbs of judgement, and change of state verbs.

Factive verbs like *regret*, *realize*, *know*, *forgive*, *remember* presuppose the truth of their complement clause. Consider the following examples, in each of which sentence a presupposes sentence b:

52) a. Smith realized that he had left his book in the classroom.
    (c.f. Smith thought that he had left his book in the classroom.)
    b. Smith left his book in the classroom.

53) a. Alice regretted eating the only orange.
    (c.f. Alice considered eating the only orange.)
    b. Alice ate the only orange.

54) a. Tom acknowledged that he had made a big mistake.
    b. Tom made a big mistake.

In each of examples 52) and 53), the sentence in the bracket does not presuppose the sentence b because the verbs *think* and *consider* are non-factive verbs.

The example below shows how verbs of judgement produce presupposition:

55) a. John blamed me for telling her.
    (c.f. John accused me of telling her.)
    b. I told her.

Once again, sentence a presupposes sentence b. As *accuse* is not a verb of judgement, the bracketed sentence does not take sentence b as its presupposition.

For a final example of verbal lexical triggers, let us consider change of state verbs, like *start*, *begin*, *stop*. These verbs have a kind of switch presupposition: the new state is both described and is presupposed not to have held prior to the change. This is exemplified in the following sentences, where sentence a presupposes sentence b in each pair:

56) a. Judy started smoking cigars.
    b. Judy used not to smoke cigars.

57) a. Susan quitted smoking.
    b. Susan used to smoking.

58) a. David resumed reading.
    b. David had stopped reading for a while.

59) a. Rose began thinking to set off early.
    b. Rose had never thought to set off early.

Besides these discussed above, there is another kind of lexical trigger which includes words like *even*, *another*, *other*, *again*, *ever*, *in spite of*, etc. The following are some examples where sentence a presupposes sentence b in each pair:

60) a. Even Mary made it.
    b. Mary is less capable than any other one.
61) a. Bill saw another lady's slipper in the woods.
    b. Bill had seen one lady's slipper in the woods.
62) a. John went fishing with other friends.
    b. John did not go fishing with us.

As mentioned in the first paragraph of this subsection, some presupposition triggers derive from syntactic structure. For example, the cleft construction in 63) and the pseudo-cleft in 64) share the presupposition in 65):

63) It was his behaviour with frogs that disgusted me.
64) What disgusted me was his behaviour with frogs.
65) Something disgusted me.

Similarly, in the following pairs of sentences a presupposes b:

66) a. It was the pearls that my future wife wished to wear at the wedding.
    b. My future wife wished to wear something at the wedding.
67) a. What amazed me was his rhetoric.
    b. Something amazed me.
68) a. It was here that I first met him.
    b. I first met him somewhere.

Other forms of subordinate clauses that may produce presuppositions are adverbial clauses and comparative clauses. 69), 70) and 71) are some of the examples in point:

69) a. He's even more clever than you are.
    b. You are clever.
70) a. I was riding motorcycles before you learned to walk.
    b. You learned to walk.
71) a. If it hadn't been for your help, we would not have succeeded.
    b. You had helped us.

Finally, interrogative structures may produce presuppositions. Here are a few examples:

72) a. Who sent the flowers to me?
    b. Someone sent the flowers to me.
73) a. Why don't pigs have wings?
    b. Pigs have no wings.
74) a. Which program is he applying for?
    b. He is applying for some program.
75) a. What is he laughing at?
    b. He is laughing at something.
76) a. Isn't it strange that the United States invaded Cambodia in 1970?
    b. The United States invaded Cambodia in 1970.

4.4.4 Presuppositions and context

As mentioned earlier, one problem for a simple truth-based account of presupposition is that often the presuppositional behaviour seems sensitive to context. While a given sentence always produces the same set of entailments, it seems that this is not true of presuppositions. Compare the two examples below:

77) a. She cried before she finished her thesis.
    b. She finished her thesis.
78) a. She died before she finished her thesis.
    b. She finished her thesis.

It is obvious that in 77), sentence a presupposes sentence b. In 78), however, when the verb *cry* is changed for *die*, the presupposition 78)b is no longer produced. Why is this? It is argued that in 78) the presupposition is blocked or cancelled by our general knowledge of the world: quite simply we know that dead people do not normally complete unfinished theses. This characteristic is sometimes known as **defeasibility**, i.e. the cancelling of presuppositions. If the arise or not of presuppositions depends on the context of knowledge, we need an account of them that can make reference to what the participants know, as in an interactional approach, rather than an account limited to formal relations between sentences.

Another example of context sensitivity occurs with sentences like 79) and

80) below:

79) It was Harry who Alice loved.

80) It was Alice who loved Harry.

These sentences seem to describe the same essential situation of Alice loving Harry; or to put it another way, we might say that they embody the same proposition. The difference between them is that they belong to different conversational contexts: whether the participants have been discussing Harry or Alice. Accordingly they seem to give rise to different presuppositions, with 79) producing 81) and 80) producing 82):

81) Alice loved someone.

82) Someone loved Harry.

The same phenomenon is found with intonation in English, where stressing different parts of the sentence can produce different presuppositions. Using capitals to show the position of this stress, we can produce the presupposition in 81) above with 83) below, and 82) above with 84) below:

83) Alice loved HARRY.

84) ALICE loved Harry.

These examples seem to provide another case where presuppositional behaviour is related to context: in this case the context of the discourse.

Another, narrower, contextual feature is traditionally called the **projection problem**. Sometimes the presupposition produced by a simple clause does not survive when the clause is incorporated into a complex sentence. Sentence 85)a below contains the factive verb *regret* and would normally produce the presupposition in 85)b:

85) a. John will regret doing linguistics.

b. John is doing/will do linguistics.

However in the context of a conditional clause like 86) below, the presupposition 85)b disappears:

86) If John does linguistics, he'll regret it.

The context here is the syntactic one provided by the adjoining clause.

So we can see that different levels of context can cause fluctuations in the presuppositional behaviour. At the most general level, the context provided by background knowledge; then, the context provided by the topic of conversation; and finally, the narrower linguistic context of the surrounding syntactic structure — all can affect the production of presuppositions. Simply giving a truth table of fixed relations between presupposing and presupposed sentences cannot adequately describe this complicated behaviour. Some more sophisticated account is required which takes account of how what participants know forms a background to the uttering of a sentence.

4.5 Summary

In this chapter we have identified a number of semantic relations that hold between sentences: synonymy, entailment and presupposition; and the sentential qualities of tautology and contradiction. We have reviewed an approach which characterizes these in terms of truth relations, using a notion of linguistic or analytic **truth**. We have seen that while this approach provides an attractive account of entailment, for example, it fails to account for the full range of presuppositional behavior, in particular presupposition's sensitivity to contextual features. We contrasted this purely semantic approach with accounts which assume a pragmatic approach: describing presupposition in terms of a speaker's strategies to package his message against his estimate of what his audience knows. We will come back to this idea of processes of packaging information again in chapter 7.

Chapter 5 Sentence semantics 1: situations

In chapter 3 we discussed aspects of word meaning. In this chapter we will investigate some aspects of meaning that belong to the level of the sentence. We will look at a number of semantic categories which belong at the sentence level and which can be seen as ways that languages allow speakers to construct different views of situations. We begin by looking in section 5.1 at how languages allow speakers to classify situations by using the semantic distinction of **situation type**. Then in section 5.2 we look at how systems of **mood** and **evidentiality** allow speakers to adopt differing attitudes towards the factuality of their sentences. Each of these are sentence-level semantic systems which enable speakers to organize descriptions of situations.

5.1 Situation types

Situation types, as we shall see in the sub-section 5.2, is a label for the typology of situations encoded in the semantics of a language. For example, languages commonly allow speakers to describe a situation as static or unchanging for its duration. Such **states** are described in the following examples:

1) David loves pizza.

2) John knows the way to the street.

In describing states the speaker gives no information about the internal structure of the state: it just holds for a certain time, unspecified in the above examples. The start point, the process and the end point of the state are not the concerns of the speaker. We can contrast this with viewing a situation as involving change, e. g.

3) Robert grew very quickly.

4) Jones is driving to New York.

These sentences describe **dynamic** situations. They imply that the action has sub-parts: Robert passed through several sites and Jones is driving through various places on the way to New York.

This distinction between static and dynamic situations is reflected in the choice of lexical items. In English, for example, adjectives are typically used for states and verbs for dynamic situations. Compare the states in the a examples below with the dynamic situations in the sentences b:

5) a. The apples are ripe.
   b. The apples ripened.

6) a. The cinema is full.
   b. The cinema filled up.

This is not an exact correlation however: as we saw above, there are a number of **stative verbs** like *be*, *have*, *know*, *remain*, *love* which can be used to describe states, e.g.

7) The book *is* on the shelf.

8) Ann *has* black hair.

9) I *know* nothing about it.

10) The amendment *remains* in force.

11) Jenny *loves* to ski.

We will say that adjectives and stative verbs are inherently static, i.e. that it is part of their lexical semantics to portray a static situation type.

5.2 Verbs and situation types

We saw in the last section that certain lexical categories, in particular verbs, inherently describe different situation types. Some describe states, others are dynamic and describe processes and events. In this section we describe elements of the meaning of verbs which correlate to differences of situation types.

5.2.1 Stative verbs

In 5.1 we saw examples of inherently stative verbs like *be*, *have*, *know*, *remain* and *love*. These verbs allow the speaker to view a situation as a steady state, with no internal phases or changes. Moreover the speaker does not overtly focus on the beginning or end of the state. Even if the speaker uses a stative in the past, e.g.

12) Catherine loved to drive sports cars.

no attention is directed to the end of the state. We do not know from 12) if or how the state ended: whether Catherine's tastes changed, or she herself is no longer around. All we are told is that the relationship described between Catherine and sports cars existed for a while. We can contrast this with a sentence like 13) below, containing a dynamic verb like *learn*:

13) Catherine learned to drive sports cars.

Here the speaker is describing a process and focusing on the end point: at the beginning Catherine didn't know how to drive sports cars, and at the end she has learnt. The process has a conclusion.

Stative verbs display some grammatical differences from dynamic verbs. For example in English progressive forms can be used of dynamic verbs like 14)a below but not of stative verbs like 14)b:

14) a. He is learning Russian.
    b.*He is knowing Russian.

This is because the progressive aspect, marked by *–ing* above, has connotations of dynamism and change which suits an activity like learn but is incompatible with a stative verb like *know*.

Similarly it usually sounds odd to use the imperative with statives; we can compare the following:

15) a. Learn Russian!
    b. ?Know Russian!

Once again, we can speculate that imperatives imply action and dynamism, and are therefore incompatible with stative verbs.

It may be however that the distinction between state and dynamic situations is not always as clear-cut. Some verbs may be more strongly stative than others;

remain for example, patterns like other stative verbs in not taking the progressive, as in 16) below, but it does allow the imperative, as in 17):

16) a. The answer remains the same: no!
    b. *The answer is remaining the same: no!

17) Remain at your posts!

It is important too to remember that verbs may have a range of meanings, some of which may be more stative than others. Let us contrast the stative and non-stative uses of *have*, for example, by looking at how they interact with the progressive:

18) a. I have a bike.
    b. *I am having a bike.
    c. I am having second thoughts about this.

19) a. She has a brother in New York.
    b. *She is having a brother in New York.
    c. She is having a baby.

In 18)a *have* means "hold in possession as one's property", and in 19)a *have* means "hold in a certain relationship", the two senses are both stative in nature. Thus when used in either of them, the verb *have* cannot take the progressive. In 18)c *have* means "engage in an activity", and in 19)c *have* has the sense of "give birth to", both senses are dynamic in nature, so the verb *have* in the two sentences can take the progressive. Similar example:

20) Have (=drink) another cup of tea.

The same explanation can be extended back to 16)a and 17). The meaning of *remain* in 16)a is "continue to be in the same state or condition", its meaning in 17) is "stay in the same place without moving away", the former is stative while the latter is dynamic. Only when used in the dynamic sense does *remain* allow the imperative. In 21) *remain* still means "to stay in the same place", and it can be used in the progressive tense.

21) He is remaining at his posts.

5.2.2 Dynamic verbs

Dynamic verbs can be classified into a number of types, based on the semantic distinctions **durative/punctual** and **telic/atelic** which will be discussed below. These different verb types correlate to different dynamic situation types. One possible distinction within dynamic situation types, for example, is between **events** and **processes**. In events, the speaker views the situation as a whole, e.g.

22) The mine blew up.

While in a process, we view, as it were, the internal structure of a dynamic situation, e.g.

23) He walked to the shop.

Processes can be subdivided into several types, for example **inchoatives** and **resultatives**. Inchoatives are processes where our attention is directed to the beginning of a new state, or to a change of state, e.g.

24) The ice melted.

25) My hair turned grey.

Resultatives are processes which are viewed as having a final point of completion: our attention is directed to this end of the process, e.g.

26) John baked a cake.

27) Joan built a yacht.

One difference between these types concerns interruption. If the action of melting is interrupted in 24) or my hair stops turning grey in 25), the actions of melting and turning grey can still be true descriptions of what went on. However if John in 26) and Joan in 27) are interrupted halfway, then it is no longer true to describe them having baked a cake or built a yacht. In some sense, to use resultatives we have to describe a successful conclusion. In this section we look at two important semantic distinctions in verbs which underlie these different dynamic situation types.

The first distinction is between **durative** and **punctual**: **durative** is applied to verbs which describe a situation or process which lasts for a period of time, while **punctual** describes an event that seems so instantaneous that it involves virtually no time. A typical comparison would be between the punctual 28) and the durative 29):

28) David coughed.

29) David slept.

What matters of course is not how much time an actual cough takes but that the typical cough is so short that conventionally speakers do not focus on the internal structure of the event.

In Slavic linguistics the equivalent of verbs like *cough* are called **semelfactive** verbs, after the Latin word *semel* "once". Other semelfactive verbs in English would include *flash*, *shoot*, *knock*, *sneeze* and *blink*. One interesting fact is that in English a clash between a semelfactive verb and a durative adverbial can trigger an **iterative** interpretation, i.e. where the event is assumed to be repeated for the period described, e.g.

30) Juan coughed all night.

31) The drunk knocked for ten minutes.

32) The cursor flashed until the battery ran down.

In each of these examples the action is interpreted as being iterative: 30) is not understood to mean that Juan spent all night uttering a single drawn out cough!

The second distinction is between **telic** and **atelic**. Telic refers to those processes which are seen as having a natural completion. Compare for example:

33) a. Harry was building a raft.

b. Harry was gazing at the sea.

If we interrupt these processes at any point then we can correctly say:

34) Harry gazed at the sea.

But we cannot necessarily say:

35) Harry built a raft.

As we saw earlier, telic verbs are also sometimes called **resultatives**. Another way of looking at this distinction is to say that *gaze* being atelic can continue indefinitely, while *build* has an implied boundary when the process will be over.

It is important to recognize that while verbs may be inherently telic or atelic, combining them with other elements in a sentence can result in a different aspect for the whole, as below:

36) a. Robert was running. (atelic)

b. Robert was running in the London Marathon. (telic)

37) a. Paul was singing songs. (atelic)

b. Harry was singing a song. (telic)

5.3 A system of situation types

Speakers use their knowledge of these semantic distinctions—stative/dynamic, durative/punctual, telic/atelic—to draw distinctions of situation types. We have seen that some verbs, like *paint*, *draw* and *build*, are inherently telic while others like *talk*, *sleep* and *walk* are atelic. Similarly some verbs are inherently stative like *know*, *love* and *resemble*, while others like *learn*, *die* and *kill* are non-stative. We have also seen from examples like 36) and 37) above that while these distinctions are principally associated with verbs, combining a verb with other elements in a sentence, like object noun phrases and adverbials, can alter the situation type depicted.

The task for the semanticists is to show how the inherent semantic distinctions carried by verbs, and verb phrases, map into a system of situation types. One influential attempt is made by Z. Vendler. In 1967, he published his well-known book *Linguistics in Philosophy* in which he identifies four types of situation, each type taking some English verbs and verb phrases as examples. The following is his system of situation types (Vendler, 1967: 97-121):

a. states
desire, want, love, hate, know, believe

b. activities (unbounded processes)
run, walk, swim, push a cart, drive a car

c. accomplishments (bounded processes)
run a mile, draw a circle, walk to school, paint a picture, grow up, deliver a sermon, recover from illness

d. achievements (point events)
recognize, find, stop, start, reach the top, win the race, spot someone

Such classification of situation types is widely accepted. In 1991, Carlotta S. Smith published his *The Parameter of Aspect* in which, building on Vendler's system, she adds the situation type **semelfactive**. Smith distinguishes semelfactive from achievements as follows (Smith, 1991: 28):

> *Semelfactives are instantaneous atelic events, e.g.* [*knock*], [*cough*]. *Achievements are instantaneous changes of states, with an outcome of a new state, e.g.* [*reach the top*], [*win a race*].

She identifies three semantic categories or features: [stative], [telic] and [duration], with roughly the characteristics we have already described, and uses these to classify five situation types, as follows (Smith, 1991: 30):

Situations	*Static*	*Durative*	*Telic*
State	[+]	[+]	*n.a.*
Activity	[−]	[+]	[−]
Accomplishment	[−]	[+]	[+]
Semelfactive	[−]	[−]	[−]
Achievement	[−]	[−]	[+]

We can provide examples of each situation type, as follows:

38) Alice hated ice cream. (state)

39) The children watched the squirrels on the grass. (activity)

40) My roommate learned Japanese. (accomplishment)

41) The door banged. (semelfactive)

42) The cease-fire began at noon yesterday. (achievement)

It is important to remember that these situation types are interpretations of real situations. Some real situations may be conventionally associated with a situation type; for example it seems unlikely that the event described in 43) below would be viewed other than as an accomplishment:

43) Rose knitted this sweater.

Other situations are more open. It happens sometimes that the same real situation is given two different interpretations. For instance:

44) Kelly was sleeping.

45) Kelly was asleep.

According to Vendler and Smith, example 44) should be defined as an activity, while example 45) as a state, though the two sentences involve the same real world situation.

5.4 Modality and evidentiality

5.4.1 Modality

Modality is another important semantic category which operates at the sentence level. It is a cover term for devices which allow speakers to express varying degrees of commitment to, or belief in a proposition. Speakers talk about factual matters such as what is true and what is not true, what has happened and what has not happened. Speakers also talk about what may or what may not be true, what ought to be true and what ought not to be true, what certain individuals are capable of and what is impossible to them, what obligations speakers have to fulfil or to refrain from fulfilling. All these notions constitute modality. Let us consider the following simple assertion:

46) Emily has gone to the railway station.

It seems that when being told 46), we assume a certain commitment on the behalf of the speaker to its truth. The speaker may be wrong of course because of his own misbelief or be lying in order to mislead us. Our conversational practice, however, seems to be built upon an assumption that speakers generally try to tell the truth, as they know it. If we discover that Emily has not gone to the railway station then our reactions will be very different depending on whether we think the speaker is simply wrong in her belief, or intentionally misleading us. We discuss this assumption of truthfulness as part of the more general issue of conversational conventions in chapter 7. We might take the opposite of the assertion 46) to be the denial 47):

47) Emily hasn't gone to the railway station.

However, without any further spoken qualification, both 46) and its negation 47) seem to carry an unspoken guarantee of "to the best of my knowledge" from the speaker's point of view.

Modal systems allow speakers to modulate this guarantee: to signal stronger and weaker commitment to the factuality of statements. There are a number of possible linguistic strategies to realize such modulation of commitment: for example the sentence can be embedded under a higher clause with an adjective or adverb of modality, e.g.

48) a. It is certain that Emily has gone to the railway station.
b. It is probable that Emily has gone to the railway station.
c. It is likely that Emily has gone to the railway station.
d. It is possible that Emily has gone to the railway station.

Here versions a-d move from strong to weak commitment to 46). Another strategy is to put into the higher clause a verb which describes the extent of the speaker's belief—what is often called in the philosophical literature his

propositional attitude:

49) a. I know that Emily has gone to the railway station.
b. I believe that Emily has gone to the railway station.
c. I think that Emily has gone to the railway station.
d. I don't know that Emily has gone to the railway station.
e. I doubt that Emily has gone to the railway station.
f. I know that Emily hasn't gone to the railway station.

In 49) we can see clearly a gradient from the certainty of the truth of the proposition expressed by the objective clause "Emily has gone to the railway station" through the certainty of its falsity.

A third strategy in English is to employ auxiliary verbs: in 51) below these mark the variations of commitment towards the assertion in 50).

50) David has paid the bill by now.

51) a. David must have paid the bill by now.
b. David might have paid the bill by now.
c. David could have paid the bill by now.
d. David needn't have paid the bill by now.
e. David couldn't have paid the bill by now.

Auxiliary verbs in this role are called **modal verbs**. Semantically, the following are modal verbs:

52) can	could	would
may	might	should
must	dare (to)	ought to
will	shall	need to
have to	have got to	

They share some distinct characteristics that grammatically and semantically differentiate them from other verbs.

It has to be pointed out that the modal verbs have numerous subtleties in what they express in different contexts. They have, on one hand, shifted semantically throughout the history of the English language. On the other hand, different speakers of the language differ somewhat in which modal verbs they prefer for what meanings.

For practical purposes, the meanings of the modal verbs are often differentiated into two classes, according to the function modal verbs perform: **epistemic** modality and **deontic** modality. The former, signaling the speaker's degrees of knowledge, reflects various judgements of factuality and expresses the possibility, probability or impossibility of a particular proposition. The examples so far have been of epistemic modality. The latter communicates judgements of moral and legal obligation, and marks the speaker's attitude to social factors of obligation, responsibility and permission. Take for example 53) below:

53) You can drive this car.

A speaker can use this to mean either of the following:

54) It is possible for you to drive this car.

55) You have my permission to drive this car.

The first is another example of epistemic modality; the second is an example of deontic modality. The following is another example of modal verbs which may express epistemic modality or deontic modality depending on the context of use:

56) The car must be ready.

Deontic modals communicate two types of social information: **obligation** as in 57) and **permission** as in 58):

57) a. You must take these books back.
b. You should take these books back.
c. You need to take these books back.
d. You ought to take these books back.

58) a. You can leave them there.
b. You could leave them there.
c. You might leave them there.

Deontic modals, like epistemic modals, signal a speaker's judgements but while with epistemics the judgement is about the way the real world is, with deontics it is about how people should behave in the world. This means that the use of denotics is tied in with all sorts of social knowledge: the speaker's belief systems about morality and legality; and her estimations of power and authority. The sentences in 57) and in 58) step down in moral strength. Thus 57)a is a stronger statement of obligation than 57)d and while 58)a for example is a bald granting of permission, 58)c is a weaker and polite version. We can imagine that deciding which of 58)a-c to use would depend on different judgements by the speaker of her authority over the listener and the degree of formality of their relationship.

Sometimes the relationship between epistemic and deontic modality is more complicated than an ambiguity resolvable in context, like 53) earlier. Speakers can use an epistemic modal to imply a deontic interpretation as in 59):

59) You could have told me you were coming.

Here the possibility of telling is used to imply a missed obligation, turning 59) into a reproof.

It has been seen that epistemic and deontic modality can be marked by the same means, for example modal verbs, and indeed that some sentences are ambiguous in form between an epistemic and deontic reading. This has led semanticists to ask what they have in common, and to speculate whether one type of modality has developed out of the other. One suggestion is that modality in general allows us to compare the real world with hypothetical versions of it. This approach derives from work on **possible world semantics**. In this view, epistemic modals allow us to set up hypothetical situations and express different strengths of prediction of their match with the real world. Thus if a speaker says 60):

60) It might be snowing in Massachusetts.

he is setting up a hypothetical situation (snow in Massachusetts) and predicting a reasonable match with reality. If on the other hand, he says:

61) It must be snowing in Massachusetts.

he is proposing a very strong match between his prediction and reality.

Deontic modality is approached in the same way. Here though the speaker is proposing a match between an ideal moral or legal situation and the real world of behaviour. So if a speaker says:

62) You should do it at once.

he is proposing a match between the ideal situation and the real situation. And when the speaker says:

63) You must do it at once.

he is proposing a more strong match between the ideal situation and the real situation.

This approach would relate modality to **conditional sentences** like 64) and 65) below, which also set up hypothetical situations:

64) If I were rich, I would be living somewhere hotter.

65) You would sleep all day, if we let you.

We can call the *if*-clause in sentences like 64) and 65), the **condition**, and the other clause, the **consequent**. This view of conditionals as part of the modal system neatly explains why we also find modal verbs used in consequent clauses, like *would* in 64) and 65) above, or *should* in the condition clauses below:

66) If you should go to London, take this to Mary.

67) Should you meet Frank, there's something I would like you to ask him.

This approach to modality is also supported by the existence of languages which have verb forms (variants of the same verb) which regularly distinguish between events in the real world and events in future or imaginary worlds. This two term modal distinction is often called a **realis/irrealis** modality (i.e. a reality/unreality distinction).

Thus far we have seen that modality distinctions in English are marked by various means including adverbs and modal verbs. It should be noted that in many other languages such distinctions are marked by verb endings which form distinct conjugations (Palmer, 1986: 47).

5.4.2 Interpretations of some modal verbs

5.4.2.1 Can/could

Both of the modals have three major distinguished meanings.

• *Possibility*

68) The teacher can be angry on hearing that.

69) The musician's performance was the best that could be hoped for.

• *Permission (less formal)*

70) In those days women could not enter Harvard University.

71) You can take the books back if you want.

• *Ability*

72) Tom could swim across Charles River when he was a child.

73) Martin can speak four languages.

5.4.2.2 May/might

• *Permission (more formal but less common)*

74) Visitors may reclaim necessary travel expenses up to a limit of $100.

75) You might stay for only one more day.

• *Possibility*

The modals, in this sense, denote the possibility of a given proposition's being or becoming true. Thus, they are termed epistemic possibility. They are often associated with fall-rise nuclear tone.

76) We may never overcome them.

77) There might be some complaints.

5.4.2.3 Must

• *Logical necessity*

Such a meaning of *must* is almost parallel to the use of *may* in the sense of epistemic possibility. It is sometimes called "epistemic necessity". It implies that the speaker judges the proposition expressed by the clause to be necessarily true, or at least to have a high likelihood of being true. Then *must* in this sense means that the speaker has drawn a conclusion from things already known or observed.

78) Jason must be sick.

79) You must be joking.

80) His uncle must have a lot of money.

• *Obligation or compulsion*

The word *must* has the implication that the speaker is advocating a certain form of behaviour. It suggests that the speaker is exercising his authority.

81) You must be back by ten o'clock.
(c.f. You have to be back by ten o'clock.)

82) Productivity must be improved, if the nation is to be prosperous.

5.4.2.4 Need/have (got) to

The quasi-modals *need, have (got) to* can be substitutes for *must* in particular cases. The word *need* (constructed as an auxiliary) is used as the negative and question form of *must*. The following two sentences are cases in point.

83) You needn't worry about your future.

84) You have to be patient.

• *Logical necessity*

85) He has to get good grades in order to get grants.

86) They have to stay till midnight.

• *Obligation or compulsion*

87) John has to work thirty hours a week.

88) The mother has to be back by five o'clock.

5.4.2.5 Should/ought to

• *Tentative inference*

The speaker does not know if his statement is true, but tentatively concludes that it is true, on the basis of whatever he knows.

89) The building should/ought to be visible from here.

90) The children should/ought to be back before four o'clock.

• *Obligation*

91) You should/ought to do as what you are told.

92) The room should/ought to be cleaned at least twice a week.

5.4.2.6 Will/would

• *Prediction*

93) I would take this advice. (future prediction in the past)

94) She will go with her roommate. (present prediction)

95) Oil will float on water. (timeless prediction)

96) In the spring the birds would return to their old haunts, and the wood would be filled with their music. (habitual prediction)

• *Volition*

97) Will/would you do me a favour? (willingness)

98) She would keep walking all the time. (insistence)

99) We won't stay longer than one night. (intention)

5.4.2.7 Shall

• *Prediction (with the first person subject)*

100) When shall we meet?

101) We shall win quite easily.

• *Volition (with the first person subject)*

102) We shall deliver it to you in time.

103) We shall uphold the wishes of the people.

5.4.3 Evidentiality

Under epistemic modality we looked at ways in which a speaker can mark different attitudes towards the factuality of a proposition. There is a related semantic category **evidentiality** which allows a speaker to communicate his attitude to the source of his information. This is possible in English of course by the use of a separate clause or by parenthetic adverbials. Compare the bare assertion in 104) with the various evidentially qualified versions in 105)a-g:

104) He was poor.

105) a. I saw that he was poor.
b. I read that he was poor.
c. He was poor, so they say.
d. I'm told he was poor.
e. Apparently he was poor.
f. He was poor, it seems.
g. Allegedly, he was poor.

These qualifications allow the speaker to say whether the statement relies on personal first-hand knowledge, or was acquired from another source; and if the latter, perhaps to say something of the source.

Some languages routinely mark such information grammatically, by special particles or specific verb forms, so that in these languages evidentiality is coded in the morphology. For example, in Makah, a Nootkan language spoken in Washington State, when a speaker offers the information of "It's bad weather", it is obligatory that he should, depending on different situations, mark the different sources of the information by using different verb forms: it is seen or experienced directly, it is inferred from physical evidence, it is heard from others, or it is quoted from someone else.

What emerges from the studies of evidential systems are differences among languages in whether the evidential markers are obligatory in ordinary speech or an optional resource for speakers. Hardman, for example, reports that among the Jaqi languages of Peru, Bolivia and Chile the identification of what she calls "data source" (i.e. the use of evidentials) is a central part of knowing how to communicate (1986: 114):

> *Accuracy on the part of the speaker is a crucial element in the public reputation of individuals; misuse of data-source is somehow somewhat less than human, or is insulting to the listener. Speakers of Jaqi languages, which include Jaqaru, Aymara and Kakwi, have obligatorily to signal whether the source of information for their statements is personal experience, or knowledge gained from other individuals by language, or comes from the remote past where no witnesses are available, i.e. from myths, history and religion. In other languages the use of evidentials is more voluntary, providing a speaker with creative resources to structure a point of view in a discourse, or perhaps to argue more convincingly.*

5.5 Summary

In this chapter we looked at aspects of sentence meaning which allow the speaker to classify situations. The category of **situation type**, for example, incorporating semantic distinctions like **static/dynamic, durative/punctual** and **telic/atelic**, allows a basic classification of situations into **states**, **activities**, **accomplishments**, etc. The semantic categories of **modality** and **evidentiality** allow the speaker to assume various attitudes towards a proposition. **Epistemic** modality reflects various judgements of factuality and **deontic** modality communicates judgements of moral and legal obligation. Both can be seen as implying a comparison between the real world and hypothetical versions of it. **Evidentiality** is a term for the ways in which a speaker qualifies a statement by referring to the source of the information. We saw that in some languages this information is grammaticalized and therefore obligatory, implying that in these communities, calculation of evidence is assumed of speakers by their hearers. We look at the role of similar hearer assumptions, e.g. that the speaker is estimating and updating her audience's state of knowledge, in chapter 7.

Chapter 6 Sentence semantics 2: thematic roles

In the last chapter we looked at aspects of sentence level semantics: how speakers may choose to characterize situations and express various degrees of commitment to the portrayal. Another set of semantic choices which face a speaker seeking to describe a situation concerns how to portray the roles of any entities involved. Let us consider the following example:

1) Jim raised the car with a jack.

This sentence identifies three entities, *Jim*, *the car*, and *a jack*, related by the action described by the verb *raise*. The sentence portrays these entities in specific roles: Jim is the entity responsible for initiating and carrying out the action, the car is acted upon and has its position changed by the action, and the jack is the means by which Jim is able to cause the action. Such roles have a number of labels in semantics, including participant roles, deep semantic cases, semantic roles, thematic relations and thematic roles. Given its wide usage in the literature of semantics, we will use the last term here: **thematic roles**.

Thematic roles concern the semantic roles of participants in a sentence. They are employed to describe aspects of the interface between semantics and syntax, in particular, to characterize the links between the semantic classification of its participants, i.e. the semantic parts of speech, that is inherent in a verb's meaning and the grammatical relations it supports. In this chapter we will look at the classification and definition of thematic roles, the relationship between thematic roles and grammatical relations, and discuss the idea that verbs must have their thematic role requirements listed in the lexicon.

6.1 Thematic roles

Linguists have proposed some lists of thematic roles. From these lists we can extract a list of thematic roles like the following (where the relevant role-bearing nominal is in bold):

AGENT: the initiator of some action, capable of acting with volition, e.g.

2) a. **David** cooked the rashers.
   b. **The fox** jumped out of the ditch.
   c. **Mary** opened the window.
   d. **Tom** drove a black car.
   e. **The ants** climbed all over the dinner table.

PATIENT: the entity undergoing the effect of some action, often undergoing some change in state, e.g.

3) a. Mr. Green mowed **the grass**.
   b. Enda cut back **these bushes**.
   c. The sun melted **the ice**.

THEME: the entity which is moved by an action, or whose location is described, e.g.

4) a. The father took **the crying boy** away.
   b. Peter passed **the ball** wide.
   c. **The book** is in the library.

EXPERIENCER: the entity which is aware of the action or state described by the predicate but which is not in control of the action or state, e.g.

5) a. **Kevin** felt ill.
   b. **Mary** saw the smoke.
   c. **Lorcan** heard the door shut.

BENEFICIARY: the entity for whose benefit the action was performed, e.g.

6) a. Robert filled in the form for **his grandmother**.
   b. They baked **me** a cake.
   c. The painter drew **the lady** a picture.

INSTRUMENT: the means by which an action is performed or something comes about, e.g.

7) a. She cleaned the wound with **an antiseptic wipe**.

b. They signed the treaty with **the same pen**.

c. Elizabeth tasted the soup with **a silver spoon**.

LOCATION: the place in which something is situated or takes place, e.g.

8) a. Those monkeys are playing **in the trees**.

b. The monster was hiding **under the bed**.

c. The band played **in a marquee**.

GOAL: the entity towards which something moves, either literally as in 9)a and c or metaphorically as in 9)b:

9) a. Sheila handed her licence **to the policeman**.

b. Pat told the joke **to his friends**.

c. He is running **towards the sea**.

SOURCE: the entity from which something moves, either literally as in 10)a and c or metaphorically as in 10)b:

10) a. The plane came back **from Paris**.

b. We got the idea **from a French magazine**.

c. The dew was blown **off the flowers**.

Thus to return to our first example, repeated below:

11) Jim raised the car with a jack.

We can describe the thematic roles by calling *Jim* the AGENT of the action, *the car* the THEME, and *a jack* the INSTRUMENT.

Besides those we have discussed, some writers have suggested some other thematic roles which include:

PERCEPT: the entity which is perceived or experienced, e.g.

12) a. The general inspected **the troops**.

b. Did you hear **that thunder**?

c. That shark frightened **the swimmers**.

RECIPIENT: a type of GOAL involved in actions describing changes of possession, e.g.

13) a. He sold **me** this wreck.

b. He left his fortune **to the church**.

6.2 Identification of thematic roles

There is some variation in the use of the terms for thematic roles: for example some linguists treat PATIENT and THEME as different names for the same role. In this book we adopt the distinction that PATIENT is reserved for entities acted upon and changed by he verb's action while THEME describes an entity moved in literal or figurative space by the action of the verb, but constitutionally changed. Thus the noun phrase *the rock* would be a PATIENT in 14) below but a THEME in 15):

14) Paul shattered *the rock.*

15) Paul threw *the rock.*

A number of tests for identifying thematic roles have been suggested. Jackendoff (1972) provides a test for AGENT: whether the phrases like *deliberately*, *on purpose*, *in order to*, etc. can be added to the sentence. This reflects the fact that an AGENT characteristically displays animacy and volition. If a sentence is still acceptable when any of the afore-mentioned phrases is added to it, the subject of the sentence is an AGENT, otherwise it is not. Look at the following examples:

16) a. *John* took the book from Bill.

b. *John* took the book from Bill in order to read it.

17) a. *John* received the book from Bill.

b. **John* received the book from Bill in order to read it.

18) a. *The boy* kicked the ball off.

b. *The boy* kicked the ball off on purpose.

19) a. *The boy* saw the cat.

b. **The boy* saw the cat on purpose.

So in the above examples, *John* in 16) and the boy in 18) act as AGENT. In 17) and 19) they do not.

The simple test proposed by Jackendoff (1990) for identifying PATIENT is to see whether a sentence can be converted to the pattern "what happened to Y was..." or "what X did to Y was...". If it can be, Y is identified as PATIENT. So for example 20) below the test would give 21), identifying *the golf club* as PATIENT:

20) Robert snapped *the golf club* in half.

21) a. What happened to *the golf club* was that Robert snapped it in half.

b. What Robert did to *the golf club* was snap it in half.

In practice, the identification of thematic roles is not as easy as what these two kinds of test have shown us. It is sometimes difficult to decide what thematic role an entity takes on. We will look at this point in 6.4.

6.3 Grammatical relations and thematic roles

It has been found that there are typical matchings between participant roles and grammatical relations: in English there is a tendency for subjects to be AGENTS, directive objects to be PATIENTS and THEMES, and INSTRUMENTS to occur as prepositional phrases. However, this need not always be the case. There are two basic situations where this is not the case: the first is where roles are simply omitted, and the grammatical relations shift to react to this, as we will discuss below; and the second is where the speaker chooses to alter the usual matching between roles and grammatical relations, a choice often marked by an accompanying change of verbal *voice*. We deal with voice later on in section 6.6.

Let's first come to a simple example of thematic role omission in 22)-24) below:

22) David broke the ice with a pickaxe.

23) The pickaxe broke the ice.

24) The ice broke.

In 22) *David* is the AGENT and subject, *the ice* is PATIENT and direct object, and *a pickaxe*, the INSTRUMENT, is in a prepositional phrase. In 23) the AGENT is omitted and now the INSTRUMENT is subject; and finally in 24) with no AGENT or INSTRUMENT expressed, the PATIENT becomes subject. The verb *break* allows all three thematic roles to occupy subject position.

The following are some more examples which show how the position of subject can be occupied by different thematic roles:

25) LOCATION subjects:

a. **This cottage** sleeps five adults.

b. **The table** seats eight.

26) AGENT subjects:

a. **The thief** stole the wallet.

b. **Fred** jumped out of the plane.

27) EXPERIENCER subjects:

a. **I** forgot the address.

b. **Your cat** is hungry.

28) RECIPIENT subjects:

a. **She** received a demand for unpaid tax.

b. **The building** suffered a direct hit.

29) PATIENT subjects:

a. **The bowl** cracked.

b. **Una** died.

30) THEME subjects:

a. **Joan** fell of the yacht.

b. **The arrow** flew through the air.

31) INSTRUMENT subjects:

a. **The key** opened the lock.

b. **The scalpel** made a very clean cut.

Some scholars have suggested that the possibility for each thematic role to occupy the subject position is not the same. It is of a hierarchical nature, not only in English but across many languages. The observation is that when speakers are constructing a sentence, they tend to place an AGENT into subject position, the next preference being for a RECIPIENT, BENEFACTIVE or EXPERIENCER, then THEME/PATIENT, then other roles. It is assumed that this is universal in almost all languages, and is therefore described as a universal subject hierarchy: AGENT > RECIPIENT/BENEFACTIVE/EXPERIENCER > THEME/PATIENT > INSTRUMENT > LOCATION.

This diagram can be read in two equivalent ways: one is that the leftmost elements are the preferred, most basic and expected subjects, while moving rightward along the string gives us less expected subjects. A second way to read this diagram is as a kind of rule of expectation, going from right to left: if a language allows the LOCATION role to be subject, we expect that it allows those roles to the left. If, however, it allows the role INSTRUMENT to be subject, we expect that it allows those roles to the left, but we don't know if it allows the LOCATION role as subject. The idea is that languages can differ in what roles they allow to occur as subject but they will obey this sequence of preference, without any gaps. So, for example, we should not find a language that allows AGENT and INSTRUMENT to be subject but not THEME/PATIENT.

The matching between thematic roles and other sentence elements (e.g. the object, adverbials, etc.) is relatively straightforward. Interested readers may give an analysis of it by themselves.

6.4 Problems with thematic roles

In 6.2 we present a list of thematic roles. While these roles, AGENT, PATIENT, EXPERIENCER, THEME, INSTRUMENT etc., may seem intuitively clear, in practice it is sometimes difficult to know which role to assign to a particular noun phrase. For example, in a sentence like 32) below is *Mary* the GOAL/RECIPIENT, or the BENEFICIARY, or both?

32) **Mary** received a gift of flowers.

And in 33), is *Mr. Wheeler* both AGENT and THEME?

33) **Mr. Wheeler** jumped off the cliff.

Examples like these raise the difficult question of whether a single entity can fulfill two or more thematic roles at the same time. This implies that the boundary between some thematic roles is not clear-cut. Earlier we defined PATIENT as the entity affected by some action, often undergoing some change in state. However, as the effect or affectedness an entity undergoes tends to vary in different degrees, from slight to great, extent of the change of state varies accordingly. The question is: where is the exact point of affectedness or change of state by which we can definitely define the role of PATIENT?

The semanticist Dixon (1991: 102-113) identifies eight types of affectedness: a range including the minimal contact of the verb *touch* in 34)a, where possibly no change occurs in the PATIENT, through *rub* in 34)b, where the surface of the PATIENT might be affected, *squeeze* in 34)c where a temporary change of shape in the PATIENT occurs, and *smash* in 34)d, where the PATIENT loses its physical integrity, to *melt* in 34)e, where the PATIENT has disappeared, as the ice has changed into water.

34) a. John touched the **lamp** with his toe.
b. The captain rubbed **the cricket ball** with dirt.
c. Henry squeezed **the rubber duck** in his hands.
d. Alison smashed **the ice cube** with her heel.
e. The sun melted **the ice**.

As the bold-faced entities from 34)a to e undergo different degrees of effect by some action, can they all be defined as PATIENT? What follows is how do we define thematic roles in general? That is, what semantic basis do we have for characterizing roles?

Facing these problems, Dowty (1991) proposes a solution where thematic roles are not semantic primitives but are defined in terms of **entailments** of the predicate. This view of semantic roles as cluster of entailments can be used to solve the problem of the fuzziness of roles. Dowty proposes that we view the roles not as discrete and bounded categories but instead as prototypical categories, where there may be different degrees of membership. He suggests that there are two basic prototypes: Proto-Agent and Proto-Patient, each of which would contain characteristic lists of entailments as shown below (Dowty, 1991: 572):

35) Properties of the Agent Proto-Role
a. volitional involvement in the event or state
b. sentience (and/or perception)
c. causing an event or change of state in another participant
d. movement (relative to the position of another participant)

36) Properties of the Patient Proto-Role
a. undergoes change of state
b. incremental theme
c. causally affected by another participant
d. stationary relative to movement of another participant

Incremental theme is one type of the THEME role proposed by Dowty (1991). It usually follows the verbs which indicate achievement and accomplishment, e.g. *mow the lawn*, *eat an egg*, *build a house*, *demolish a building*. The observation is that the action (for example, the mowing action) and the state of the associated THEME/PATIENT (e.g. the lawn) are in a proportional relationship: some mowing cuts some of the grass, more mowing, more of the grass, etc. until completing the action cuts all of the grass.

The idea behind 35) and 36) is that thematic roles are composed of lists of entailments and the clusters of entailments for Agent Proto-Role and Patient Proto-Role would allow various kinds of shading. For example some participants might have more of the entailments than others. So, for example, *John* in *John cleaned the house* would include all four of the entailments in 35) above: volition, sentience, causation and movement. By contrast *John* in *John fainted and dropped the vase* would involve no volition, and *the storm* in *The storm destroyed the house* would involve neither sentience nor volition. We can see that this approach allows variation amongst AGENTS: some will be more typical and involve a greater number of characteristic entailments; others will be more marginal. Similar variation would hold for PATIENTS.

This way of describing thematic roles allows flexibility in defining the roles. One result of the classification of Agent Proto-Role and Patient Proto-Role is that traditional role-types fall out as more-or-less prototypical versions of the two main categories, as 37) shows.

37) a. **Maggie** pruned **the roses**.
 b. **Joan** felt the heat as the aircraft door opened.
 c. **The knife** cut through the bag.
 d. Roberto watched **the game**.

In 37)a *Maggie* involves all four entailments in 35): volition, sentience, causation and movement, so it is a centrally prototypical AGENT; in 37)b *Joan*, an EXPERIENCER, can be seen as a more marginal AGENT, including sentience but not volition or causation; *the knife* in 37)c, an INSTRUMENT, only includes causation and movement but not volition or sentience.

Similarly *the roses* in 37)a involves all four entailments in 36) above, so it is a centrally prototypical PATIENT, but *the game* in 37)d, a PERCET, does not undergo a change of state nor is causally affected, it can only be considered to be a marginal PATIENT.

6.5 The motivation for identifying thematic roles

In the above sections, we discussed issues related to thematic roles. People may ask why it is necessary for linguists to identify thematic roles. From our discussion so far we can conclude some reasons to identify thematic roles.

Firstly, thematic roles can be employed to describe aspects of the interface between semantics and syntax, in particular to characterize the links between the semantic classification of its participants that is inherent in a verb's meaning and the grammatical relations it supports. For example, when we use an English verb *feel* in *Mary felt the heat as soon as the aircraft door was opened*, we identify a relationship between an EXPERIENCER and a PERCEPT. This can be viewed as one of many conventional ways of viewing relations that is coded in the language. Grammatically the verb *feel* is transitive, taking a subject and direct object. As we have seen, one fact we have to account for is that there is a conventional linkage between the participant roles and the grammatical relations, such that in this case the EXPERIENCER will be subject and the PERCEPT, direct object.

Secondly, thematic roles can be used to help characterize semantic verbal classes. For example we can identify in English two classes of psychological verbs both of which take two arguments (i.e. are transitive), one of which is an EXPERIENCER and the other a STIMULUS. The classes differ however in their linking between these two roles and subject and object position. The first class has the thematic role grid or theta grid, a term from Generative Grammar, in 38)a below, and can be exemplified by the verbs in 38)b, while the second class has the theta grid in 39)a and includes verbs like those in 39)b:

38) Psychological verbs type 1

a. V: <EXPERIENCER, STIMULUS>

b. *admire*, *enjoy*, *fear*, *like*, *love*, *relish*, *savour*

39) Psychological verbs type 2

a. V: <STIMULUS, EXPERIENCER>

b. *amuse*, *entertain*, *frighten*, *interest*, *please*, *surprise*, *thrill*

Thus we say *Jim liked the result* but *The result pleased Jim*.

Thirdly, the classifications of verbs exemplified above can help predict the grammatical processes individual verbs will undergo. Thus, though the motivation for grammatical rules is often multifactorial, theta-role grids have been used to describe argument changing processes like **passive**, as we shall discuss in the next section, or argument structure alternations like those in 40) and 41) below, where in each case the example sentences are in a, the link between theta-grids and syntactic arguments is given in b, and some example verbs in c:

40) a. He banged the broom-handle on the ceiling.
He banged the ceiling with the broom-handle.
She tapped the can against the window.
She tapped the window with the can.

b. V: <AGENT, INSTRUMENT & THEME, LOCATION>
NP NP PP

V: <AGENT, LOCATION, INSTRUMENT & THEME>
NP NP PP

c. *bang*, *bash*, *beat*, *hit*, *knock*, *pound*, *rap*, *tap*, *whack*

41) a. The whole community will benefit from the peace process.
The peace process will benefit the whole community.

b. V: <BENEFICIARY, SOURCE>
NP PP

V: <SOURCE, BENEFICIARY>
NP NP

c. *benefit*, *profit*

These alternations are just two of a large range that have been identified for English. The conditional factors for such alternations are often a mix of semantic information, such as the verb's meaning and its theta-grid, and its syntactic environment.

6.6 Voice

The category of **voice** adds new dimensions to the relationship between thematic roles and grammatical relations. It affords speakers some flexibility in viewing thematic roles. Let us observe and compare the following sentences:

42) a. The girl watered the flowers.
b. The flowers were watered by the girl.

c. The flowers were watered.

In 42)a *the girl*, the AGENT, is the subject, and *the flowers*, the PATIENT, is the object. In the passive version 42)b, the PATIENT becomes the subject and the AGENT is in a prepositional phrase. This is a typical active-passive voice alternation: the passive sentence has a verb in a different form — the past participle with the auxiliary verb *be* — and it allows the speaker a different perspective on the situation described. This passive sentence allows the speaker to describe the situation from the point of view of the PATIENT rather than that of the AGENT. In 42)c the AGENT is omitted to obscure the identity of an AGENT.

Passive constructions also allow the foregrounding of a role that is not PATIENT. Or they allow the speaker to view a situation from the perspective of other thematic roles. In the following examples, THEME, PERCEPT, BENEFICIARY and RECIPIENT roles act as the subject of the passive constructions:

43) **This money** was donated to the church. (THEME subject)

44) **The explosion** was seen by just three people. (PERCEPT subject)

45) **He** was given a camera by his grandmother. (RECIPIENT subject)

46) **Monica** was voted for last year. (BENEFICIARY subject)

It should be noted subject and thematic role are not the same thing. Jackendoff (1990: 49) points out that there is no thematic role of subject. Subject is a syntactic relation, not a conceptual one, and syntactic subjects can hold a variety of different thematic roles. The thematic roles function in terms of the meanings of verbs and prepositions.

6.7 Summary

In this chapter we talked about the ways in which a speaker may portray the roles of participants in a situation. We outlined a classification of such semantic roles, termed **thematic roles** or **theta-roles**, including AGENT, PATIENT, THEME, etc. and described the relationship between these roles and grammatical relations like **subject** and **object**. It has been claimed that as part of its inherent lexical specification a verb requires its arguments to be in specific thematic roles, and that this can be reflected by formulating thematic role **grids**, or **theta-grids**. We discussed the difficulties there are in fixing tight definitions for individual thematic roles, and presented one approach, from Dowty (1991), which seeks to provide a solution in terms of fuzzy categories. We also presented several reasons for identifying thematic roles.

The last point we came to concerns how the grammatical category of **voice** allows speakers different strategies for relating thematic roles and grammatical relations. We mainly focused on relations with **subject** position, in particular the way in which **passive voice** allows the foregrounding of non-AGENT roles to subject and the backgrounding of AGENT roles away from subject.

Chapter 7 Context and inference: a pragmatic study of meaning 1

In chapter 1, we discussed the relationship between semantics and pragmatics. One suggested proposal is that while both areas of study are concerned with meaning, semantics is the study of conventional, linguistic meaning and pragmatics is the study of how we use this linguistic knowledge in context. In this view, pragmatics is the study of how hearers, for example, have to combine semantic knowledge with other types of knowledge and make inferences in order to interpret a speaker' s meaning. In this chapter we focus on areas of meaning where there is a very clear evidence of this combination of different types of knowledge. By doing this we move our attention to the study of language use and to what are therefore, for many linguists, pragmatic aspects of meaning. We begin with deixis.

7.1 Deixis

The term **deixis**, a noun, derives from classical Greek *deiknymi*, which means "to show, point out". This term, as defined by J. Lyons (1977: 636), refers to "the function of personal and demonstrative pronouns, of tense and of a variety of other grammatical and lexical features which relate utterances to the spatio-temporal co-ordinates of the act of utterance". That is, deixis is the function of grammatical as well as lexical means relating a piece of language to its context in terms of its users, the time and place of its occurrence, and the people and objects it refers to. The words used in this function are known as **deictics**. Typical examples are pronouns, demonstratives, time and place adverbs, and some grammatical categories such as tense.

The interpretation of deictics relies heavily on context. In sentence 1), the pronouns *I, it* and *him* are expressions that refer to some people and objects respectively.

1) I gave it to him.

The information who and what they refer to can be retrieved only from the context of utterance rather from the sentence alone. Likewise, if sentence 2) is said in pitch-darkness, it will be hard to determine the referents of the deictics *you* and *this*:

2) Listen, I'm not agreeing with you but with you and not about this but about this.

Every language in the world has a deictic system. In terms of the semantic content of deictic words, deixis has been classified into five types: place deixis, person deixis, time deixis, discourse deixis and social deixis.

7.1.1 Place deixis

Place deixis is also called spatial deixis. It is used to indicate the spatial relations between the speaker and the referred object or place. Typical place deictics include place adverbs *here, there, in(side), out(side), up(stairs), down(stairs), nearby, far away, opposite, behind*, etc. Such deictic devices in a language commit a speaker to set up a frame of reference around himself. Every language carries an implicit division of space around the current speaker, a division of time relative to the act of speaking, and, via pronouns, a referring system for the participants involved in the talk.

Adverbs of location can be used deictically as in 3):

3) You stand *here*, Jim stand *there* — twenty meters away from here.

The adverbs *here* and *there* pick out places according to their proximity to the location of the speaker.

Demonstratives work in a similar way: English has a two-term opposition between *this/these*, and *that/those*. Once again the current speaker occupies the reference point: items closer to him will be described as *this/these*, items further away as *that/those*. While languages contain such deictic divisions of space, their use has to be calculated by the participants in actual contexts. For example, how big an area is meant by *here* depends on context: a speaker might use *here* to refer to a country, a city, a room, a part of a room, a particular point, etc. This plasticity is inherent: the use of *here* does not even always have to include the location of the speaker. We can use *here* pointing to locations on a map, but there will be an actual or implicit contrast with *there*, a place further way from the speaker.

Other languages divide the space around the speaker differently, for example Spanish has a three-term distinction: *esto* "this", *eso* "that" (just there), and *aquello* "that" (over there). These demonstratives can be used to give three zones of proximity to the speaker as shown in 4). They can also be used to relate to the position of an addressee as in 5):

4) *speaker

near speaker	further away	furthest from speaker →
esto	*eso*	*aquello*

5) *esto* "close to the speaker"
eso "close to the addressee"
aquello "distant from both"

Languages differ in both how many divisions of space are coded in their demonstratives and what other information is obligatorily included. The cross-linguistic differences demonstrate that different semantic information is grammaticalized or lexicalized in different languages (Saeed, 1997: 175-177).

The examples so far have been of deictic elements relating to location and proximity relative to the speaker. Deictic elements may also include information about motion towards and away from the speaker. For example, the comparison between *come* and *go* in 6) and 7) below tells us something about the location of the speaker:

6) Don't come into my bedroom. (The speaker is in the bedroom.)

7) Don't go into my bedroom. (The speaker is not in the bedroom.)

Some languages have specific deictic motion morphemes: Somali for example has two: *soo* "towards the speaker" and *sii* "away from the speaker", which combine freely with verbs, as in 8):

8) a. *Soo soco*!
DEIC walk
"Come this way! Approach!"

b. *Sii soco*!
DEIC walk
"Go on over there! Go away!"

From examples 6) and 7) we can see that the different information conveyed by the deictic motion morphemes *soo* and *sii* in 8) has been incorporated respectively into the meanings of the English verbs *come* and *go*.

7.1.2 Person deixis

Person deixis grammaticalizes the roles of participants: the current speaker, addressee(s) and others. This information is grammaticalized by pronouns: typically a first person singular pronoun is used for the speaker, second person pronouns for addressee(s) and minimally, a third person category for a category "neither-speaker-nor-addressee(s)". This basic three-way system is the basis of most pronoun systems but once again languages differ in the amount of other contextual information that is included in pronouns. We can show this with a comparison of Arabic and English person pronoun systems, using just subject pronouns for brevity.

English pronouns:

Singular	**Plural**	**Singular or Plural**
I	we	you
he	they	
she		
it		

Arabic pronouns:

Singular	**Dual**	**Plural**
'anna "I"		*nahnu* "we"
'anta "thou (m)"	*'antumaa* "you (two)"	*'antum* "you (m)"
'anti "thou (f)"		*'antunna* "you (f)"
huwa "he, it"	*humaa* "they (two)"	*hum* "they (m)"
hiya "she, it"	*hunna* "they (f)"	

We can see that the Arabic pronouns encode more information about number than the English pronouns: there is an extra category *dual*, which is used for "exactly two". The coding of gender is also different: English has a neuter pronoun "it" which does not occur in Arabic, where all third persons have to have either masculine or feminine gender. On the other hand, Arabic pronouns encode gender more widely: English only distinguishes between *he* and *she*, so both languages have an economic and "portable" reference system for participants that can be used in any context, but we can see that the packaging of information about participants differs.

One point worth mentioning here is that in English the first person plural *we* differs from the second and third person plurals in that it does not stand in the same relationship to *I* as *they* to *he/she/it* or singular *you* to plural *you*. It is to be interpreted as "I, in addition to one or more other persons" (I + he/she/it), not as "more than one I" (I + I + I...). There can be only one speaker. It is impossible for many people to say exactly the same thing at the same time. When a speaker uses *we*, what he means is that he is acting as the spokesman, there are others who share his position.

Also, the English *we* can be inclusive or exclusive of the addressee. For example,

9) If *we* don't teach well you can refuse to attend our class. (exclusive *we*)

10) *We* complemented ourselves too soon, John. (inclusive *we*)

Obviously, in English to determine whether *we* includes the addressee or not, we must resort to the context in which it is used. This kind of information, however, is conveyed in two different first person plural pronouns in some languages. The Ethiopian Omotic language Zayse, for example, has two distinct first person plural pronouns, as shown below (Hayward, 1990):

núy "we" (including the addressee(s))

níi "we" (not including the addressee(s))

Thus in Zayse, saying the equivalent of "We're going to the party" overtly communicates whether the addressee is included, whereas English speakers have to rely on the context.

7.1.3 Time deixis

Time deixis is used to indicate time relations relative to the time of speaking. Time deixis is mainly performed by time adverbials like *now, then, today, tomorrow*, and expressions formed by units of time *morning, afternoon, week, month*, or their names *Monday, January* together with *this, that, last, next.* It is impossible to specify the time for the deictic expressions unless we know the exact time when the expressions are uttered.

In languages like English where there is a tense system, tense is also said to be a means of time deixis, since the reference point for the system is usually the act of speaking. So in English, we have the three tenses: past, future and present.

More complicated time references are possible. For example the speaker can locate an event in the past or future and use that event as the reference point for its own past, present and future. To do this in English complex tenses are used. If a speaker in 1945 said, for example:

11) By 1939 my father had seen several arrests.

the verb *had seen* is one of these complex tenses, called the **pluperfect**. The year 1939 is in the past of the utterance of course, but the speaker has made it the anchoring point for its own past. The father's acts of seeing are marked as being in this secondary past, as well as in the past relative to the act of speaking.

Complex future tenses like *will have been* allow a similar creation of a past-of-a-future-event, as in an utterance like 12):

12) By 2050 we will have experienced at least two major earthquakes.

Here of course the earthquakes are portrayed as in the past relative to 2050, but in the future relative to the act of speaking.

7.1.4 Discourse deixis

Discourse deixis, also known as textual deixis, is not one of the basic deictic categories. By means of this device we can refer to portions of discourse. Expressions like *in the last paragraph, in the next chapter, this story*, sentence-initial *therefore, in conclusion, anyway, all in all*, are discourse deictics, where the reference is relative to the utterance. There are also cases of the use of pronouns such as *it* in 13), which, for the lack of a better category, we call discourse-deictic:

13) I keep *my car* in the garage but my next-door neighbour keeps *it* in his drive.

It, the so-called **pronoun of laziness**, is in a sloppy relation to the antecedent; there is no referential identity here. It is sometimes called discourse-deictic as it refers to the chunk of discourse, the noun phrase that would otherwise have to be repeated with the necessary qualifications (*his car*).

7.1.5 Social deixis

Social deixis is the use of deictic terms for indicating social status of the participants in a discourse, and their relations determined thereupon. The terms mainly used in social deixis are personal pronouns and terms of address.

The pronoun systems of some languages have grammaticalized information about the social identities or relationships of the participants in the conversation. The most obvious example is the distinction in many languages between "familiar" and "polite" pronouns, e.g. *tu/vous* in French, *tu/usted* in Spanish, *du/sie* in German, *dei/vei* in Russian, and *ni*（你）/*nin*（您）in Chinese. Speakers of these languages are committed to revealing their calculations of relative intimacy and formality to their addressees.

Vocatives are another area in which the social relations between participants are clearly manifested. Whether you call somebody by the official title, the full name, the first name, or the nickname, reflects directly the social distance between you two.

7.1.6 Grammaticalization of contextual information

So far we have discussed the different types of deixis. From the discussion we can see that languages vary in the type of semantic information that is obligatorily included in deictic terms. When semantic distinctions are obligatory in this way we will say that they are **grammaticalized**. An informal distinction has been made between, on the one hand, the obligatory "wired-in" ways a language divides up space, time, person, etc. in its function words (like demonstratives and pronouns) or its morphology, and on the other hand, the ability which seems to exist in all languages to talk about any division of space, time, person, etc. by paraphrase. Thus we can use the latter ability to provide English translations for a single addressee in Arabic (i.e. '*anta* or '*anti*) which obligatorily includes information about gender. In Arabic there is no "you (singular)" pronoun which does not include a gender specification and the two pronouns for a single addressee (i.e. '*anta* and '*anti*) also have corresponding verbal forms. English on the other hand does not distinguish the gender of the addressee in its pronouns and verbal morphology. To come back to our distinction, this does not mean, of course, that English speakers cannot make reference to the gender of an addressee, merely that this information is not obligatory, i.e. grammaticalized. It can be seen that in our discussion of deixis above we are only concerned with cases where contextual features are grammaticalized in language.

7.1.7 Metaphorical relationship between space, time and discourse deixis

Space deixis, time deixis and discourse deixis are closely related. It is now widely accepted that time deixis and discourse deixis are metaphorical extensions of place deixis. Systems of spatial deixis are commonly used in other domains. Firstly, systems of spatial deixis are often used as a form of orientation within a discourse, where they are called **discourse** or **textual deixis** (see 7.1.4). For example,

14) **Here** our argument runs into some difficulties.

15) **At this point** we have to look back to our initial premises.

16) "High" and "tall" are synonymous: **this** may be used in speaking of what grows — a tree; **that** in speaking of what does not grow — a mountain.

17) Struggle and submission are before the colonial people: **this** leads to slavery, **that** to freedom.

Secondly, spatial deixis terms, such as demonstratives, are extended to refer to time. An example of this use of the demonstratives is below:

18) **That** year was much hotter than **this** one is.

This transference is often described as a metaphorical shift from the more concrete domain of physical space to the more abstract domain of time and discourse. It is a general human tendency to extend spatial terms in this way to a range of other linguistic domains. A commonly used example is languages where semantic notions like possession and states are expressed spatially, as in the Irish examples below:

19) Tá Porsche agam.
is Porsche at me
"I have a Porsche."

20) Tá slaghdán orm.
is cold on me
"I have a cold."

21) Tá gliondar orm.
is delight on me
"I am delighted."

In 19) possession is expressed spatially, while in 20) and 21) physical and emotional states are so expressed. A more complicated example which is sometimes quoted is the use of the verb *go* in English and other languages for immediate future tenses as in the future tense reading of *He is going to call a meeting to discuss it*, where the idea of spatial movement away from the speaker is mapped into time as a future event.

The extension of space to other domains is systematically investigated in cognitive linguistics, a relatively young branch of study, under topics such as conceptual metaphor and image schema. We will come to this point again in chapter 10.

7.2 Reference and context

Deictic expressions have been extensively studied, but it would be wrong to see their context-dependence as exceptional, as a special part of language. Much of reference involves reliance on context, together with some calculation on the part of the speaker and hearers. A clear example of this is the use of what Clark (1978) calls **short-hands**. The following is an example of Saeed (1997) from his own experience:

22) It's a struggle keeping the barnacles from off the crops.

This is a sentence he heard when he turned on the radio. At first the referent of the noun phrase *the barnacles* was a confusion to him. After a while of listening it became clear that *the barnacles* was a short-hand for *the barnacle geese*. The reference would have been clear, of course, if he had listened from the beginning of the programme. This example, on the one hand, shows that information from linguistic context plays an essential role in determining the reference of a linguistic expression, and on the other hand, reveals what is characteristic of normal language use: speakers calculate how much their hearers need to make successful references, and where they can, they economize. Let us look at two more examples:

23) Dickens is on the top shelf.

24) He's got two reds left.

The speaker of 23) obviously feels that *Dickens* is sufficient for the hearer to identify *the books by Dickens*. 24) is said during a snooker game. Also the speaker is confident that the hearer can infer from the game situation what *two reds* refers to.

Short-hands are sometimes grouped with the rhetorical devices **metonymy** and **synecdoche**. The former is where we identify the referent by something associated with it, as in 25) below:

25) a. **The kettle**'s boiling.
    b. Who were all **those suits** drinking in the pub last night?
    c. **Washington** is negotiating with **Moscow**.
    d. Have you cleared this deal with **the top floor**?

Synecdoche is a form of reference where the part stands for the whole, as in 26):

26) a. All of his cattle are affected; he'll lose more than fifty **head**.
    b. We need some new **faces** around here.
    c. We need a couple of strong **bodies** for our team.

The use of technical terms like **short-hands**, **metonymy** and **synecdoche** has the advantage that it suggests that these are rhetorical devices, special uses of language, whereas they are just specific examples of the routine calculation involved in making reference. They seem to be produced and understood naturally and spontaneously. In cognitive linguistics metonymy and synecdoche are listed under the general term **metonymy** or **conceptual metonymy** which is considered to be conceptual in nature, conventionalized and can be explained as mapping processes. We shall turn to this in chapter 10.

We can further illustrate the above use of context and calculation with a hypothetical situation where someone wants to buy two bottles of Qingdao beer. In a pub, he might say *Two bottles of Qingdao, please!* In a theatre bar, where only bottled beer is available, his order might be: *Two Qingdaos, please!*

At a sponsor's stall at an open-air concert, which only serves Qingdao beer, in bottle or on draught, he could say: *Two bottles, please!* If the stall only sold bottles, he might say just *Two please!*. The point here is that the ordinary use of referring expressions involves calculations of retrievability, which take account of contextual information.

7.3 Knowledge as context

These calculations of retrievability are really guesses about knowledge: a speaker choosing how to make reference to an entity must make estimations of what his hearers know. So if someone were to rush up to you and shout:

27) The baby's swallowed the canary!

his choice of words reveals that he thinks you can identify both the baby and the canary involved (Note "the canary" is ambiguous here!). To discuss the role of knowledge it is useful to divide it into different types. We might distinguish between three different sources for the knowledge a speaker has to estimate:

(1) that computable from the physical or situational context;

(2) that available from what has already been said, i.e. from the linguistic or discoursal context;

(3) that available from background or common knowledge.

Let us examine them one by one.

7.3.1 Situation as context

Under this heading we can put the knowledge gained from filling in the deictic expressions, i.e. who is speaking to whom, the time and location of the conversation. For example,

28) I don't like her, I like her.

In this example, if the two "hers" refer to two different girls, situational information will be of vital importance for making clear which girl each "girl" identifies. And the speaker may have to resort to gestures if he wants to refer successfully. Similarly, in example 29) the reference has to be made with a certain movement of the hands and arms indicating the desired size of the room; usually, this presupposes that one can see the speaker and identify his movements.

29) I need a room this big.

Example 30) also illustrates how situational context determines the interpretation of a lexical item:

30) Mother: Haven't you got a knife, Billy?
Billy: (at table, fingering his meat: has penknife in his pocket, but no knife of the appropriate type)

Although Billy does have a knife (a penknife), the context (sitting at the meal table) stipulates that it is not a knife of the appropriate kind. In other words, the situational context narrows down the meaning of knife to CUTLERY KNIFE.

7.3.2 Discourse as context

Discourse itself serves as a context, affecting sentence and word-level interpretation, tipping the interpretation of what would otherwise be ambiguous words or phrases in a certain direction. For example, some sentences can be interpreted literally (according to the standard usage of the words) or figuratively (by deviating from what we understand to be the standard significance of the words for some special meaning or effect). Discourse as a context can prompt readers to engage in one or the other.

When we are trying to understand a sentence, we often make use of information that is not contained directly within the sentence itself. As mentioned above the information may come from a linguistic or discoursal context, situational context, or background knowledge context. Here we, of course, will only consider the role of information from linguistic or discoursal context in the interpretation of linguistic expressions. Let us first look at the following examples:

31) a. Who broke the window?
b. John did.

32) a. I'm thirsting.
b. Me too.

In isolation, sentence fragments like *John did* or *Me too* cannot be interpreted, but in the right conversational context they are meaningful. Participants would have no difficulty interpreting *John did* as *John broke the window*; or *Me too* as *I'm thirsting too*. Clearly the preceding discourse licenses these interpretations.

We can see another example of the role of the discourse itself as context when we look at the notion of **discourse topic**. It seems clear that in conversing, participants construct a notion of what the discourse is about — a kind of current topic. This topic is a form of knowledge which then influences the way they interpret the meaning of what they subsequently hear. There have been a number of experiments which support this picture. One simple one is described by Brown and Yule (1983: 139-140), from a study by Anderson et al. (1977). Subjects were asked to read the story in 33) below, with the "prisoner" title, then asked questions about it.

33) A Prisoner Plans His Escape

Rocky slowly got up from the mat, planning his escape. He hesitated a moment and thought. Things were not going well. What bothered him was being held, especially since the charge against him had been weak. He considered his present situation. The lock that held him was strong, but he thought he could break it.

We can read this text with the interpretation that Rocky is a prisoner, in a cell, planning to break the lock on the door and escape. The answers of the subjects to the questions about the text revealed that there was a general interpretation among them that Rocky was alone, that he had been arrested by the police, and that he disliked being in prison. When the same text was presented under another title, the "Wrestler" title in 34) below, other subjects gave quite different answers to questions on this fragment. They indicated that they thought Rocky was a wrestler who was being held in some kind of wrestling "hold" and was planning to get out of this hold. In this interpretation there is no prison-cell and no police.

34) A Wrestler in a Tight Corner

Rocky slowly got up from the mat, planning his escape. He hesitated a moment and thought. Things were not going well. What bothered him was being held, especially since the charge against him had been weak. He considered his present situation. The lock that held him was strong, but he thought he could break it.

The main point here is that listeners add their own inferences when they interpret utterances, fleshing out the materials in ways that depend on knowledge provided by the discourse topic.

John Bransford and Johnson (1973: 400) did a similar experiment. They gave their subjects the passage in the panel below:

35) The procedure is actually quite simple. First you arrange items into different groups. Of course one pile may be sufficient depending on how much there is to do. If you have to go somewhere else due to lack of facilities, that is the next step; otherwise, you are pretty well set. It is important not to overdo things. That is, it is better to do too few things at once rather than too many. In the short run this may not seem important but complications can easily arise. A mistake can be expensive as well. At first, the whole procedure will seem complicated. Soon, however, it will become just another facet of life. It is difficult to foresee any end to the necessity for this task in the immediate future, but then, one never can tell. After the procedure is completed one arranges the materials into their appropriate places. Eventually, they will be used once more and the whole cycle will then have to be repeated. However, that is part of life.

Subjects who were given this passage on its own found it (as you probably did) difficult to comprehend. Those who were provided with an appropriate context in the form of the title, "Washing Clothes", on the other hand, found the same passage reasonably easy to understand.

Evans (2006) introduced the concept of **facet** when discussing the effect of linguistic context, or to use Evans's term, sentential context on the interpretation of a particular expression. A facet is a sense that is due to the part-whole structure of an entity, and is selected by a specific sentential context. Facets are context-dependent because the distinctions between facets only arise in certain sentential contexts. For example, consider the lexical item *book*. By virtue of its structure, the concept BOOK consists of both TEXT (the informational content of a book) and TOME (the physical entity consisting of pages and binding). These two meanings are facets which only become apparent in certain sentential contexts. Consider the examples in 36).

36) a. That book is really thick.

b. That book is really interesting.

The example in 36)a refers to the TOME facet of *book* while 36)b refers to the TEXT facet. Observe that it is sentential context (the presence of the expressions *thick* versus *interesting*) rather than context of use that induces a particular facet.

7.3.3 Background knowledge as context

This type of knowledge has been called many things, including background, common-sense, encyclopaedic, socio-cultural, and real-world knowledge. What is usually meant is the knowledge a speaker might calculate others would have before, or independently of, a particular conversation, by virtue of membership in a community. Each community implies certain types of knowledge that are shared by all the members in it and which conversationalists must seek to calculate as they interact. We can use an example that is so obvious that we may not notice its reliance on cultural knowledge:

37) A: I'm hungry.

B: I'll lend you some money.

This exchange gains coherence from the knowledge that money can be exchanged for food, which is cultural knowledge not present in any reasonable dictionary entry for the words *food* or *money*. Much of the fleshing out of an utterance via inference that we mentioned above relies on this kind of background knowledge. To take another invented exchange, in 38):

38) A: Shall we go and get some ice cream?

B: I'm on a diet.

Here speaker A might be reasonably infer that B's reply is a refusal; that B's reply implies "No". We will look at the use of such implications in section 7.6, but what's important here is that the implication and inference both rely on cultural knowledge about diets and ice cream. The fact that it is cultural knowledge which is providing the basis for the inference can be shown by using an example that is less familiar to English speakers, like the exchange in 39) below:

39) A: Come over next week for lunch.

B: It's Ramadan.

If A and B are Muslims then A will probably infer that B's reply means "No". If A is not a Muslim then he will probably have some difficulty in catching B's real intention.

Background knowledge also plays an important role in resolving ambiguity in a sentence. This point has been discussed in detail in chapter 3, so we will not go any further with it here. Interested readers may turn to 3.2 for what they want to know.

7.3.4 Giving background knowledge to computers

The importance of background knowledge to language understanding was quickly recognized in the field of Artificial Intelligence (AI). One typical application is the design of computer programs to process and store information from texts, e.g. newspaper articles, so that users can later interrogate the databases. These programs quickly revealed the extent to which human readers make inferences to gain an understanding of a text; inferences that are often based on background knowledge. Various forms of knowledge representation have been proposed to model this background information. Roger Schank and his colleagues (Schank and Abelson, 1977; Cullingford, 1978) devised scripts to do this. Scripts are descriptions of what typically goes on in various social settings. One well-known example is a restaurant **script** of which 40) below is a simplified version (written in English rather than a computer language) (Schank and Kass, 1988: 190):

40) a. Actor goes to a restaurant.
   b. Actor is seated.
   c. Actor orders a meal from waiter.
   d. Waiter brings meal to the actor.
   e. Actor eats the meal.
   f. Actor gives money to the restaurant.
   g. Actor leaves the restaurant.

In this very basic script the underlined elements are variables that have to be filled in from any specific restaurant text the script is applied to. A fuller script than 40), with more details of what goes on in a typical restaurant, allowed the computer program Script Applier Mechanism (SAM), to interpret a text about a restaurant visit by using inferences to fill in the gaps in the text. Such a text is in 41) below with an interpretation in 42) (both based on Schank and Abelson, 1977), which includes inferences based on the script in 40):

41) John went to a restaurant. The waiter gave John a menu. The waiter came to the table. John ordered a lobster. John was served quickly. John left a large tip.

42) John went to a restaurant. John looked for a table. John went to the table. John sat down in the chair. John got the menu from the waiter. John read the menu. The waiter went to the table. John ordered lobster. The cook prepared the lobster. The waiter got the lobster from the cook. The waiter served John the lobster. John ate the lobster. John indicated to the waiter he would like to get the bill from him. John got the bill from the waiter. John left the waiter a large tip. John paid the bill. John left the restaurant.

As can be seen, inferences based on a script allow a much fuller version of what went on in the visit than is explicit in the text, and SAM is then able to respond to questions about the visit, as shown in an example interrogation 43) (based on Schank and Abelson, 1977):

43) Q: What did John eat?
A: LOBSTER.
Q: Who gave John the menu?
A: THE WAITER.
Q: Who gave John the lobster?
A: PROBABLY THE WAITER.
Q: Who paid the bill?
A: PROBABLY JOHN.
Q: What happened when John went to the table?
A: JOHN SAT DOWN AND THE WAITER GAVE HIM A MENU.
Q: Why did John get a menu?
A: SO HE COULD ORDER.
Q: Why did John give the waiter a large tip?
A: BECAUSE HE WAS SERVED QUICKLY.

In subsequent work Schank and his colleagues have developed this approach further, replacing scripts with knowledge representations which are more flexible and which share components more easily; see Schank and Kass (1988) for a brief overview.

7.4 Information structure

We have been looking at how different types of knowledge provide a contextual background for understanding utterances, and at how speakers routinely make guesses about the knowledge accessible to their listeners. In this section we will briefly examine how linguistic structure reflects these guesses, or to put it another way: how these estimates of knowledge are grammaticalized. We will see that speakers "package" their utterances to take account of these estimates of knowledge. This packaging is often called **information structure** or, alternatively, **thematic structure**.

Perhaps the most universally grammaticalized distinction is the basic one between the information which the speaker assumes his hearers already know and the information that the speaker is presenting as additional or new. This distinction is ubiquitous and grammaticalized in so many different ways that there are a number of different terminologies describing it. Two of the terminologies most frequently used for the distinction are **given information** and **new information**. The former, the already present knowledge, is what the speaker believes to be known to the hearer (either because it is physically present in the context or because it has already been mentioned in the discourse); the latter, the additional information, is what the speaker believes to be not known to the hearer.

One basic way for a speaker to convey his assumption that something is given is to use a definite nominal. One way to do this in English is to use the definite article *the*; compare for example:

44) a. I'm going to the concert.
    b. I'm going to a concert.

The definite article in 44)a signals that the speaker assumes the hearer can identify the referent, the concert. The normal conversation pattern is for items to be introduced by an indefinite nominal, remain conversationally salient for a time, then fade from salience, perhaps latter to be reintroduced. This is a very complicated and little understood process but a simple sketch might go as follows: a nominal will be introduced with a marker that it is new, perhaps an indefinite noun phrase, as in 45) below:

45) I'm going to **a concert** tonight.

Thereafter a definite article can be used to show that it is now given:

46) **The concert** begins at seven.

If the concert is not mentioned again, it fades from salience and will need to be referred to by various support structures: *that concert, that concert you mentioned*, etc. While an entity is accessible, it can be referred to by pronouns, e.g.

47) The concert begins at seven and **it**'ll go on for hours.

The reference of *it* in 47) is supported by the preceding nominal *the concert*. This relationship of indirect reference is called **anaphora**. The nominal *the concert* is termed the antecedent and the pronoun *it* is termed an **anaphoric pronoun**. There is another kind of relationship of indirect reference which is called **cataphora** where, instead of looking back in a discourse for the interpretation of a pronoun, we look forward for its interpretation. This relationship is exemplified in 48):

48) It's going down quickly, the sun. (*It* refers forwards to *the sun*.)

It should be noted that for hearers to be able to make inference on the basis of such abbreviatory forms as pronouns, they have to be maximally accessible. We can see the parallel between this anaphoric use of pronouns and the **deictic** or **exophoric** use of pronouns, where the referents are also maximally accessible because they are physically present in the context of the utterance, e.g. if the speaker points to someone and says:

49) Look at **him**.

Another marker of information structure in English is intonation, where the assignment of primary stress can be used to bring parts of the sentence into prominence. One of the main functions of this prominence is to mark new information. In the following examples, capitals show this primary stress, and we divide the given and new elements of the sentence:

50) a. JOHN repaired the bicycle.

b. Given: Someone repaired the bicycle.

c. New: It was John.

51) a. John repaired THE BICYCLE.

b. Given: John repaired something.

c. New: It was the bicycle.

52) a. John REPAIRED the bicycle.

b. Given: John did something to the bicycle.

c. New: He repaired it.

What the English intonation system is doing here is allowing the speaker to partition the sentence into two elements: a prominent part and the rest. This prominent part is usually called the **focus**. As we see here, one function of focus is to mark new information. Another function allows the speaker to pick out one of a number of alternatives, as in:

53) a. Did HARRY take the car?

b. No, GOERGE did.

Here both nominals may be activated in the conversation and the focus now has a **contrastive** function.

In other languages this function of intonation is taken over by specific, otherwise meaningless, words which mark elements of the sentence as in focus or not. Somali, for example, has focus words which include the nominal focus particle *baa*, as shown in 53)a and b:

54) a. *Amina baa wargeyskii keentay.*

Amina FOCUS newspaper brought

"**Amina** brought the newspaper, It was Amina who brought the newspaper."

b. *Amina wargeyskii bay keentay.*

baa + ay

Amina newspaper FOCUS + she brought

"Amina brought **the newspaper**, It was the newspaper Amina brought."

This word *baa* follows a nominal and places it in focus. Once again one of the primary uses of this focus system is to mark new information: sentence 54)a fits a conversational context where is was known that someone brought the newspaper and the sentence asserts it was Amina, while in 54)b, it was known that Amina brought something, and the sentence asserts that it was the newspaper she brought.

Another way of marking information structure in English is by syntactic constructions. Certain constructions serve to place parts of the sentence in focus, for example the constructions known as clefts in 55), and the pseudo-cleft in 56), where the focus elements are capitalized:

55) a. It is THE BOY who is petting the cat.
(Given: X is petting the cat; New: X = the boy)
b. It is THE CAT which the boy is petting.
(Given: the boy is petting X; New: X = the cat)

56) What the boy is petting is THE CAT.
(Given: the boy is petting X; New: X = the cat)

Once again we can see that focus is part of information structure: in 55)a and b the basic situation described is the same: *the boy is petting the cat*, but the information is packaged differently to fit different states of participants' knowledge at the specific point in the conversation.

Another way of grammaticalizing given information is achieved through ellipsis. It is quite often that in a discourse what is accessible or known to the hearer will not be verbally expressed any more, as 57) shows:

57) Slice a onion finely, brown ø in the butter and then place ø in a small dish.

The two slots represented by ø can be filled in with the pronoun *it*. If necessary, it is easy for the hearer to tell that the first ø refers to "the onion which has been cut finely" and the second refers to "the onion which has been cut finely and browned in the butter".

Halliday, at a Systemic Workshop in the early seventies of the last century, presented a passage which shows the importance of thematic or information structure to comprehension. The passage is a US radio report describing an official welcome for three astronauts who have completed a successful mission.

58) The sun's shining, it's a perfect day. Here come the astronauts. They're just passing the Great Hall; perhaps the President will come out to greet them. No, it's the admiral who's taking the ceremony...

Halliday then altered the markers of information structure to produce the text in 59):

59) It's the sun that's shining, the day that's perfect. The astronauts come here. The Great Hall they are just passing; he'll come out to greet them the President. No, it's the ceremony that the admiral's taking...

As can be seen, the use of inappropriate markers of information structure, in effect disregarding the reader's evolving state of knowledge, make it hard for the reader to construct a coherent model of what is going on from the text, even though the propositional content is the same as that in 58) and the cohesive links are maintained. The point is of course that in reality speakers continually assess their audience's knowledge, and package their utterances accordingly.

7.5 Inference

Throughout our discussion of the role of context in interpretation, we have seen examples of the way that listeners actively participate in the construction of meaning, in particular by using inferences to fill out the text towards an interpretation of speaker meaning. We now turn to look at examples of conversational inference, first with a general discussion in this section, then with a look at one important approach to inference, conversational implicature, in section 7.6.

We can begin our examples of inference with anaphora. As described above, this is a special sub-type of **co-reference**, a referential relation between expressions where they both refer to the same entity. There are many types of co-reference: a nominal may be repeated as in 60); there may be an independent nominal, used as an epithet as in 61), or very commonly, anaphoric pronoun may be used as in 62). As mentioned earlier, anaphoric pronouns differ from full nominals in that they have no independent reference and must rely on an antecedent for their interpretation.

60) I fell down a hole yesterday. **The hole** was very deep.

61) I saw your uncle this afternoon. **The old fool** still doesn't recognize me.

62) I trod on a slug this morning. **It** died.

Very commonly interpreting anaphora across sentences involves inference.

Take for example the interpretation of the pronoun **it** (shown in bold) in 63) below:

63) The plane was late, the hotel wasn't fully built, there were crowds everywhere she went. I think **it** really disappointed her.

If we are to look for a nominal antecedent for the pronoun *it* in 63), possible candidates are *the plane, the hotel, crowds*. It seems more likely though that it is the whole situation that *it* refers back to: a kind of composite antecedent we could call something like *the holiday*. This cumulative antecedent has to be constructed by the listener. This kind of "sloppy" use of pronouns is very common, but seems to cause listeners no difficulty.

In discussing the phenomenon of co-reference, Halliday and Hasan (1976) proposed a simple substitution view where an expression may simply be replaced by another in the text. Consider their comment on text 64):

64) Wash and core six cooking apples. Put them into a fireproof dish.

"It is clear that *them* in the second sentence refers back to (is ANAPHORIC to) the *six cooking apples* in the first sentence."(1976: 2) However, if we are interested in how readers proceed through such a text, we have to ask whether the expression *them* in the second sentence really simply refers to the *six cooking apples* in the first sentence. Whereas it is indeed those same "six cooking apples" which are at issue in the second sentence, it is relevant to note, and for the reader to understand, that they have undergone a change of state. Whereas in the first sentence they are pristine apples, straight from the supermarket, in the second they are "washed and cored". Their **description** has changed. In order for the reader to understand this, he is unlikely to base his interpretation on the substitution principle. Consider a more violent, constructed example:

65) Kill an active, plump chicken. Prepare it for the oven, cut it into four pieces and roast it with thyme for one hour.

Presumably the **identity** of the chicken is preserved, at least until it is dismembered, but its description has certainly changed. A reader who simply went back up the endophoric chain and substituted the expression *an active*, *plump chicken* for the *it* in the last clause would, in a significant sense, have failed to understand the text.

From the above we can conclude Halliday and Hasan's substitution view is not adequate for explaining co-reference. It is true that in anaphoric reference the anaphoric pronoun may refer to an entity identical in every aspect with the one referred to by its antecedent, but in many cases the referent of an anaphoric pronoun is one that has undergone some change of state. We may say that the explanation Halliday and Hasan gave to co-reference is formal rather than semantic.

Another similar example:

66) I've just had my hair curled and *it* (= my hair which I've just had curled) looks windblown all the time.

Besides the problem we have just mentioned, Halliday and Hasan's substitution view also meets difficulty in interpreting the following texts:

67) STOP BUS VANDALS
by reporting *it* at once
to the driver or conductor
(sign displayed in Edinburgh buses)

68) There're two different ladies going up to the whist and both have a wig and *they*'re most natural.

69) Even an apprentice can make over twenty pound a week and *they* don't get much tax (taken) from that.

70) There's a car going up the road and *he* comes to a crossroads.

71) The second car hasn't got time to avoid the person who swerved away to avoid the car that was pulling out and *he* hits *it*.

72) (Talking about the First World War) I used to go about with a chap — I don't know whether he's still alive now or not — but — there was nine — ten — eleven in the family altogether — two girls — and nine boys — and *she* lost eight sons one after the other.

73) One of our main jobs in the Botanics is writing on the flora of Turkey. *They* don't have the scientists to do *it*.

74) Oh I was on the bus and *he* didn't stop at the right stop.

75) In the middle of the page there's a square quite large — and near the bottom of *it* there's number five in red.

In 67) we cannot find a ready antecedent for *it* to substitute for. We can only assume that *it* is an "act of vandalism" which should be reported. (Examples like this shows that Halliday and Hasan are not concerned to produce a description which accounts for how texts are understood. They are, rather, concerned to examine the linguistic resources available to the speaker or writer to mark cohesive relationships.)

The correct interpretation of the reference of *they* in 68) depends on the hearer's understanding that there are two wigs and not one, as the nominal antecedent (*a wig*) by itself would suggest. In 69), there is a similar problem, with a singular nominal antecedent and a plural pronoun. By itself, the expression *an apprentice* might be interpreted as introducing a particular individual into the discourse. However, when interpreted in the context of the predicate *can make over twenty pound a week*, it has to be taken, not as a particular individual, but as *any* individual from a set of individuals to whom the lexical expression *apprentice* can be applied. The choice of subsequent pronoun (e.g. *he* or *they*) then simply reflects the speaker's perspective on whether he is considering a typical individual or a set of such individuals. The speaker of 69) chooses the latter. Examples 68) and 69) present a grammatical mismatch in terms of number disagreement between antecedent nominal and subsequent pronoun. Examples 70) and 71), both taken from descriptions of traffic accidents, seem to present a mismatch in terms of gender agreement. In 70), the hearer is clearly required to infer that a car moving along a road must have a driver and that it is this inferred driver who the *he* is used to refer to. Example 71) presents a more complex problem. Despite the presence of both a human and a non-human antecedent for *he* and *it*, the most natural interpretation of what happened requires us to match the grammatically "human" pronoun with the "non-human" antecedent, and the "non-human" pronoun with the "human" antecedent. This explanation does not seem to be on the basis of an antecedent nominal/anaphoric pronominal substitution relationship.

The inadequacy of the substitution approach is even more apparent in those situations where a pronoun occurs in a discourse with no antecedent nominal at all. The use of the pronoun *she* near the end of the extract 72) provides such an example. In this extract there is no linguistic expression which could be treated as the direct antecedent for *she*. Of course, we can propose that if the speaker is talking about a *family* and there is a female referent (*she*) who *lost eight sons*, then we can infer that it is "the mother" the speaker is referring to. Notice that, if the hearer does follow this procedure, then he is using "new" information to determine a "given" referent. Obviously, example 72) raises a serious problem for any analysis of pronouns as conveying "given" information which depends on a referential assignment via information in the preceding discourse.

The interpretation of the reference of the italicized pronouns in 73) and 74) depends on what is predicated of them, and is not solely determined by information in the preceding discourse. In example 73), it seems that the speaker has assumed that, if he is talking about a country, he can refer to a group of people in that country without having to assert explicitly that "Turkey has people in it". If that is a required inference on the hearer's part, then it can only take place after the hearer has heard the "new" predicate attached to the pronoun *they*. As for example 74), just as a car involved in a car crash is most likely to have a driver, as in 70), so too is a bus carrying passengers. The referent of the pronoun *he* is the implied entity, the driver. These two examples have illustrated the fact that we need to take "new" predicate into account when assigning an interpretation to some "given" elements, such as pronouns in discourse.

Example 75) reveals the fact that in some types of discourse pronouns are most typically used to refer to "current" entities, and hearers can use this type of regularity as a basis for their referential assignments. This explains why, in extract 75), the hearer can interpret the pronoun *it* as a reference to the "current entity" (*a square*) and not to the "displaced entity" (*the page*), even though the grammatical categories (number and gender) do not provide distinguishing clues.

In 7.3.2, we introduced Evans' concept of **facet** when discussing the effect of linguistic context on the interpretation of a particular expression, and we used example 36) to elaborate this point.

Now let's extend the example in which we use the pronoun *it* to refer back to "that book" in 36)a and b.

76) a. That book is really thick. I cannot put it into the paper bag.
b. That book is really interesting. Everyone is eager to read it.

Obviously, the pronoun *it* in 76)a and b relates respectively to the TOME facet and the TEXT facet of the book.

Sometimes the two facets appear in the same sentence, as illustrated in 77):

77) Although it's an expensive book, it's well worth reading.

While formally both the first *it* and the second *it* refer to "an expensive book", semantically the former relates to the TOME facet of the book and the later to the TEXT facet. This example shows that contextual information plays a vital role in determining the specific referent of an anaphoric pronoun. It also reveals that co-reference is not just a matter of form but also a matter of meaning.

There are other referential links routinely made between sentences. Some have been called **bridging inferences** by Clark (1977). Below are a few examples:

78) a. I looked into the room. **The ceiling** was very high.
   b. I walked into the room. **The windows** looked out to the bay.
   c. I walked into the room. **The chandeliers** sparkled brightly.
   d. John went walking out at noon. **The park** was beautiful.
   e. Mary got some picnic supplies out of the car. **The beer** was warm.
   f. Robert found an old car. **The steering wheel** had broken off.
   g. I bought a bicycle yesterday. **The frame** is extra large.
   h. There was a car approaching the junction, but **the driver** didn't stop at the give way sign.
   i. I got on a bus yesterday and **the driver** was drunk.
   j. Mary dressed the baby's arm. **The bandage** was made of white cotton.

In each of these examples, the nominal in bold occurs with a definite article, showing that the speaker assumes that the referent is accessible to the listener, i.e. that it is given. In each case the question is: how, if it has not been mentioned earlier, nor is physically present at the utterance, did this nominal become part of given information? The answer seems to be that the listener makes a bridging inference which links the nominal to the preceding sentence and create coherence. In these examples the basis for the inferences seems to be background knowledge. People know from their own experience that rooms usually have ceilings, commonly have windows, may have chandeliers, a car or a bus must have a steering wheel and a driver to drive it, a bicycle must have a frame, the supplies of a picnic may include beer, bandage is what mostly used to dress a wound, and that one of the conventional places to go for a walk is in a park. With this knowledge as a bridge, the listener can infer what the bold-faced noun phrases specifically refer to.

What the listeners seem to be doing here is making inferences to preserve a notion of coherence in what they are told. Speakers seem confident that their listeners will do this and they take advantage of it to speak less explicitly than they might. The following are examples of where the speaker seems to rely on the listener inferences:

79) I left early. I had a meeting to attend.

INFERENCE: Speaker left because of having to attend the meeting.

80) A: Have you returned the book to the library?

B: I'm reading it now.

INFERENCE: B has not returned the book to the library.

Knowing that their listeners will flesh out their utterances with inferences gives speakers the freedom to imply something rather than state it. In the next section we look at one particular type of implication identified in the pragmatics literature, **conversational implicature**.

Before ending up this section, it is possibly worthwhile to mention the achievements of cognitive linguistics, a new branch of language study established in the 80s of the last century, in the study of anaphora and bridging inferences. Cognitive linguists approach such language phenomena from the perspective of metonymy. Metonymy, in the cognitive linguistics literature, is defined as a cognitive process in which the vehicle provides mental access to the target within the same domain. Metonymy in cognitive linguistics is modeled as idealized cognitive models (ICMs) by Lakoff (1987), conceptual mappings by Radden and Kövecses (1999), domain highlighting by Croft (2000), combinations of mappings and highlighting by Ruiz de Mendoza (2000), scenarios by Panther and Thornbury (1999) and more generally as reference-point activation by Langacker (1999) and Barcelona (2000). Here we will just give a short introduction of this topic. We begin with examples 81) and 82):

81) a. The room has two doors.

b. Open the door.

c. We took the door off its hinges and then walked through it.

82) a. The workmen delivered the window.

b. Close the window.

c. I painted the window while she was standing in it.

According to the interpretation by cognitive linguists, the referents of "the door" in 81)a and "the window" in 82)a are conceptualized as unitary structures, while their referents in 81)b and 82)b are conceptualized as the moving parts of the unitary structures, not including the frame of the door or window. In 81)c and 82)c, the anaphoric pronoun "it" refers respectively to the aperture created when the moving part of the door as a unitary structure is opened or the space within the frame of the window. The different senses of *door* and *window* illustrated above are related to each other through metonymy, in our understanding of the term. A speaker of English has a good deal of common-sense or background knowledge about *doors* and *windows*. He knows, for example, about their usual shape, size, and manner of construction, and about their function and usual location. This kind of knowledge is held together in what we might call (with apologies for the pun) our "door" and "window" frames. Different uses of *door* and *window* merely perspectivize different components of the respective frames. It is perhaps significant that most speakers of English need to think twice before becoming aware of the polysemy of *door* and *window*. This is undoubtedly because the frames, and the background cultural knowledge they embody, are so much taken for granted. Of course, our discussion here is mainly focused on the problem of determining the referent of the anaphoric pronoun to show that the relation between an anaphoric pronoun and its antecedent is not merely a relation of formal substitution. There are many other elements that need to be taken into account.

The following are some more examples of anaphora which will be analyzed from the perspective of conceptual metonymy in chapter 10:

83) Paul went to *the theatre, they* were playing Shakespeare.

84) *Plato* is on the top shelf. *It* is bound in leather.

85) *This* is parked out back and *it* won't start. (spoken while giving the key to the hearer)

86) *I* am parked out back.

87) *The French fries* is waiting and *he* is getting upset.

88) I need to call *the garage* — *they* said they'd have my car ready.

89) *Ringo* was hit in the fender when *he* was momentarily distracted by a motor cycle.

90) *Finland* phoned, *they* sent their love.

7.6 Conversational implicature

The term conversational implicature was introduced by the philosopher H. Paul Grice. It refers to something that is implied in conversation, that is, something that is left implicit in actual language use. In lectures and a couple of very influential articles (Grice, 1975, 1978), Grice proposed an approach to the speaker's and hearer's cooperative use of inference. As we suggested above, there seems to be enough regularity in the inference-forming behavior of listeners for speakers to exploit this by implying something, rather than stating it. Grice argued that this predictability of inference information could be explained by postulating a **cooperative principle**: a kind of tacit agreement by speakers and listeners to cooperate in communication. Grice's observations are focused at such a level of language use: if I am in conflict with you, I still may want to communicate my intentions to you, and assume you will work out the implications of my utterances. It is at the underlying level of linguistic communication that Grice identifies this cooperation between speakers and listeners.

7.6.1 Grice's Cooperative Principle

Grice's Cooperative Principle goes as follows:

Make your conversational contribution such as required at the stage at which it occurs by the accepted purpose or direction of the talk exchange in which you are engaged.

To be more specific, there are four maxims under this general principle:

The maxim of quantity

a. Make your contribution as informative as required (for the current purpose of the exchange).

b. Do not make your contribution more informative than is required.

The maxim of quality

a. Do not say what you believe to be false.

b. Do not say that for which you lack adequate evidence.

The maxim of relation

Be relevant.

The maxim of manner

a. Avoid obscurity of expression.

b. Avoid ambiguity.

c. Be brief (avoid unnecessary prolixity).

d. Be orderly.

Grice phrased the cooperative principle and its component maxims as if they were injunctions: *Do thus*! This can be misleading: it is important to realize that the conversational principles that Grice proposed are not rules, like phonological or morphological rules, which people have to follow to speak a language; nor are they moral principles. Perhaps the best way to interpret a maxim *Do X!* is to translate it into a descriptive statement: the hearer seems to assume that the speaker is doing X in communicating.

The cooperative principle and its maxims are just basic assumptions, not rules, and they can be broken. They are not followed by everybody all the time. Grice distinguished between the speaker secretly breaking them, e.g. lying, which he termed **violating** the maxims; and overtly breaking them to convey the speaker's real intention, which he called **flouting**.

In Grice's view, conversational implicatures can only be worked out on the basis of the cooperative principle. If somebody deliberately conceals facts from his hearers, the basis for accurate interpretation is lost, though a liar succeeds only when his hearers assume that he is observing the cooperative principle. In other words, lies do not have implicatures proper. So the cases Grice discusses are all blatant, apparent violations. The speaker has shown it clearly that some maxims are violated, yet at a deeper level the cooperative principle can still be thought to be upheld. The following examples illustrate how the maxims can be flouted and what conversational implicature will come from the flouting.

91) A: When is Susan's farewell party?

B: Sometime next month.

This is said when it is known to both A and B that B knows exactly when Susan is going to give her farewell party. Thus B is withholding some of the information required at this stage of conversation and is thus flouting the maxim of quantity. The implicature that results is "I do not wish to tell you when the party is going to be held".

Also for the first maxim of quantity, Grice uses as an example an imagined reference letter by A for his past student X, who is applying for a lectureship in philosophy, and it reads: "Dear Sir, Mr. X's command of English is excellent, and his attendance at tutorials has been regular. Yours, etc." Grice comments "A cannot be opting out, since if he wished to be uncooperative, why write at all? He cannot be unable, through ignorance, to say more, since the man is his pupil; moreover, he knows that more information than this is wanted. He must, therefore, be wishing to impart information that he is reluctant to write down. This supposition is tenable only on the assumption that he thinks Mr. X is no good at philosophy. This, then, is what he is implicating." (Grice, 1975: 52)

And tautologies like *Boys are boys* and *War is war* are extreme examples in which the first quantity maxim is violated. At the superficial level, the level of what is said, they are totally uninformative. At a deeper level, the level of what is implicated, however, they are informative. They may convey implicatures like "Boys are naughty and mischievous by nature" "It's no use lamenting the tragedies of war. Terrible things always happen in it. That's its nature".

An example in which the second maxim of quantity is violated will be:

92) A: Where is X?

B: He's gone to the library. He said so when he left.

In a sense, the first part of B's answer is enough for A's question. But by adding the second part, the speaker may implicate that he is not sure whether X has really gone to the library.

The examples Grice provides for the violation of the first quality maxim are all traditional figures of speech like 93) and 94).

93) He is made of iron.

94) Every nice girl loves a sailor.

That is, at the level of what is said, they are false statements. No natural human being is made of iron, unless he is a robot. So 93) cannot be taken literally. Instead we will interpret it as a metaphor, meaning this man has a character like iron. In the case of 94), the implicature is that many girls love sailors. The following is an example of non-figurative nature which violates the first quality maxim:

95) A: Would you like to join us for the picnic on Sunday?
B: I'm afraid I have got a class on Sunday.

This is said when it is known to both A and B that B is not having any class that will prevent him from going for the picnic. Thus B is saying something that he himself knows to be false and is flouting the maxim of quality. His implied message is "I do not want to join you for the picnic on Sunday".

In cases when we do not have adequate evidence, we will usually qualify our utterances by "It may be the case that..." or "I'm not sure but...".

The following is an example which illustrates the violation of the maxim of relation and the resultant implicature:

96) A: How did the math exam go today, Jonnie?
B: We had a basketball match with the other class and we beat them.

This is said when it is known to both A and B that it is entirely possible for B to tell A how well or how poorly he did in the math exam. B's response is thus totally irrelevant to A's question. Therefore he is flouting the maxim of relation. The implicature is "I don't wish to talk about the math exam".

97) A: Shall we get something for the kids?
B: Yes. But I veto I-C-E C-R-E-A-M.

This is an example in which B is being deliberately obscure, so that the children will not be able to understand what A and B are talking about. It is said when it is known to both A and B that B has no difficulty in pronouncing the word "ice-cream". Thus B has flouted the maxim of manner. B's utterance has the implicature that "I don't want the kids to know we are talking about getting them some ice creams".

When illustrating the violation of the ambiguity avoidance maxim, Grice uses as an example William Blake's lines "*Never seek to tell thy love, love that never told can be*". In this case, *love* may refer to an emotion or the person one loves. And "Love that never told can be" may mean either "Love that cannot be told" or "Love that if told cannot continue to exist".

And if a reviewer has chosen 98)b rather than 98)a, then the prolixity implicates that Miss X's performance is so poor that the word "sing" cannot be applied.

98) a. Miss X sang “Home sweet home”.

b. Miss X produced a series of sounds that corresponded closely with the score of “Home sweet home”.

Next is another example showing the creative flouting of the maxim of manner from Flann O’Brien’s novel *At-Swim-Two-Birds* (1967: 38). Readers may think it over and try to understand why the author employs such a technique of language use.

99) The three of us were occupied in putting glasses of stout into the interior of our bodies and expressing by fine disputation the resulting sense of physical and mental well being.

Grice did not give any example of disorder, which is understandable in that generally a disordered utterance will not convey any thing but the fact that the speaker is mentally unsound. *They had a baby and got married* is not a disordered version of *They got married and had a baby*. They are both ordered, though, in their own different ways. But the Chinese example “屡败屡战” may be seen as an instance of the exploitation of this maxim.

Toward the end of his “*Logic and Conversation*”, Grice mentioned briefly some characteristics of conversational implicature. In what follows we summarize Grice’s ideas in the light of other linguists’elaborations.

Calculability

The fact that speakers try to convey conversational implicatures and hearers are able to understand them suggests that implicatures are calculable. They can be worked out on the basis of some previous information. In his paper, Grice lists the necessary data as follows:

(1) the conventional meaning of the words used, together with the identity of any references that may be involved;

(2) the CP and its maxims;

(3) the context, linguistic or otherwise, of the utterance;

(4) other items of background knowledge; and

(5) the fact (or supposed fact) that all relevant items falling under the previous headings are available to both participants and both participants know or assume this to be the case.

And he suggests there is a general pattern for the working out of a conversation implicapture. That is, when somebody says something, which apparently does not make sense at the superficial level, the level of what is said, you will not simply think that he is talking nonsense and stop thinking about it any more. You will instead try to find out its implied meaning at a deeper level. And if on the basis of every information available, there is one interpretation which may support your previous assumptions, then you will take it as the real point the speaker is trying to get across. For example, in the case of the reference letter, the reader will not simply think it utterly useless and throw it away immediately after the first reading. He will assume that the writer is still following some normal practices like the cooperative principle and tries to say something true and relevant. Since the most important thing is whether Mr. X is qualified for the job, about which the letter includes nothing explicitly, the reader will have to assume that the writer has some negative views on that.

Cancellability

Cancellability is also known as defeasibility. We said that the presence of a conversational implicature relies on a number of factors: the conventional meaning of words used, the cooperative principle, the linguistic and situational contexts, etc. So if any of them changes, the implicature will also change. For example, 100)a usually implicates 100)b. But if the speaker add "if not more" to 100)a, to change it to 100)c, then the previous implicature 100)b is cancelled, or defeated. And 100)c means 100)d.

100) a. John has three cows.

b. John has only three cows.

c. John has three cows, if not more.

d. John has at least three cows.

In the case of the reference letter, if the writer adds "though I don't mean he's no good at philosophy", then the original implicature is no longer there.

A conversational implicature may even be cancelled simply by the situational context. If to have three cows is a condition for anyone to get a subsidy from the government, then when the inspector asks John's neighbour 100)e, he could very well answer 100)f, without implicating 100)b.

e. Has John really got the requisite number of cows?

f. Oh sure, he's got three cows all right.

Again in the case of the reference letter, if the student is applying for a lectureship in English, then this letter becomes a favourable comment.

In the following two examples, when 101) is expanded into 102) by adding more information, the implicature in 101) is cancelled:

101) A: Can I borrow five pounds?
B: My purse in the hall.
(B's implicature: Yes.)

102) A: Can I borrow five pounds?
B: My purse in the hall. But don't you dare touch it. I'm not lending you any more money.

Non-detachability

By non-detachability is meant that a conversational implicature is attached to the semantic content of what is said, not to the linguistic form. Therefore it is possible to use a synonym and keep the implicature intact. In other words, an implicature will not be detached, separated from the utterance as a whole, even though the specific words may be changed. For example, 103)a-e said ironically will all implicate 104).

103) a. John's a genius.
b. John's a mental prodigy.
c. John's an exceptionally clever human being.
d. John's an enormous intellect.
e. John's a big brain.

104) John's an idiot.

In response to "How did the math exam go today, Jonnie?", which is used for the violation of the relation maxim, any utterance which is not directly related to it will generate the implicature *I don't wish to talk about the math exam.* One does not have to say "We had a basketball match with the other class and we beat them". Utterances like "We saw a good film yesterday, don't you want to see it?" "You look pretty in this new dress" will all do.

Conversational implicatures related to the manner maxims, however, are an exception to this characteristic, as they rely on the form rather the content. "But I veto I-C-E C-R-E-A-M" replaced by "But don't give them ice creams" would give the game away.

Non-conventionality

Conversational implicature is by definition different from the conventional meaning of words. To show the differences more clearly, we can have a look at some examples of entailment. In chapter 4 when discussing sentence relations and truth, we said that **entailment** is a logical relationship between two sentences in which the truth of the second necessarily follows from the truth of the first, while the falsity of the first follows from the falsity of the second. We may exemplify it with sentences like the pair in 105). Now sentence 100)a, which has implicatures like 100)b, also has entailments as shown in 106)a-g.

105) a. I saw a boy.

b. I saw a child.

106) a. John has some cows.

b. John has some animals.

c. John has something.

d. Somebody has three cows.

e. Somebody has some cows.

f. Somebody has some animals.

g. Somebody has something.

As is clear from the examples, entailment is part of the conventional meaning. Part of the meaning of *cow* is "It refers to an animal". To know the meaning of *John* partly means to know "It is a name of a person", so it can be replaced by *somebody.* If you do not know the entailment of a word, you simply have to look it up in a dictionary. There is no way to work out an entailment on the basis of the cooperative principle and the context.

Another consequence of its being conventional is that entailment is constant in all contexts. There is no context in which while *I saw a boy* is true but *I saw a child* is not true. In this sense, entailment is determinate. In contrast, implicature is indeterminate, which varies with the context. And this is sometimes seen as another characteristic of conversational implicature.

At the end of the discussion, we may summarize **conversational implicature** as a type of implied meaning, which is deduced on the basis of the conventional meaning of words together with the context, under the guidance of the cooperative principle and its maxims. In this sense, implicature is comparable to illocutionary force (or illocutionary act) in speech act theory in that they are both concerned with the contextual side of meaning, or "言外之意" in Chinese. And these two theories differ only in the mechanisms they offer for explaining the generation of contextual meaning.

7.6.2 Post-Gricean developments

The theory of conversational implicature has opened up a new way of explaining the use of language. However, there is some inconsistency and redundancy among the CP and its maxims. Linguists of the post-Gricean period, therefore, have sought to boil down Grice's original four maxims (and eight sub-maxims) to a set of principles, which are truly indispensable and do not overlap at the same time. In this section, we shall discuss two such suggestions.

7.6.2.1 The Q- and R-principles

These two principles were proposed and developed by Laurence Horn (1984, 1989, 1996). They are held to be in tension with each other. The Q-principle draws together Grice's first quantity maxim and the first two sub-maxims of manner. It is a kind of guarantee of informational adequacy to the hearer. In Zipf's least-effort principle, this is essentially out of the hearer's economy. It may be informally characterized as:

Q-principle: say as much as you can, balancing against the R-principle.

The R-principle is a principle of speaker economy; it subsumes the relevance or relation maxim and the last two maxims of manner, and can be represented as:

R-principle: say no more than you must, balancing against the Q-principle.

One area where the Q-principle is held to operate is in scalar implicatures (Horn, 1989; Gazdar, 1979). This is the claim that certain linguistic expressions form a scale of strength, <X, Y>, where X is stronger than Y, for example:

107) Q-principle scales

a. <all, some>

b. <be certain that, think that>

c. <succeed in, try to>

Strength here is a notion of informational content and also involves an asymmetrical relation of entailment, the semantic relation discussed in chapter

4. The stronger expression X entails Y, but Y does not entail X. Thus *all* entails *some* but *some* does not entail *all*. The idea is that when a speaker utters a weaker expression from a scale, the Q-principle ensures that the hearer infers that the speaker believes the stronger expression does not hold. This explains the following implicatures:

108) a. Jane ate some of the biscuits IMPLICATES Jane didn't eat all of them.
b. I think she's at home IMPLICATES I'm not certain she's at home.
c. I tried to buy you some flowers IMPLICATES I didn't buy you some flowers.

In simple terms, though if Jane in 108)a did eat all the biscuits she surely ate some of them, to use *some* when *all* would apply is held to be a violation of the Q-principle and therefore uncooperative, in Gricean terms.

The R-principle is used to explain why longer forms have different interpretation than shorter ones, when they seem to be paraphrases of each other. See for example the pairs:

109) a. Leonora caused her husband to die.
b. Leonora killed her husband.

110) a. I don't not like you.
b. I like you.

In 109)a the periphrastic use of two clauses weakens the chain of cause and effect relative to 109)b. It would be odd to use 109)a if for example Leonora stabbed her husband to death in a violent rage. The sentences in 110) show that a double negative often has a different interpretation than a corresponding positive: in ordinary use 110)a doesn't quite mean the same as 110)b. In both these examples the shorter form (i.e. the unmarked form) is assumed to be the expected form because of the R-principle; the longer forms (i.e. the marked forms) as violations, will therefore carry extra levels of meaning.

Similarly, the use of the unmarked lexical causative in 111)a implicates that the action was brought about in an unmarked way, perhaps by stepping on the brake pedal, while the choice of the morphologically more complex from as in 111)b implicates that some unusual method was used, by pulling the emergency brake.

111) a. Lee stopped the car.

b. Lee got the car to stop.

Obviously, the use of a marked (relatively complex and/or prolix) expression when a corresponding unmarked (simpler, less "effortful") alternate expression is available tends to be interpreted as conveying a marked message (one which the unmarked alternative would not or could not have conveyed).

7.6.2.2 Relevance Theory

A more radical development of Grice's maxims is Relevance Theory (Sperber and Wilson, 1995). This approach seeks to unify the Gricean cooperative principle and conversational maxims into a single principle of relevance that will motivate a hearer's inferential strategy:

> *Principle of relevance (Sperber and Wilson, 1995:158)*
>
> *Every act of ostensive communication communicates the presumption of its own optimal relevance.*

To understand this definition, we need to be clear about the key notions in it: "ostensive communication" and "presumption of optimal relevance". Sperber and Wilson agree with Grice that communication is not simply a matter of encoding and decoding, it also involves inference. But they maintain that inference has only to do with the hearer. From the speaker's side, communication should be seen as an act of making clear one's intention to express something. This act they call ostensive act. In other words, a complete characterization of communication is that it is ostensive-inferential. And "ostensive communication" or "inferential communication", is a shorthand.

Evans (2006: 459) claims Relevance Theory is a theoretical approach to communication in general, which views **verbal communication** as one instance of ostensive-inferential communication. According to Sperber and Wilson, the defining characteristic of communication is that it involves revealing or making manifest a particular communicative intention. In other words, the communicator's intention is revealed by some kind of ostensive behavior. For example, in response to the question *How are you getting home?* you can perform a manual gesture representing a car's steering wheel. This is a form of ostensive behavior signaling a specific communicative intention, namely that the "addressee" should infer that you will be driving home. Equally, if you are at a party that you wish to leave, you can raise you arm and tap your watch to indicate to your partner that it's time to go. In both cases, the act would fail as an instance of communication if it were not ostensive. For example, if you were sitting in the bathroom by yourself, the act of tapping your watch would fail to achieve ostensive-inferential communication.

Of course, for speaker and hearer to communicate successfully, particularly where inference is concerned, they must rely upon shared information. For example, the person in our earlier example who indicates that he will be driving home relies upon the assumption that his "addressee" knows that cars have steering wheels and can recognize the gesture that represents this. Sperber and Wilson describe this shared knowledge upon which inferences depend as the "**mutual cognitive environment**". Consider the following excerpts from Sperber and Wilson.

> *The cognitive environment of an individual is a set of facts that are manifest to him ... A fact is manifest to an individual at a given time iff [if and only if] he is capable at that time of representing it mentally and accepting its representation as true or probably true ... an individual's total cognitive environment is the set of all the facts he can perceive or infer ... a function of his physical environment and his cognitive abilities ... The total shared environment of two people is the intersection of their two total cognitive environments, i.e. the set of all facts that are manifest to them both.* (Sperber and Wilson, 1995: 39–41)

As these excerpts make explicit, inference depends upon the speaker's knowledge, and the knowledge he can assume on the part of the hearer.

To explain "presumption of optimal relevance", we shall first look at what the notion of relevance by Sperber and Wilson means.

According to Sperber and Wilson, human cognition is driven by relevance in the sense that information (whether sensory-perceptual or linguistic) is selectively processed on the basis of the search for contextual effects: information that will affect our existing knowledge in some useful way or will allow us to construct an inference. For example, imagine driving down the road in your car with the radio on. In this context, you are bombarded with sensory-perceptual stimuli including visual stimuli as well as linguistic and non-linguistic sounds. Suppose that you have been worried about your car lately. In this context, you might "tune out" the linguistic sounds coming from the radio and focus your attention on the sounds coming from under the bonnet. Depending on whether these sounds are out of the ordinary or not, this information will interact with what you already know about your car and allow you to draw some conclusions. In this context, the car's sounds are more relevant than the radio's sounds. Now imagine that you are late for work and concerned about the time. You transfer your attention to the linguistic sounds coming from the radio and listen for the newsreader to announce the time. In this context, the radio's sounds are more relevant than the car's sounds. As this simple example illustrates, the human mind constantly searches for relevant information. This idea is captured by the "**Cognitive Principle of Relevance**", which states that "Human cognition tends to be geared to the maximization of relevance". (Sperber and Wilson, 1995:158)

Sperber and Wilson argue that ostensive-inferential communication is driven by the presumption of relevance. In other words, a hearer will assume that any act of (linguistic or non-linguistic) ostensive-inferential communication is relevant, and moreover will search for the optimally relevant interpretation. It is this assumption that allows us to deduce or infer the communicative intention signaled by an act of ostensive communication. This idea is captured by the "**Communicative Principle of Relevance**", which states that "Every act of ostensive communication communicates a presumption of its own optimal relevance" (Sperber and Wilson, 1995: 260). "Optimal relevance" is defined in the following way:

> *Presumption of optimal relevance* (*Sperber and Wilson*, 1995: 158)
>
> *a. The set of assumptions {I} which the communicator intends to make manifest to the addressee is relevant enough to make it worth the addressee's while to process the ostensive stimulus.*
>
> *b. The ostensive stimulus is the most relevant one the communicator could have used to communicate {I}.*[①]

That is, every utterance comes with a presumption of the best balance of

---

① Later on, Sperber and Wilson revised the presumption of optimal relevance as follows:

a. The ostensive stimulus is relevant enough for it to be worth the addressee's effort to process it.

b. The ostensive stimulus is the most relevant one compatible with the communicator's abilities and preferences.

effort against effect. On the one hand, the effects achievable will never be less than is needed to make it worth processing. On the other hand, the effort required will never be more than is needed to achieve these effects. In comparison to the effects achieved, the effort needed is always the smallest. This accounts to saying "of all the interpretations of the stimulus which confirm the presumption, it is the first interpretation to occur to the addressee that is the one the communicator intended to convey". For example, the first interpretation of 112) to occur to the hearer will usually be that George has a big domestic cat.

112) George has a big cat.

As the word *cat* is ambiguous, it may also refer to other animals of the species *felid* in some situations. That is, 112) may be used to mean 113).

113) George has a tiger, a lion, a jaguar, etc.

But Sperber and Wilson argue that even if interpretation 113) is correct, thus verifying the first part of the presumption of optimal relevance, i.e. 113) is relevant enough; the second part would invariably be falsified, i.e. 113) will not be the most relevant on account of the increased processing effort involved. In other words, if 113) were the intended interpretation, the speaker should have, instead, used something like 114), or, if he lacked the necessary information, something like 115) or 116):

114) George has a tiger.

115) George has a tiger or a lion, I'm not sure which.

116) George has a felid.

These utterances would have saved the hearer the effort of first accessing and considering interpretation 113), and then having to compare the two. Hence, they assure the hearer that he need not worry. The first interpretation consistent with the principle of relevance is always the best hypothesis. All other interpretations would manifestly falsify the second part of the presumption of relevance.

Let us consider one more example from Sperber and Wilson (1995: 189). Imagine that this utterance is made in a jeweler's shop in response to an enquiry from a customer about how long they might expect to wait for the watch to be repaired.

117) It will take some time to repair your watch.

It is obvious that a watch repair must take "some time" (as opposed to no time), so the customer assumes that the communicative intention behind the utterance cannot be to convey this uninformative and therefore irrelevant interpretation. Sperber and Wilson argue that our presumption of relevance in everyday communication guides us to a more appropriate interpretation of the utterance. If the customer knows that it usually takes about a week to get a watch repaired, then the most relevant reason for mentioning the time it will take is probably because the repair will take significantly longer than a week.

Finally, let us look at the two terms distinguished by Sperber and Wilson: **explicature** and **implicature**. The term "explicature" describes an assumption that is explicitly communicated. In relating to explicit or context-independent meaning, this term roughly corresponds to the traditional idea of semantic meaning. The term "implicature", which is adopted from Grice (1975), relates to implicit or inferential (context-dependent) meaning, and corresponds to the traditional view of pragmatic meaning. Sperber and Wilson also follow the standard formal view in assuming that semantic "decoding" takes place prior to the calculation of pragmatic inferences. However, they depart from the standard formal view in arguing that meaning construction relies to considerable extent upon inference, even in the "decoding" of explicatures. This idea is illustrated by example 118) from Sperber and Wilson (1995: 186).

118) The child left the straw in the glass.

This sentence is straightforwardly interpreted to mean that a child left a "drinking tube" in a glass drinking vessel. This meaning is the explicature expressed by the sentence. However, as Sperber and Wilson observe, even this straightforward sentence requires some inferential work, because the expression *straw* is lexically ambiguous: it could mean the child left a "cereal stalk" in the glass. To derive the more likely or accessible "drinking tube" interpretation, the hearer has to access encyclopaedic information relating to children and the typical scenarios involving a "straw" and a "glass". The availability of the most salient interpretation might also depend on contextual information, such as whether the child in question was in a kitchen or a farmyard. As this example illustrates, many explicatures will rely upon inference on the part of the hearer in order to retrieve the intended meaning. Sperber and Wilson's model therefore departs from the standard formal model in emphasizing the role of inference in deriving explicit meaning. Blakemore(1992: 58) discusses a traditional example of implicature in 119) below, where B's answer produces the implicature shown.

119) A: Did you enjoy your holiday?

B: The beaches were crowded and the hotel was full of bugs.

(B's implicature: No, I didn't enjoy my holiday.)

Blakemore argues that pragmatic processes of another more basic sort are involved in the interpretation of B's utterance. The hearer A has a number of problems to solve because of the sketchiness of the linguistic input. For example, what were the beaches crowded with? Which hotel is referred to? Which meaning of the word *bug* is involved, e.g. electronic listening device, or insect? She argues that we get the answers to these by pragmatic processes, and that these processes necessarily produce an intervening phase which underlies the production of implicatures. This two-phase interpretation gives us 120)a and b from B's reply in 119):

120) a. The beaches at the holiday resort that the speaker went to were crowded with people and the hotel he stayed at was full of insects.

b. The speaker did not enjoy his holiday.

To get to 120)a the hearer must perform certain tasks, including for example determining which hotel is referred to. In the relevance theory the correct target for reference will be the one that makes the resulting proposition maximally relevant to the accessible context. Clearly the most relevant hotel to B's holiday story is the one he stayed in. This information being accessible in the context relies on the real-world knowledge that beach holidays often involve staying in hotels. Other tasks involve expanding elliptical expressions: that the beaches were crowded with people; and resolving lexical ambiguity: that the bugs are insects. Clearly in a context where A and B are spies, the most accessible interpretation might have bugs as listening devices. These interpretations, which are expansions of the original underspecified linguistic input, are called explicatures. They too are licensed by the principle of relevance and they form the basis for further inferential steps to arrive at the conversational implicature in 120)b.

These processes of expanding to explicit content are seen as operating at the word level in what is termed **lexical pragmatics**. The contextual plasticity of words is seen as a product of a number of inferential processes, including **narrowing**, as in Wilson and Carston's (2006: 409) example:

121) All politicians drink.

Here the meaning of drink has been narrowed from the meaning "drinks liquid" to mean "drinks alcohol" and possibly further, to "drinks alcohol in sufficient quantities to be worth commenting on". In relevance theory terms, drinking liquid is clearly necessary for staying alive and in most contexts the fact that a person drinks liquid has no obvious relevance. Thus in many contexts the expected interpretation of 122) below:

122) Brian doesn't drink.

is that Brian doesn't drink alcohol. Other processes include **broadening** or approximation (Sperber and Wilson, 2004) where the sense of word is extended, as the word *square* in:

123) His father has a square face too.

In this example it is unlikely that the speaker intends the usual dictionary meaning of *square*. In this view, lexical narrowing and broadening are types of pragmatic enrichment that contribute to explicatures.

The exchange in example 124) illustrates how an implicature is derived (Sperber and Wilson, 1995:194).

124) Peter: Would you drive a Mercedes?
Mary: I wouldn't drive ANY expensive car.

In this exchange, Mary fails to answer Peter's question directly (because Peter's utterance is a "yes-no question", a straightforward "yes" or "no" would provide a direct answer). The presumption of relevance allows Peter to assume that Mary has answered the question in the most relevant way possible and to infer her intended meaning. Mary's utterance interacts with Peter's encyclopaedic knowledge and gives rise to the fact that a Mercedes is an expensive car. This fact interacts with Mary's assertion that she wouldn't drive ANY expensive car, and by a process of logical deduction gives rise to the explicature that Mary wouldn't drive a Mercedes. Mary's utterance counts as the optimally relevant way of answering Peter's question because it is maximally informative. Her utterance gives rise to a greater number of contextual effects than a direct "no" response, because Peter now knows not only that Mary wouldn't drive a Mercedes, but also that she wouldn't drive a BMW, a Bentley, a Jaguar and so on. From this perspective, the extra effort or processing "cost" involved in the retrieval of the implicature(s) is rewarded by the "benefit" of a greater number of contextual effects.

In their account of implicature, some linguists make a distinction between **implicated premises** and **implicated conclusions**. We can illustrate these terms with a modification of 124):

125) Peter: Would you drive a Saab?
Mary: I wouldn't drive ANY Swedish car.
(Mary's implicature: I would not drive a Saab.)

Mary's implicature is called an implicated conclusion and fits what is traditionally called a conversational implicature. However for it to be derived, Mary has introduced into the context the linking assumption:

126) A Saab is a Swedish car.

In the relevance theory 126) is called an implicated premise. It is not directly stated and therefore is implicated but it is provided as an inferential support for the final implicature, or implicated conclusion. Note that the implicated premise 126) need not be known by the hearer; in 125) if Peter doesn't know a Saab is Swedish he will infer it in order to preserve the relevance of Mary's reply.

In summary, in the relevance theory one overarching principle of relevance is used to describe a whole range of inferential behavior. The theory stresses the under-determination of meaning and its reliance on context and inference. Through the notion of explicatures these writers take the process of inference in understanding deep into traditional areas of semantics and reduce the importance of literal or context-free meaning.

Table 7-1 summarizes the main assumptions of Relevance Theory.

Table 7-1 Relevance Theory

Primarily concerned with accounting for ostensive-inferential communication; language is just one form of this.
Shared knowledge is the "mutual cognitive environment".

Continued

Cognition is driven by the search for relevance (Cognitive Principle of Relevance); relevance yields contextual effects.
Acts of ostensive communication (including utterances) presume their own optimal relevance.
Optimal relevance means that the information is worth retrieving and that the hearer has chosen the most relevant means of communicating.
While explicature and implicature roughly correspond to semantic and pragmatic meaning, respectively, both rely upon inference, which is relevance-driven.

7.7 Summary

One basic conclusion from this chapter is that to understand an utterance, hearers have to access and use contextual information of different types. We have seen, for example, that a hearer has to be able to perform the interpretative tasks in 127):

127) a. Fill in the deictic expressions;
b. Fix the reference of nominals;
c. Access background knowledge;
d. Make inference.

Each of these tasks involves calculation. Hearers have to create meaning by combining linguistic and contextual information; in doing so, they make inferences as a matter of course. We have seen several examples of this, including short-hand expressions and conversational implicatures. These tasks draw upon different types of knowledge, which can be classified as in 128).

128) a. the language used (e.g. English, French, Chinese)
b. the local contextual information (e.g. when and where uttered, and by whom)
c. background knowledge (e.g. cultural practices)

In this chapter we have concentrated on fleshing out the second and third types of knowledge. This does not mean that the first type of knowledge is not so important as the second and third types in understanding an utterance. Actually it is the basis for understanding almost all utterances as it would be difficult to understand someone if you do not first understand the literal meaning of what he has said.

This distinction between types of knowledge brings us back to the issue of the division between semantics and pragmatics, discussed in chapter one. Is only the use of the first type of knowledge in 128) above properly part of semantics, leaving the use of the second and third types to pragmatics? If so, and many linguists would accept this, many of the processes of interpreting meaning that we have discussed in this chapter, for example interpreting deictic expressions and forming conversational implicatures, are part of pragmatics. One related problem is what to call this first type of knowledge: if we call it "meaning", then what do we call the result of combining it with contextual information to get the final message?

One response is to distinguish between three types of meaning: the conventional meaning of words and sentences in the language, the speaker's intended meaning, and the hearer's constructed meaning. Another possibility is to call the sentence meaning, simply **meaning**; the speaker meaning, **content**; and the hearer meaning, **interpretation**. If we use these latter terms, then our basic observation in this chapter has been that meaning under-represents content and that the hearer must enrich meaning to get an interpretation. The extent to which this interpretation corresponds to content will determine the success of the communication. As pointed out by the American linguist W. D. Whitney over a hundred years ago, communication is a process of interpretation (1971 [1867]: 15):

> *Sentences are not images of thoughts, reflected in a faultless mirror; or even photographs, needing only to have the color added: they are but imperfect and fragmentary sketches, giving just outlines enough to enable the sense before which they are set up to seize the view intended, and to fill it out to a complete picture; while yet, as regards the completeness of the filling out, the details of the work, and the finer shades of coloring, no two minds will produce pictures perfectly accordant with one another, nor will any precisely reproduce the original.*

Chapter 8 *Speech act theory: a pragmatic study of meaning 2*

In this chapter we maintain our focus on language use and we look at the idea that part of the meaning of an utterance is its intended social function. It seems clear that learning to communicate in a language involves more than acquiring the pronunciation and grammar. We need to learn how to ask questions, make suggestions, greet and thank other speakers. In other words we need to learn the uses to which utterances are conventionally put in the new language community and how these uses are signaled, if we are to use the language in a realistic way. Similarly, as hearers, part of understanding the meaning of an utterance is knowing whether we have been asked a question, invited to do something, etc. In a terminology introduced by J. L. Austin (1975), which we will discuss in section 8.1, such functions of language are called **speech acts**.

In the last chapter we discussed areas of meaning which highlight the role of context and speaker-hearer interpretation. We recognized that if we admit a distinction between semantics and pragmatics, some of these topics, e.g. conversational implicature, seem to fall under pragmatics, while others, like reference and deixis, seem to straddle the semantics-pragmatics divide. The study of speech acts occupies a similar border area. In many cases the intended function is linguistically coded: languages often have, for example, specific morphemes, intonation and sentence patterns to mark questions, wishes, orders, etc. However, as we shall see, communicating functions also rely on both general knowledge of social conventions and specific knowledge of the local context of utterance. This area, then, reveals the pattern we saw in the last chapter: hearers have to coordinate linguistic and non-linguistic knowledge to interpret a speaker's intended meaning.

We can begin our discussion by identifying two important characteristics of speech acts: **interactivity** and **context-dependence**. The first is a crucial feature: communicating functions involve the speaker in a coordinated activity with other language users. For example, a bet only comes into existence when two or more parties interact. If I say to someone *I bet you five pounds he doesn't get elected*, a bet is not performed unless my addressee makes some response like *Okay* or *You're on*. While other speech acts like asking a question or greeting someone do not need explicit responses to make them questions or greetings, they nonetheless set up the expectation for an interactive response. Studies in the discourse analysis approach known as **conversational analysis** have revealed that failure to respond to a question, say by silence, triggers certain types of compensatory behaviour: the speaker may repeat the question, seek to evade the perceived rejection, or others may try to repair the lapse.

The second feature, context-dependence, has two aspects. The first is that many speech acts rely on social conventions to support them. Sometimes this is very explicit, where the speech act is supported by what Searle (1969) called **institutional facts**. Thus every society has procedures and ceremonies where some participants' words carry a special function. Examples commonly used in the literature include a judge saying *I sentence you to hang by the neck until dead*, a country's president announcing *I declare a state of national emergency*, a priest in the marriage ceremony saying *I now pronounce you man and wife*, and so on. These speech acts of sentencing prisoners, pronouncing a couple married, etc. can only be performed by the relevant people in the right situations, where both are sanctioned by social laws and conventions. Again though these are just the most explicit cases, it is clear that social conventions also govern ordinary uses of language in society. Sociolinguistic and ethnographical studies have shown us how the forms of asking questions, making greetings, etc. are influenced by a particular society's conventions for the participants' age, gender, relative social status, degree of intimacy, etc.

The second aspect of context dependence is the local context of a speech act. An utterance may signal one speech act in one situation and another elsewhere.

Questions in English are notoriously flexible in this way. If the asker already knows the answer then an utterance with the form of a question can be, for example a request, as when I see you are wearing a watch and I say *Can you tell me the time?* Or the question might have the force of a statement *No* as in B's possible replies in the invented exchange in 1) below:

1) A: Are you going to marry her?
  B: a. Are you crazy?
    b. Do you think I'm crazy?

We can find a parallel use of questions with known answers in the popular use of sentences like *Is the Pope a catholic? Do dogs have fleas?* or *Do bears shit in the woods?* as livelier and more informal ways of saying *Yes, of course.*

Because of this flexibility, we have to be careful about terminology. Some sentences have a particular grammatical form which is conventionally associated with a certain speech act. Thus questions in English, which of course include several types, usually have a special rising intonation pattern and an inverted subject-verb word order which differentiates them from statements, as 2)b and c below are distinguished from 2)a:

2) a. She is leaving.
  b. Is she leaving?
  c. When is she leaving?

When there is a conventional match between grammatical form and speech act function we can identify a **sentence type**. We need to use separate terms for sentence types and speech acts though, so that we can identify cases where the matching does not hold. Thus we might identify the sentence types in 3) below:

3) a. declarative, e.g. *John will paint the window.*
  b. interrogative, e.g. *Will John paint the window?*
  c. imperative, e.g. *John, paint the window!*
  d. optative, e.g. *If only John would paint the window!*

The conventional, or literal, use of these sentence types will be to perform the speech acts with the corresponding letter in 4) below:

4) a. assertions
  b. questions

c. orders

d. wishes

However, as we have already seen, interrogatives can be used for other speech acts than asking questions, and the same is true to a greater or lesser degree of the other sentence types. We will discuss this variability in section 8.3.

Both of the features we have outlined, interactivity and context dependence, emphasize that in discussing speech acts we are examining the union of linguistic and social behaviour. We will begin our discussion of this behaviour by reviewing J. L. Austin's theory of speech acts in section 8.1, then go on to examine revisions of the theory by J. R. Searle and others in 8.2. Thereafter in section 8.3 we will look at an interesting and difficult area for the theory: variability and indirect speech acts. Finally, in section 8.4 we will come back to the relationship between indirect speech acts and politeness.

8.1 Austin's Speech Act Theory

Speech act theory is an important theory in the pragmatic study of language. It was initially proposed by the British philosopher John Langshaw Austin in the late 50s of the 20th century and widely discussed in the 60s and 70s. There is an enormous literature on it from both the philosophical and linguistic point of view. In this chapter, however, we will mainly focus our attention on the ideas of J. L. Austin and J. R. Searle, another important writer on speech acts. We look at Austin's proposals in this section and discuss Searle's developments in section 8.2.

8.1.1 The performative-constative dichotomy

Austin's work is in many respects a reaction to some traditional and influential attitudes to language. We can risk simplifying these as a starting point. The attitudes can be said to involve three related assumptions, as follows:

5) a. that the basic sentence type in language is declarative (i.e. a statement or assertion)

b. that the principal use of language is to describe states of affairs (by using statements)

c. that the meaning of utterances can be described in terms of their truth or falsity

Among Austin's contemporaries the assumptions are associated with the philosophers known as **logical positivists**, or **logical empiricists**. Logical positivists argue that unless a sentence can be verified, i.e. tested for its truth or falsity, it is meaningless. And they have developed a theory of meaning on the basis of truth conditions.

Austin's opposition to these views is the "common-sense" one that language is used for far more than making statements and that for the most part utterances cannot be said to be either true or false. He makes two important observations. The first is that not all sentences are statements and that much of conversation is made up of questions, exclamations, commands, and expressions of whishes etc., like the examples in 6) below:

6) a. Excuse me!
   b. Are you free next Monday afternoon?
   c. Hello.
   d. Six pints of stout and a packet of peanuts, please!
   e. Read me the letter.
   f. What a girl (she is)!
   g. If only you'd asked me earlier!

Such sentences are not descriptions and cannot be said to be true or false.

Austin's second observation was that even in sentences with the grammatical form of declaratives, not all are used to make statements. Austin identified a subset of declaratives that are not used to make true or false statements, such as the examples in 7) below:

7) a. I promise to finish it in time.
   b. I bet you six pence it will rain tomorrow.
   c. I declare this meeting open.
   d. I warn you that the bull will charge.
   e. I name this ship the Queen Elizabeth.
   f. I bequeath my watch to my brother.
   g. I apologize.

Austin claimed of these sentences that they were in themselves a kind of action: thus by uttering 7)a a speaker makes a promise rather than just describing one.

Based on these two observations, Austin concluded that there are two types of sentences: **performatives** and **constatives**. In his *How to Do Things With Words* (1962), Austin argues that sentences like those in 7) do not state a fact or describe a state. They cannot be said to be true or false. The uttering of these sentences is, or is part of, the doing of an action. So they are called performatives. The action performed in each sentence is named by the first verb in the sentence, so the verbs are called performative verbs.

In contrast, example 8) said by a chemistry teacher in a demonstration of an experiment is not a performative. It is a description of what the speaker is doing at the time of speaking. The speaker cannot pour any liquid into a tube by simply uttering these words. He must accompany his words with the actual pouring. Otherwise one can accuse him of making a false statement. Sentences of this type are known as constatives. Constatives are statements that either state or describe, and are thus verifiable.

8) I pour some liquid into the tube.

8.1.2 Felicity conditions

Austin argued that it is not useful to ask whether performative utterances like those in 7) are true or not, rather we should ask whether they work or not: do they constitute a successful warning, bet, ship-naming, etc.? In Austin's terminology a performative that works is called **felicitous** and one that does not is **infelicitous**. For them to work, such performatives have to satisfy the social conventions that we mentioned earlier when we were discussing the context-dependence feature of speech acts. For a very obvious example, I cannot rename a ship by walking up to it in dock and saying *I name this ship the Flying Dutchman*. Less explicitly, there are social conventions governing the giving of orders to co-workers, greeting strangers, etc. Austin's name for the enabling conditions for a performative is **felicity conditions**. The felicity conditions suggested by Austin are as follows:

> A1 *There must exist an accepted conventional procedure having a certain conventional effect, the procedure to include the uttering of certain words by certain persons in certain circumstances, and further,*
>
> A2 *the particular persons and circumstances in a given case must be appropriate for the invocation of the particular procedure invoked.*

B1 *The procedure must be executed by all participants both correctly and*

B2 *completely.*

Austin went on to add **sincerity** clauses: firstly that participants must have the requisite thoughts, feelings and intentions, as specified by the procedure, and secondly, that if subsequent conduct is called for, the participants must so conduct themselves.

When illustrating condition A1, Levinson (1983: 229f) says in Muslim cultures, a man may achieve a divorce by saying to his wife "I hereby divorce you" three times in succession. The utterance of these words constitutes the performance of divorce. As a British citizen, however, he cannot divorce his wife in this way. There is no such a conventional procedure in British society. To explain condition A2, we may continue with the case of the Muslim divorce. That is, according to the Muslim tradition only the man has the right to divorce his wife in this way, and he has to address it to his wife, otherwise it will still be infelicitous. As for the conditions of the second class, the Muslim man must use the correct sentence. If he does not, then it will not have the expected effect. And he must say it three times in succession. One or twice is not enough to bring it off. To adhere to the sincerity clauses, the speaker must mean what he says. When promising, for example, he must be prepared to fulfill it. And he must do so subsequently. Austin described the unsuccessful performance of a speech act because of the violation of any of the four rules in A and B as a **misfire**. Thus my casually renaming any ship visiting Dublin docks is a misfire because A2 above is not adhered to. If a speech act is insincerely performed, that is, if the sincerity clauses are violated, then what will be resulted in is described by Austin as an **abuse** of the speech act, as for example saying *I bet*...with no intention to pay, or *I promise*... when I already intend to break the promise. Linguists, as opposed to philosophers, have tended not to be so interested in this second type of infelicity, since the primary speech act has, in these cases, been successfully communicated.

In the discussion of these conditions, however, Austin gradually realized that they are not really useful for separating performatives from constatives. For example, it is true that with some performatives, there will be a conventional procedure and the procedure must be executed correctly and completely. So at the wedding ceremony in Britain, when the priest asks the bridegroom, "Wilt thou have this woman to thy wedded wife... and, forsaking all other, keep thee only unto her, so long as ye both shall live", he could only answer "Yes, I will". He cannot use other expressions, even if they are synonymous. But it is also true that with some performatives, there may not be such a strict restriction. To make a promise, for example, one can either say "I promise" or "I give my word for it". On the other hand, the so-called constatives may also be infelicitous in these ways. "The present King of France is bald" is infelicitous in the same way as "I bequeath my watch to my brother" said by someone who does not have a watch. They both presuppose the existence of something, which does not actually exist. And the person who makes a statement must also have the requisite thoughts, feelings and intentions. To make a promise one must have the intention to carry it out. Similarly, to state that something is the case, one must believe it. One cannot say "The cat is on the mat, but I don't believe it".

8.1.3 Collapse of the dichotomy

Having failed to separate performatives from constatives by means of felicity conditions, Austin tried to explore the possibility of distinguishing them on grammatical and lexical criteria. He noticed that typical examples of performatives have some common features, namely, they use first person singular subject, simple present tense, indicative mood, active voice, and performative verbs. And generally their performative nature can be emphasized by inserting the adverb *hereby*, e.g. *I hereby request that you leave my property*. Judged with these new criteria, sentences in 9) are not performatives:

9) a. She names this ship the Queen Elizabeth.
   b. I'm naming this ship the Queen Elizabeth.
   c. Name this ship the Queen Elizabeth.
   d. This ship is named the Queen Elizabeth.

However, he immediately refuted it on the ground that they are neither sufficient nor necessary conditions for a performative. Performatives may take other forms as well. The subject may be first person plural, second person, third person, or a noun, and the voice may be passive like those in 10) below:

10) a. We promise to clean the room afterwards.

b. You are (hereby) charged with treason.

c. Pedestrians are requested to keep off the grass.

d. Notice is hereby given that trespassers will be prosecuted.

e. Five pounds says he doesn't make the semi-final.

(= I bet you five pounds that he doesn't make the semi-final.)

In informal situations, other moods and tenses are also possible. Instead of "I order turn right" and "I invite you to come up and see me sometime", one can simply say "Turn right" and "Come up and see me sometime". In place of "I find you guilty" the jury may say "You did it". The clearest example is, perhaps, "Thank you". It apparently looks like an imperative, without a subject. Yet it is a performative. By uttering these words, you have expressed your gratitude to the hearer. There is no need to do any other things, though people sometimes jokingly say "You can't just thank me with words".

On the other hand, constatives may also take the form of a performative as is shown in 8). And even the most typical constative verb *state*, which is used to describe things, may be used to do things. In uttering "I state that I'm alone responsible", the speaker has made a statement and undertaken the responsibility. It seems that none of the above-mentioned special characteristics of performative utterances is indispensable to their performance and therefore the distinction between performatives and constatives cannot be maintained. All sentences can be used to do things. The original performatives are only a special type of sentences in which the speaker's intention is made explicit by the performative verb.

8.1.4 A theory of illocutionary act

As Austin found there is no theoretically sound way to distinguish between performatives and constatives, he finally collapsed his distinction between the two kinds of sentences. He set up another model to explain the way acts were performed by means of language. According to his new model, a speaker might be performing three acts simultaneously when making an utterance: **locutionary act**, **illocutionary act**, and **perlocutionary act**.

A locutionary act is the act of uttering words, phrases and clauses. It is the act of conveying literal meaning by means of syntax, lexicon and phonology. An illocutionary act is the act of expressing the speaker's intention; it is the act performed in saying something. In fact, the term **speech act** is often used with just this meaning of illocutionary act. A perlocutionary act is the act performed by or resulting from saying something; it is concerned with what follows an utterance; it is the consequence of, or the change brought about by the utterance; it is the act performed by saying something. By telling somebody something the speaker may change the opinion of the hearer on something, or mislead him, or surprise him, or induce him to do something, etc. Whether or not these effects are intended by the speaker, they can be regarded as part of the act that the speaker has performed. Let's look at an example:

11) You have left the door wide open.

The locutionary act performed by the speaker is his utterance of all the words *you*, *have*, *door*, *open*, etc. thus expressing what the words literally mean.

The illocutionary act performed by the speaker is that by making such an utterance he has expressed his intention of speaking, i.e. asking someone to close the door, or making a complaint, depending on the context.

The perlocutionary act refers to the effect of the utterance. If the hearer gets the speaker's message and sees that the speaker means to tell him to close the door, the speaker has successfully brought about the change in the real world he has intended to; then the perlocutionary act is successfully performed.

Of the three speech acts, linguists are most interested in the illocutionary act because this kind of speech act is identical with the speaker's intention, and in their study of language communication, linguists are most interested in how a speaker expresses his intention and also how his intention is recognized by the hearer. In this sense, speech act theory is in fact a theory of the illocutionary act.

8.2 Searle's theory of speech acts

The speech act theory provided great philosophical insight into the nature of linguistic communication. In the light of this theory, when we are speaking a language, we are doing something, or in other words performing acts; and the process of linguistic communication consists of a sequence of acts. The theory aroused great interest among scholars in the 1960s and 1970s. One of those who made notable contributions to it is the American philosopher-linguist John Rogers Searle.

One of the contributions Searle has made is his classification of speech acts. This is something Austin himself had tried to do but did not do very successfully. According to Searle, speech acts fall into five general categories, i.e. there are five general types of things we do with language. Specific acts that fall into each type share the same **illocutionary point**, but differ in their strength. The term illocutionary point here refers to the purpose or aim of a speech act, thus the point of directives is to get the hearer to do something. The five basic categories of speech acts suggested by Searle include **representatives**, **directives**, **commissives**, **expressives**, and **declarations**.

Representatives (or **assertives**): these are speech acts which commit the speaker to the truth of the expressed proposition, and thus carry the values "true" or "false". Stating, asserting, concluding, describing, etc. are among the most typical of the representatives, e.g.

12) a. The earth is a globe.
b. It was a warm sunny day.
c. Chomsky didn't write about music.
d. I have never seen the man before.

In using a representative, the speaker makes words fit the world (of belief).

Directives: these are speech acts that the speaker uses to get the hearer to do something. Commanding, ordering, requesting, suggesting, begging, pleading, inviting, advising, warning, threatening are all specific instances of this type of speech act, e.g.

13) a. Open the window!
b. You'd better go to the clinic.
c. Your money or your life!
d. Could you lend me a pen, please?
e. I expect you to give us a favorable reply.
f. Have another glass of beer please.

In using a directive, the speaker attempts to make the world fit the words (via the hearer).

Commissives: these are speech acts whose point is to commit the speaker to some future course of action, i.e. when speaking the speaker puts himself under a certain obligation. Promising, vowing, pledging, guaranteeing, swearing, offering, undertaking are the most typical cases. Commissives can be performed by the speaker alone, or by the speaker as a member of a group.

14) a. I promise to come.

b. I will bring you the book tomorrow without fail.

c. We will not do that.

In using a commissive, the speaker undertakes to make the world fit the words (via the speaker).

Expressives: these are speech acts whose illocutionary point is to express the psychological state specified in the utterance. The speaker is expressing his feelings or attitude towards an existing state of affairs. Apologizing, thanking, congratulating, welcoming are paradigm cases of this type of speech acts, e.g.

15) a. I'm sorry for the mess I have made.

b. It's really kind of you to have thought of me.

c. Congratulations!

In using an expressive, the speaker makes words fit the world (of feeling).

Declarations: these are speech acts which bring about immediate changes in the institutional state of affairs and which tend to rely on elaborate exlinguistic institutions. Paradigm cases include excommunicating, declaring war, christening, marrying, firing from employment, etc. This reminds us of Austin's famous classical examples of speech act. The following are some other examples.

16) a. I now declare the meeting open.

b. I appoint you chairman of the committee.

c. I fire you!

d. Priest: I now pronounce you husband and wife.

e. Jury Foreman: We find the defendant guilty.

In using a declaration, the speaker changes the world via words.

As has been said earlier, all the acts that belong to the same category share the same purpose but differ in their strength or force. For instance, there are various ways to let others know what you believe in. You can say "I guess he has stolen the car", or "I believe/think he has stolen the car", or "I solemnly swear he has stolen the car". Here the degree of commitment varies from the first utterance to the third utterance. The commitment is small in the first utterance, stronger in the second, and the strongest in the third. In addition, all the utterances that can be made to perform the same act may vary in their syntactic form. For example, in order to get someone to do something, we can use the imperative form "Close the door"; we can also choose one from a variety of other forms such as these in 17):

17) a. Will you close the door!
    b. Can you close the door!
    c. Do you mind closing the door?
    d. I would be very grateful if you could close the door!
    e. The door is open!
    f. The door please!

In distinguishing these acts, Searle further developed Austin's notion of felicity conditions into a classification of conditions that must hold for a successful speech act. Searle (1969) distinguishes between **preparatory**, **propositional**, **sincerity** and **essential** conditions for an act. Here we just look at Searle's classification of felicity conditions for promise and warning.

In Searle's further development of Austin's felicity conditions, the preparatory conditions for a promise are significantly different from those for a warning. When I promise to do something, there are two preparatory conditions: first, the event will not happen by itself, and second, the event will have a beneficial effect. When I utter a warning, there are the following preparatory conditions: it isn't clear that the hearer knows the event will occur, the speaker does think the event will occur, and the event will not have a beneficial effect. Related to these conditions is the sincerity condition that, for a promise, the speaker genuinely intends to carry out the future action, and, for a warning, the speaker genuinely believes that the future event will not have a beneficial effect. The propositional conditions, also called content conditions, for both a promise and a warning, prescribe the content of the utterance must be about a future event, that is, something that has already happened cannot be promised or warned. A further content condition for a promise requires that the future event will be a future act of the speaker.

Finally, there is the essential condition, which covers the fact that by the act of uttering a promise, I hereby intend to create an obligation to carry out the action as promised. In other words, the utterance changes my state from non-obligation to obligation. Similarly, with a warning, under the essential condition, the utterance changes my state from non-informing of a bad future event to informing. This essential condition thus combines with a specification of what must be in the utterance content, the context, and the speaker's intentions, in order for a specific speech act to be appropriately (felicitously) performed.

Searle provides felicity conditions like those for a promise and a warning for each type of speech act. We shall be satisfied for now with looking at just these two. Interested readers may refer to Searle (1969).

8.3 Indirect speech acts

A different approach to distinguishing types of speech acts can be made on the basis of structure. A fairly simple structural distinction between three general types of speech acts is provided, in English, by the three basic sentence types. As shown in 18), there is an easily recognized relationship between the three structural forms (declarative, interrogative, imperative) and the three general communicative functions (statement, question, command/request).

18) a. You wear a seat belt. (declarative)
b. Do you wear a seat belt? (interrogative)
c. Wear a seat belt! (imperative)

Whenever there is a direct relationship between a structure and a function, we have a **direct speech act**. Whenever there is an indirect relationship between a structure and a function, we have an **indirect speech act**. Thus, a declarative used to make a statement is a direct speech act, but a declarative used to make a request is an indirect speech act. As illustrated in 19), the utterance in 19)a is a declarative. When it is used to make a statement, as paraphrased in 19)b, it is functioning as a direct speech act. When it is used to make a command/request, as paraphrased in 19)c, it is functioning as an indirect speech act.

19) a. It's cold outside.
b. I hereby tell you about the weather.
c. I hereby request of you that you close the door.

Different structures can be used to accomplish the same basic function, as in 20), where the speaker wants the addressee not to stand in front of the TV. The basic function of all the utterances in 20) is a command/request, but only the imperative structure in 20)a represents a direct speech act. The interrogative structure in 20)b is not being used only as a question, hence it is an indirect speech act. The declarative structures in 20)c and 20)d are also indirect requests.

20) a. Move out of the way!
    b. Do you have to stand in front of the TV?
    c. You're standing in front of the TV.
    d. You'd make a better door than a window.

One of the most common types of indirect speech in English, as shown in 21), has the form of an interrogative, but is not typically used to ask a question (i.e. we don't expect only an answer, we expect action). The examples in 21) are normally understood as requests.

21) a. Could you pass the salt?
    b. Would you open this for me?

Indeed, there is a typical pattern in English whereby asking a question about the hearer's assumed ability ("Can you?" "Could you?") or future likelihood with regard to doing something ("Will you?" "Would you?") normally counts as a request to actually do something.

Requests are often performed indirectly. Their indirectness has certain characteristics that tend to group requests into the following types:

Group 1 Sentences concerning the hearer's ability to do something (some examples below are quoted from Searle):

22) a. Can you pass the book over?
    b. Could you type this paper for me?

Group 2 Sentences concerning the speaker's wish or want that the hearer will do something:

23) a. I would like you to write this down.
    b. I would appreciate it if you could do it for me.
    c. I'd rather you didn't do that any more.
    d. I'd very much obliged if you would take me there.

Group 3 Sentences concerning the hearer's doing something:

24) a. Would you kindly pick that up for me?
    b. Wouldn't you turn the TV down a little?

Group 4 Sentences concerning the hearer's desire or willingness to do something:

25) a. Do you want to return these books for me now?

b. Would it be convenient for you to come over on Friday afternoon?

c. Would it be too much trouble for you to type the paper for me?

Group 5 Sentences concerning reasons for doing something:

26) a. You should write to them every now and then.

b. Must you make that noise when you are reading?

c. You'd better book the tickets two weeks in advance.

Sometimes sentences are used that have more than one of these elements, with one inside another:

27) Would it be too much trouble if I suggested that you could possibly return these books for me?

Indirect speech acts are generally associated with greater politeness in English than direct speech acts. In order to understand why, we have to look at a bigger picture than just a single utterance performing a single speech act.

According to Thomas (1995: 124), the indirectness of language depends on four parameters: (1) the relative power between the speaker and the hearer, (2) the relative social distance between the speaker and the hearer, (3) the degree of imposition of the action involved in a particular culture, and (4) the relative right and obligation between the speaker and the hearer.

How indirect speech acts are understood? Searle's view of how we understand indirect speech acts is that we combine our knowledge of three elements to support a chain of inference. The elements are: the felicity conditions of direct speech acts, the context of the utterance, and principles of conversational cooperation, such as the Gricean maxims of relevance, quality, etc. that we discussed in chapter 7. We can briefly sketch how these three types of knowledge are used in this chain of reasoning by looking at the example of *Can you pass the salt?* In an everyday situation, the context will tell the hearer that the speaker should already know that he can pass the salt, and thus he recognizes that the question violates the felicity conditions for a question (i.e. the speaker does not know the answer for a yes/no question in terms of the literal meaning of the question). The assumption of cooperative principles however leads the hearer to search for some other point for the utterance. This is essentially the search for an indirect speech act, i.e. the hearer asks himself, as it were, if it can't be a genuine question, what is the purpose of this utterance? The hearer knows that a condition for requests is that the hearer can actually carry out the desired act, and also recognizes that to say *yes* here is to confirm that a preparatory condition for doing the desired act has been met. The hearer also knows as part of general background knowledge that passing salt around at table is a usual part of meals, so this is a reasonable goal for the speaker to entertain. From these pieces of knowledge the hearer infers that the speaker's utterance is likely to be a request.

8.4 Indirect speech acts and politeness

Researchers of indirect speech acts have found that in many cases a speaker's use of indirect speech acts is motivated by considerations of politeness. Searle (1975: 64), for example, writes: "In the field of indirect illocutionary acts, the area of directives is the most useful to study because ordinary conversational requirements of politeness normally makes it awkward to issue flat imperative statements (e.g. *Leave the room*) or explicit performatives (e.g. *I order you to leave the room*), and we therefore seek to find indirect means to our illocutionary ends (e.g. *I wonder if you would mind leaving the room*). In directives, politeness is the chief motivation for indirectness."

Politeness is usually regarded by most pragmatists as a means or strategy which is used by a speaker to achieve various purposes, such as saving face, establishing and maintaining harmonious social relations in conversation. Leech (1983b: 80) looks on politeness as crucial in accounting for "why people are often so indirect in conveying what they mean".

The role of politeness in social interaction and conversation has been an important topic in sociology and conversational studies: we cannot hope to review this large literature here but a few remarks might shed useful light on the issue of indirect speech acts. We can begin by noting that work of the sociologist Ervin Goffman (1967, 1971, 1981) on the social construction of the self, and his notion of **face** (roughly, the public image an individual seeks to project) has influenced a number of linguistic studies which have dealt with politeness, including Brown and Levinson (1978, 1987), Leech (1983) and some others.

In Brown and Levinson's version, face is "the public self image that every member of society wants to claim for himself" (1978: 66). For them, face has two components: **positive face**, which represents an individual's desire to seem worthy and deserving of approval, and **negative face**, which represents an individual's desire to be autonomous, unimpeded by others. In George Yule's words, "A person's **negative face** is the need to be independent, to have freedom of action, and not to be imposed on by others. The word 'negative' here doesn't mean 'bad', it's just the opposite pole from 'positive'. A person's **positive face** is the need to be accepted, even liked, by others, to be treated as a member of the same group, and to know that his or her wants are shared by others. In simple terms, negative face is the need to be independent and positive face is the need to be connected." A kind of mutual self-interest requires that conversational participants maintain both their own face and their interactors' face. In this view, many verbal interactions are potential threats to face. Threats to negative face, which potentially damage an individual's autonomy, include orders, requests, suggestions and advice. Threats to positive face, which potentially lower an individual's self and social esteem, include expressions of disapproval, disagreements, accusations and interruptions. Speakers can threaten their own face by words: such self-threats to positive face include apologies and confessions.

In the continual interactive balancing of one's own and other's face, politeness serves to diminish potential threats. In other words, speakers seek to weaken face threatening acts by using a series of strategies, which together can be called politeness or tact. One of these strategies is the use of indirect speech acts. These indirect acts can be seen to follow the distinction between positive and negative face. Negative indirectness helps to diminish the threat of orders and requests: examples would include giving an explanation for a request rather than the request itself, e.g. saying *It's very hot in here* instead of *Please open the window*; or querying a preparatory condition for a request, as in *Could you open the window?* Positive indirectness weakens the threat provided by disagreements, interruptions, etc.: for example, by prefacing them with apologies or explanation as in *I'm sorry but you're wrong* instead of simply *You're wrong*, or *I have to say that I don't agree* instead of *I don't agree*.

While the notion of politeness does seem to have explanatory value for the study of indirect speech acts, one important issue which it raises is cross-cultural variation. Researchers have applied the notion of politeness to a number of different languages and some have argued that the account of politeness strategies we have outlined, including the use of indirect speech acts, is too firmly based on the European and North American cultural norms. The notion of face, according to Brown and Levinson, is universal; every language community will have a system of politeness but the details of the system will vary because face is related to "the most fundamental cultural ideas about the nature of the social persona, honour and virtue, shame and redemption, and thus to religious concepts" (Brown and Levinson, 1987: 13). Thus politeness strategies, and individual speech acts, will vary from culture to culture.

8.5 Summary

In this chapter we have seen that the social function of an utterance is an important part of its meaning. We reviewed J. L. Austin's very influential theory of **speech acts**, which emphasizes the role of language in communicating social acts like requesting, questioning, promising, thanking, stating, as well as more institutional verbal acts like pronouncing sentence in court, or performing ceremonies of baptizing, marrying, etc.

We say that understanding the speech act force, or **illocutionary force** in Austin's terms, of an utterance involves the hearer in combining linguistic knowledge about grammatical marking with both background cultural knowledge and knowledge of the immediate local context. The determination of the linguistic marking of speech act force is in itself not a simple task: we saw that the markers may have other roles to perform in the grammar. Moreover, even when we can identify sentence types, the correlation between these and speech acts is not a steady one: the investigation of indirect speech acts reveals that inference and conversational principles play a role in hearers' recognition of a speech act.

Overall the study of speech acts is a fascinating area: partly because their role is so crucial to the social interaction in a speech community (so that we have no choice but to study them) but also because they give us another glimpse of the interpretive powers that interactants routinely employ in order to communicate: unconsciously and seamlessly combining linguistic and other forms of knowledge in order to reach meaning.

Chapter 9 Decomposition of meaning

In the study of phonology, phonologists found that a phoneme is not the smallest, indivisible unit of speech sound. It can be decomposed into its constituents — distinctive features. For example, the phoneme /p/ in English can be dissected into its distinctive features **bilabial**, **stop** and **voiceless**, the phoneme /b/ into the distinctive features **bilabial**, **stop** and **voiced**, the phoneme /t/ into **alveolar**, **stop** and **voiceless**, and the phoneme /k/ into **velar**, **stop** and **voiceless**. Obviously, the first two and the second two phonemes differ from each other in only one distinctive feature. Thus the dissecting of phonemes into their distinctive features can show clearly where a phoneme is different from and where it is similar to another phoneme. This method of analyzing phonemes is taken over by semanticists and philosophers for their study of word meaning and sentence meaning. What follows from their study are two ways of analyzing lexical meaning and sentence meaning which are called respectively **componential analysis** and **predication analysis**. This chapter is an introduction of these two ways of meaning analysis.

9.1 Componential analysis

In chapter 3 we reviewed a range of lexical relations which reveal the fact that lexical items in a language are semantically interrelated to each other in one way or another. This networking feature of words in the lexicon leads semanticists to hypothesize that words are not the smallest semantic units but are built up of smaller components of meaning which are combined differently (or **lexicalized**) to form different words. Thus, words like *woman*, *bachelor*, *spinster* and *wife* are viewed as being composed of elements such as [ADULT], [HUMAN], etc.:

1) woman	[FEMALE] [ADULT] [HUMAN]
bachelor	[MALE] [ADULT] [HUMAN] [UNMARRIED]
spinster	[FEMALE] [ADULT] [HUMAN] [UNMARRIED]
wife	[FEMALE] [ADULT] [HUMAN] [MARRIED]

The elements in square brackets are called **semantic components**, **semantic features**, or **semantic primitives** and this kind of analysis is often called **componential analysis** (CA for short).

To be economical, many linguists use a binary feature format for these components. This is, plus and minus signs are used to indicate whether a certain semantic feature is present or absent in the meaning of a word. Example 2) will in this format be as below:

2) woman	[-MALE] [+ADULT] [+HUMAN]
bachelor	[+MALE] [+ADULT] [+HUMAN] [-MARRIED]
spinster	[-MALE] [+ADULT] [+HUMAN] [-MARRIED]
wife	[-MALE] [+ADULT] [+HUMAN] [+MARRIED]

Words like *father*, *mother*, *son* and *daughter*, which involve a relation between two entities, may be shown as follows:

3) father	PARENT (x, y) & MALE (x)①
mother	PARENT (x, y) & -MALE (x)
son	CHILD (x, y) & MALE (x)
daughter	CHILD (x, y) & -MALE (x)

Verbs can also be analyzed in this way:

4) take	CAUSE (x, (HAVE(x, y)))②
give	CAUSE (x, (-HAVE(x, y)))
die	BECOME (x, (-ALIVE(x)))
kill	CAUSE (x, (BECOME(y, (-ALIVE(y)))))
murder	INTEND (x, (CAUSE (x, (BECOME(y, (-ALIVE(y)))))))

The statement of semantic components is also more economical if we

① This is a usual expression in logic. In plain English, it means "x is a parent of y, and x is male".

② This expression means "x causes x to have y".

include some redundancy rules which predict the automatic relationships between components. An example of such a role is:

5) HUMAN → ANIMATE
ADULT → ANIMATE
ANIMATE → CONCRETE
MARRIED → ADULT
Etc.

With this relationship of implication we can reduce the number of components in our semantic description of a word. For example, the semantic description for *wife* in 6)a can be stated more economically as in 6)b:

6) a. wife [-MALE] [+HUMAN] [+ADULT] [+MARRIED] [+ANIMATE] [+CONCRETE], etc.
b. wife [-MALE] [+ADULT] [+MARRIED]

Componential analysis has a number of striking advantages.

Firstly, by showing the semantic components of different words we may better account for the sense relations between words and those between sentences. A pair or a group of words are synonymous if they share a number of common semantic features. A pair or a group of words are antonymous if they share all the other common semantic features except one crucial contrasting semantic feature. Pairs of antonyms include *man* and *woman*, *boy* and *girl*, *give* and *take*, and many others. Words which have all the semantic components of another are hyponyms of the latter, e.g. *boy* and *girl* are hyponyms of *child* since they have all the semantic components of their superordinate, namely, [HUMAN] and [–ADULT].

Secondly, componential analysis throws new light on sense relations between sentences, which may allow an economic characterization of these relations. In example 7) below, 7)a-c are all self-contradictory, as there are words or expressions, which have contradictory semantic components in them.

7) a. *John killed Bill but Bill didn't die.
b. *John killed Bill but he was not the cause of Bill's death.
c. *John murdered Bill without intending to.

Examples 8) and 9) are similar examples of contradiction which can be explained with semantic components.

8) a. John is married to Mary.

b. John is a bachelor.

9) a. I am an orphan.

b. I have a father.

But a more important sense relation between sentences is entailment, exemplified by the pairs of sentences in examples 10), 11), 12) and 13).

10) a. Smith cooked some lambchops.

b. Smith cooked some meat.

11) a. John killed Bill.

b. Bill died.

12) a. I saw a dog.

b. I saw an animal.

13) a. John is a bachelor.

b. John is unmarried.

The member sentences of each pair are in such a relationship that the truth of the second sentence necessarily follows from the truth of the first sentence, while the falsity of the first follows from the falsity of the second. In terms of semantic components, we can say it is because the first sentence in each pair contains words which have all the semantic components of a word used in the second sentence.①

Despite its advantages, componential analysis also faces some problems when analyzing the meaning of a word in terms of semantic components. One problem is that many words are polysemous. They have more than one meaning, consequently they will have different sets of semantic components. A case in point is the word *man*, which is usually said to have a component [MALE]. But it may also be used in a generic sense as in *Man is mortal*, which applies to both sexes. Secondly, some semantic components are seen as binary taxonomies. [MALE] and [FEMALE] is one, and [ADULT] and [YOUNG] is another. But as we have learnt

---

① There seems to be an exception as shown by the sentences in 1) below. 1)a entails 1)b, but *boys* has all the semantic components of *children*, not the other way round. However, this exception is more apparent than real. This entailment comes from the use of *all* rather than the sense relation between *boys* and *children*. If *some children*, or *children*, is used in 1)a, it will no longer entail 1)b, which is also born out by the sentences in 2).

1) a. All children are a nuisance.

b. Boys are a nuisance.

2) a. He likes all fruit.

b. He likes apples.

in the discussion of antonymy in chapter 3, the opposition between [MALE] and [FEMALE] is different from that between [ADULT] and [YOUNG]. The former is absolute while the latter is relative. In English, though both *boy* and *girl* are marked as [YOUNG] or [–ADULT], the distinction between *boy* and *man* is very different from that between *girl* and *woman*. Very often, the former distinction is relatively clear-cut while the latter is rather vague. There is a considerable overlap between *girl* and *woman*. A female person may often be referred to by both. The third problem with this analysis is that there is a class of words that do not seem to have any semantic features, such as *the*, *of*, and *ah*. They are generally referred to as function words, as opposed to content words. The fourth problem concerns the identification of semantic primitives. These primitives have been attacked from both philosophical and psychological perspectives. The former claims that these semantic components are simply a variation of, and equivalent to, the necessary and sufficient conditions approach to word meaning that we discussed in chapter 2. As we saw there, it proves impossible to agree on precise definitions of word meaning. The resulting practical difficulties for the decompositional semanticists include knowing how to validate any proposed set of primitives, and when to stop identifying them, e.g. knowing what are the right features and how many is enough. The criticisms from the psychological perspective claim that there is no experimental evidence for semantic primitives. Experiments have shown little or no support for varying degrees of internal complexity in words. These studies seem to show that in processing language we seem to treat words as atoms of meaning, and therefore do not divide them into subcomponents in order to understand them. The fifth problem goes around how to explain the semantic components themselves. As it stands, semantic components like [HUMAN] [ADULT] [MALE] are not ordinary words of English, they belong to a **metalanguage**, a language used for talking about another language. The attempt to explain the meaning of *man* in terms of these components is simply a translation from English into the metalanguage. To someone who does not know the metalanguage, this translation explains nothing.

To decompositional semanticists, none of these attacks seems fatal. Responses to the psychological attack, e.g. Jackendoff (1990: 37ff), point out that we would expect words to be the relevant unit for processing, not components.

After all, goes this reply, that's why semantic features are bunched into word units: because these particular bunchings have cognitive utility, i.e. they are useful sizes and mixtures for thinking and talking about the world. In reply to the complaint about the never-ending identification of primitives, these linguists tend to claim that this is an empirical question, not solvable in advance by stipulation. "There should eventually come a point when increasing the complexity of a semantic theory by adding new markers no longer yields enough advantage in precision and scope to warrant the increase. At that point the system of markers should reflect the systematic features of the semantic structure of the language." (Katz and Fodor, 1963: 190) Responses to the criticism of metalanguages have varied: some semanticists agree with it and conduct their inquiry through the medium of a natural language like English. This is in effect to give up the search for a neutral metalanguage. Another response is to rely more firmly on tried and tested metalanguages from other disciplines like logic. Still others rely on empirical justification for the formalisms they use: in this view the machinery is justified to the extent it allows the analyst to capture significant generalizations.

9.2 Katz's semantic theory

One of the earliest approaches to semantics within generative grammar was componential: it appeared in Katz and Fodor (1963), and has been refined since, notably in Katz and Postal (1964) and Katz (1972). For simplicity we will refer to it as **Katz's theory**. Two central ideas of this theory are:

(1) Semantic rules have to be **recursive** for the same reasons as syntactic rules: that the number of possible sentences in a language is very large, possibly infinite.

(2) That the relationship between a sentence and its meaning is not arbitrary and unitary, i.e. that syntactic structure and lexical content interact so that *John killed Fred* and *Fred killed John* do not have the same meaning despite containing the same lexical elements; nor do *The snake frightened Mary* and *The movie delighted Horace* despite having the same syntactic structure. In other words that meaning is **compositional**. The way words are combined into phrases and phrases into sentences determines the meaning of the sentences.

Katz's theory reflects this by having rules which take input from both the syntactic component of the grammar, and from the vocabulary. For these linguists the aims of the semantic component, paralleling the aims of syntax, are:

(1) to give specifications of the meanings of lexical items;

(2) to give rules showing how the meanings of lexical items build up into the meanings of phrases and so on up to sentences;

(3) to do this in a universally applicable metalanguage.

The first two aims are met by having two components: firstly, a dictionary which pairs lexical items with a semantic representation; and secondly, a set of **projection rules**, which show how the meanings of sentences are built up from the meanings of lexical items. The third aim is partially met by the use of semantic components. We can look at the dictionary and the projection rules in turn.

9.2.1 The Katzian dictionary

The details of the form of dictionary entries changed considerably during the development of this theory; we can risk abstracting a kind of typical entry for the most famous example: the word *bachelor* (Katz and Fodor, 1963; Katz and Postal, 1964).

14) bachelor {N}

a. (human) (male) [one who has never been married]

b. (human) (male) [young knight serving under the standard of another knight]

c. (human) [one who has the first or lowest academic degree]

d. (animal) (male) [young fur seal without a mate in the breeding season]

The conventions for this entry are as follows. Information within curly brackets {*i*} is grammatical information; here simply that the four readings are all nouns. Our entry in 14) contains two types of semantic component: the first, the elements within parentheses (*i*), are **semantic markers**. These are the links which bind the vocabulary together, and are responsible for the lexical relations we looked at earlier. The second type, shown in square brackets [*i*], are **distinguishers**. This is idiosyncratic semantic information that identifies the lexical item. So Katz and his colleagues built into their theory the common-sense idea that part of a word's meaning is shared with other words, but part is unique to that word.

9.2.2 Projection rules

These rules are responsible for showing how the meaning of words combines into larger structures. Since this theory was designed to be part of a Chomskyan generative grammar, the rules interfaced with a generative syntactic component. So typically the projection rules operated on syntactic phrase markers, or "trees", as in Fig. 9.1. The projection rules used these trees to structure the amalgamation of word meanings into phrase meanings, and then phrase meanings into the sentence's meaning. Again we can select a standard example from Katz and Fodor (1963) in Fig. 9-1. In this figure the subscripts (1-4) on the syntactic labels show the order of amalgamation of semantic readings, once the individual words had been attached to the bottom of the tree. To keep the figure readable, we just include the words, not their associated dictionary entries, which are of course what is actually being amalgamated; we'll look at this fuller version a little later. Thus the projection rules begin at the bottom of the syntactic tree by amalgamating the semantic readings of *the* and *man* to give the semantics of the NP *the man*. Similarly, the rules combine the semantics of *colorful* and *ball*, then add the semantics of *the*, to form the NP *the colorful ball*. Thereafter the rules move up the tree combining elements until a semantic representation for the whole sentence *The man hits the colorful ball* is reached. We can see that these projection rules are clearly designed to reflect the compositionality of meaning and they effectively provide a solution to the integration of syntax and semantics. Sentences made up of the same words but in different orders will surely be given different semantic interpretations.

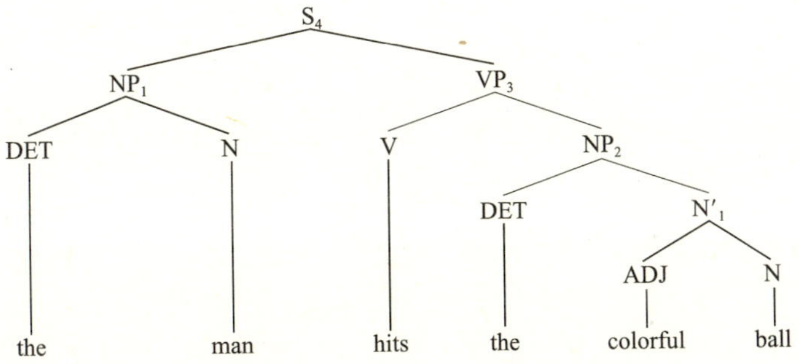

Fig. 9-1 Projection rules

The main constraint on the amalgamation processes involved in these rules is provided by **selection restrictions**. These are designed to reflect some of the contextual effects on word meaning. We can stay with the same example and look at the dictionary entries for *colorful* and *ball* in 15) and 16) below, with the selection restrictions shown on the adjective in angle brackets 〈 〉:

15) colorful {ADJ}

a. (color) [abounding in contrast or variety of bright colors] 〈(physical object) or (social activity)〉

b. (evaluative) [having distinctive character, vividness, or picturesqueness] 〈(aesthetic object) or (social activity)〉

16) ball {N}

a. (social activity) (large) (assembly) [for the purpose of social dancing]

b. (physical object) [having globular shape]

c. (physical object) [solid missile for projection by engine of war]

Thus the dictionary provides two readings for *colorful* and three for *ball*; and as we noted, the selection restrictions which restrict co-occurrence are attached to the adjective. To see how this works we can observe that by simple arithmetic the two readings for *colorful* and the three for *ball* should produce six combinations for *colorful ball*. However some combinations are blocked by the selection restrictions: the second reading of *colorful*, being restricted to (aesthetic object) or (social activity) will not match the second or third readings for *ball*.

As the projection rules successively amalgamate readings, the selection restrictions will limit the final output. We will not spell out the process in any great detail here except to show one legal output of the amalgamation rules for Fig. 9.1:

17) The man hits the colorful ball.

[some contextually definite](physical object)(human)(adult)(male)(action)(instancy)(intensity)[strikes with a blow or missile][some contextually definite](physical object)(color)[[abounding in contrast or variety of bright colors][having globular shape]]

From this brief outline of the Katzian approach to meaning, we can see that an essential part of the theory is the attempt to establish a semantic metalanguage through the identification of semantic components: in simple terms, the theory is **decompositional**. It is these components that Katz (1972) uses to try to characterize the semantic relations of hyponymy, antonymy, synonymy, contradiction, entailment, etc. We can take just one example of this: Katz (1972: 40) provides the simplified dictionary entry for *chair* in 18):

18) chair

(object)(physical)(non-living)(artifact)(furniture)(portable) (something with legs)(something with a back)(something with a seat)(seat for one)

Katz argues that the internal structure of components in 18) can explain the entailment relation between 19) below and each of 20)a-h:

19) There is a chair in the room.

20) a. There is a physical object in the room.

b. There is something non-living in the room.

c. There is an artifact in the room.

d. There is a piece of furniture in the room.

e. There is something portable in the room.

f. There is something having legs in the room.

g. There is something with a back in the room.

h. There is a seat for one in the room.

This then is a semantic justification for meaning components.

However, there are problems in this theory. First, the distinction between semantic marker and distinguisher is not very clear. Katz and Fodor themselves pointed out that the feature (young) in the dictionary entry for *bachelor*, which we quoted earlier, was included in a distinguisher, but it could be regarded as a semantic marker, since it represents something general. In Katz and Postal (1964: 14), even (never married)(knight)(seal) are treated as semantic markers. And eventually Katz dropped this distinction completely.

Second, there are cases in which the collocation of words cannot be accounted for by grammatical markers, semantic markers or selection restrictions. Katz and Fodor (1971[1963]: 513) argue that features (male)(female) are involved in the different acceptability of *The girl gave her own dress away* and **The girl gave his own dress away*. Presumably, they would also say the acceptability of *He* *said hello to the nurse and she greeted back* shows that *nurse* has a feature (female). But *My cousin is a male nurse* is a perfectly normal sentence while *My cousin is a female nurse* is decidedly odd.

The most serious defect concerns the use of semantic markers like (human) and (male), which, more usually called semantic components as we mentioned in the last section, are elements of an artificial metalanguage. To explain the meaning of man in terms of (human)(male) and (adult), one must go on to explain the meaning of these semantic markers themselves, otherwise it means nothing.

9.3 Components and conflation patterns

The notion of semantic component is also used by Leonard Talmy (1975, 1983, 1985), who has studied how elements of meaning are combined not only in single words but cross phrases. Talmy has for example identified semantic components associated with verbs of motion. These include the following (Talmy, 1985: 60-61):

21) the **Figure**: an object moving or located with respect to another object (the **Ground)**;
the **Motion**: the presence *per se* of motion or location in the event;
the **Path**: the course followed or the site occupied by the Figure object with respect to the Ground object;
the **Manner**: the type of motion.

Thus in 22), *Henry* is the Figure; the Ground is *the crocodile*; the Path is *away from*; and the verb encodes the Manner of motion: *swam*.

22) Henry swam away from the crocodile.

In 23) below, *the banana* is the Figure; *the tree* is the Ground; *from* is the Path; and Manner is again expressed in the verb *hung*.

23) The banana hung from the tree.

Talmy has pointed out differences between languages in how these semantic components are typically combined or **conflated** in verbs and verb phrases. Comparing for example how Path and Manner information is conflated in English, as in 24) below, and Spanish, as in 25):

24) a. He ran out of the house.
b. He ran up the stairs.

25) a. Salió de la casa corriendo.
left from the house running
"He ran out of the house."
b. Subió las ecaleras corriendo.
went-up the stairs running
"He ran up the stairs."

In the English sentences in 24) the Manner, "running", is incorporated in the verbs while the direction, or the Path, is encoded in an external prepositional phrase. This strategy for the verb is schematically represented as in 26) below:

26) Conflation of Motion with Manner (Talmy, 1985: 62)

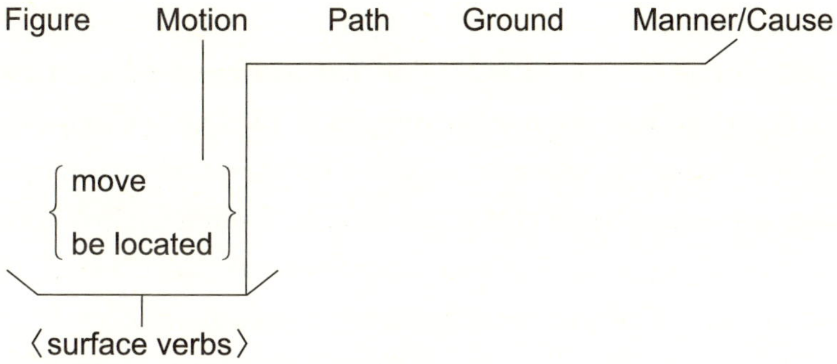

Other examples of this pattern from English are in 27):

27) a. The flag *drooped* on the mast.
b. The ball *spun* across the line.
c. She *pirouetted* out of the lecture hall.
d. They *rolled* the beer keg into the seminar.

In the Spanish sentences in 25) the information is differently packaged: the Path is encoded in the verb and the Manner is encoded in external phrases. The conflation in the verb can be represented as in 28):

28) Conflation of Motion with Path (Talmy, 1985: 69)

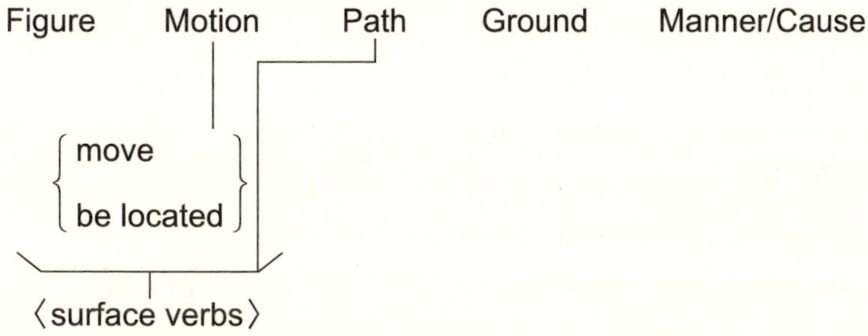

Some further examples of this from Spanish are in 29) (Talmy, 1975, 1985):

29) a. La botella *entró* a la cueva (flotando).
the bottle moved-in to the cave (floating)
"The bottle floated into the cave."

b. La botella *salió* de la cueva (flotando).
the bottle moved-out from the cave (floating)
"The bottle floated out of the cave."

c. *Metí* el barril a la bodega rodandolo.
I moved in the keg to the storeroom rolling it
"I rolled the keg into the storeroom."

A third possible pattern of conflation combines the Figure with the Motion: that is, instead of information about Manner — about *how* something is moving — being incorporated into the motion verb, as in English *running/swimming/hopping/cartwheeling etc. into the cave*, such a pattern would include information about *what* is moving. Talmy (1985) identifies the Californian Hokan language, Atsugewi as a clear instance of this pattern and concludes that in Atsugewi semantic features of the Figure are encoded in the verbs of motion.

This pattern of conflation is represented schematically as in 30):

30) Conflation of Motion with Figure(Talmy, 1985: 73)

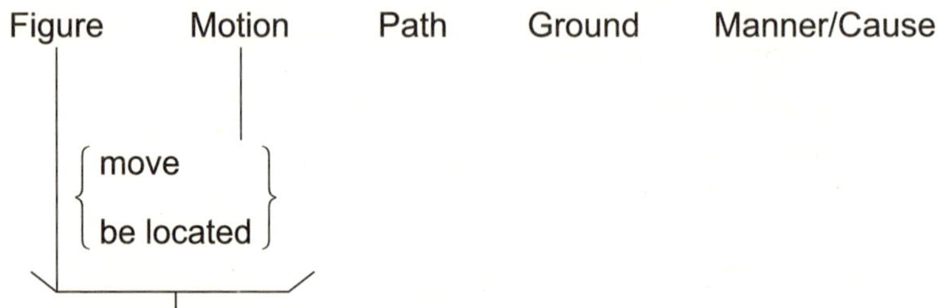

Talmy (1985) suggests that languages can be classified into different types, depending upon how their semantic components characteristically map into grammatical categories such as verbs. The word *characteristically* is used here to identify a normal or **unmarked** pattern in the language:

Any language uses only one of these types for the verb in its most characteristic expression of Motion. Here, "characteristic" means that: (1) It is colloquial in style, rather than literary, stilted, etc. (2) It is frequent in occurrence in speech, rather than only occasional. (3) It is pervasive, rather than limited, that is, a wide range of semantic notions are expressed in this type. (Talmy, 1985: 62)

The idea is that languages fall into different types on the basis of their patterns of conflation, and thus a classification or **typology** can be set up, as in Table 9-1 (Talmy, 1985: 75).

Table 9-1 Language family in terms of verb conflation patterns

Language/Language family	Verb conflation patterns
Romance, Semitic, Polynesian, Nez Perce, Caddo	Path + fact-of-Motion
Indo-European except Romance, Chinese	Manner/ Cause + fact-of-Motion
Atsugewi and all of North Hokan, Navajo	Figure + fact-of-Motion

Talmy's work has led to a number of cross-linguistic studies of how semantic components are conflated into lexical and grammatical structures. Scholars in China have done some contrastive studies of motion verbs and other kinds of verb in English and Chinese, and have found that the conflation patterns of semantic components of motion verbs and other kinds of verb in the two languages are not the same in every way though, according to Talmy, both of them fall into the same type of language, that is, the **manner language** or **satellite-framed language**. In the next section we will give a brief introduction of their studies.

9.4 Conflation patterns of motion verbs in English and Chinese

This section is a contrastive study on the similarities and differences between English and Chinese motion verbs in conflation or lexicalization patterns. The introduction is mainly based on Li Xue's *A Contrastive Study of Lexicalization Patterns in Motion Verbs Between English and Chinese*, published in 2011.

9.4.1 Conflation patterns of manner verbs in English and Chinese

9.4.1.1 Similarities

Roughly speaking, English and Chinese manner verbs are similar in two aspects. In the first aspect, English and Chinese have many similar domains of manner verbs, like *walk*（走）, *run*（跑）, *climb*（爬）, etc. This can be shown by comparing the lists of English and Chinese manner verbs in the following Table 9-2 (domains are capitalized).

Table 9-2 Similar domains of manner verbs in English and Chinese

Domain	English	Chinese
WALK	*walk*	走
CLIMB	*climb*	爬
RUN	*run*	跑
JUMP	*jump*	跳
FAST MOTION	*rush, plunge, race*	冲，扑，疾驰
SMOOTH MOTION	*glide, slide*	滑
FURTIVE MOTION	*slip*	溜
(LIQUID) MOVE	*flow, splash*	流，溅
MOVE IN WATER	*swim, float*	游，漂
(BIRDS) MOVE	*fly, flit*	飞，掠
SUDDEN MOTION	*flash*	闪
MOVE DOWNWARD	*dive, fall*	俯冲，跌
MOVE IN LARGE NUMBERS	*crowd, stream, swarm*	拥，涌，蜂拥
MOVE BY VEHICLES	*drive, paddle*	驶，划
MOVE AROUND	*roll*	滚
(WIND) MOVE QUICKLY	*sweep*	扫
GO HURRIEDLY	*hurry*	赶
MOVE LIKE A WORM	*wriggle*	蠕动

How to explain this similarity in manner verbs between English and Chinese? The answer lies in human capacity for basic-level categorization.

Categorization is the most fundamental of all human cognitive abilities; it's the ability to categorize, i.e. to see similarity in diversity (Taylor, 2001: F42). The contemporary cognitive science has challenged the traditional views on categorization and proposed new theories of categorization, which center on the idea that human beings categorize the world on the basis of prototypes and basic-level categories. We will not go further with this point here. For details of categorization, prototypes and basic-level categories, see 10.4.1.

Initial research on basic level and other levels of categorization had been mainly made on objects and organisms. Later, discussions about levels and basicness of activities or actions began to appear. For example, in motion verb category, there is the hierarchy of MOVE, WALK, STRIDE at the superordinate, basic and subordinate levels respectively, as presented in the following Fig. 9-2.

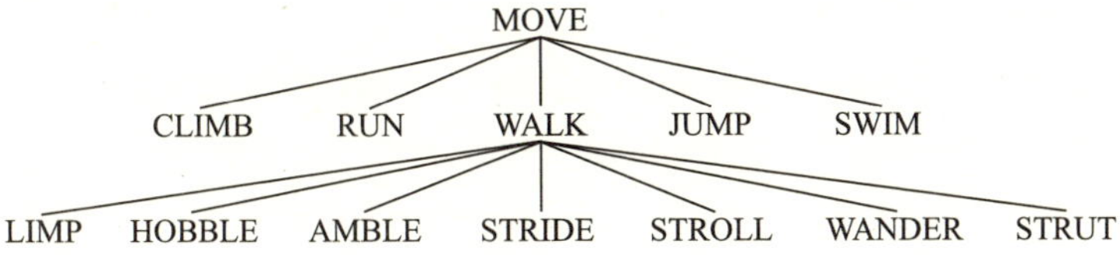

Fig. 9-2 Hierarchy of motion verbs

Though it is sometimes problematic to define the superordinate or subordinate status of some actions, most people would agree that actions like *walk*（走）, *run*（跑）, *climb*（爬）, *jump*（跳）, *swim*（游）belong to basic-level categories in motion domain. Since motion is one of the most basic human experiences, we can conclude that basic-level categorization in motion domain should be the same for all human beings, including English and Chinese people. This can explain why English and Chinese have many similar domains of manner verbs. It is the common basic-level categorization in English and Chinese people's conceptualization of motion domain that leads to similar lexicalizations of these basic concepts.

The rationality of this explanation can also be proved by the fact that most of these domains of manner verbs also exist in many other languages, such as Turkish, Spanish, Japanese, Korean and Thai. Turkish, Spanish, Japanese, Korean and Thai are path languages, in which manner verbs are not the preponderant group of motion verbs. However, some basic domains of manner verbs also exist in these languages. This fact shows that basic-level categorizations in the conceptualizations of motion domain are similar for most human beings.

Now we turn to the second aspect concerning the similarities between English and Chinese manner verbs. According to the result of a quantitative study by Li Xue (2011), manner verbs are used with a frequency of 76.22% in English and 70.23% in Chinese. Contrasted with the frequency of 22.52% and 29.48% of path verbs used in English and Chinese respectively, manner verbs are used with a much higher frequency than path verbs in both English and Chinese. The underlying reason for this phenomenon is that manner is a salient domain in both English and Chinese speakers' conceptualizations of motion events. This is the second similarity in manner verbs between English and Chinese, and this similarity seems to support Talmy's typological classification of Chinese as a manner language.

9.4.1.2 Differences

Through a comparison of English and Chinese manner verbs, it is found that the major difference between them is that there is a great discrepancy in the number of types of manner verbs between English and Chinese. English has 198 types of manner verbs, whereas in Chinese the number is only 66 (Li Xue, 2011: 100). The great discrepancy in the number of types of manner verbs between English and Chinese can be attributed to two differences in the construction of manner verb lexicon in English and Chinese.

The first difference is that for many basic domains of manner, Chinese does not have as diverse manner verbs which belong to the subordinate categories as English. We will take the domains of "walking, jumping, climbing and running" for illustration.

In the domain of "walking", English has more than thirty motion verbs of subordinate categories expressing various specific manners of walking, whereas Chinese has only a few such verbs, as presented in the following Table 9-3.

Table 9-3 Manner verbs of "walking" in English and Chinese

Manners of walking	English	Chinese
with big steps	*stride, march*	—
unevenly, due to injury	*limp, hobble*	—
unsteadily, esp. due to illness, drink, etc.	*lurch, stumble, reel, totter, stagger, falter*	蹒跚，趔趄，踉跄
heavily	*clump, plod, trudge, lumber, trundle*	—
heavily and angrily	*stamp, stomp, stump*	—
awkwardly, without lifting the feet	*shuffle, shamble, waddle*	—
quietly, trying to avoid being noticed	*tiptoe, pad*	—
proudly and confidently	*strut, prance, swagger*	—
shakily, usu. from age	*toddle, dodder*	—
up and down	*pace*	踱，踅

Continued

Manners of walking	English	Chinese
lightly	*patter, trip*	—
uncertainly or secretively	*sidle*	蹭
quickly	*trot*	—
with one foot in front of the other	*step*	迈，跨

As is shown in Table 9-3, Chinese has only a few motion verbs expressing specific manners of walking, which are equivalent to those in English. For many other motion verbs which express specific manners of walking in English, there are no counterparts in Chinese. Chinese usually uses the combination of "adverbial expressions＋走" to express those specific manners of walking, such as 一瘸一拐地走(limp)，拖拖拉拉地走(shuffle)，摇摇晃晃地走(dodder)，踮着脚尖走(tiptoe)，瑟瑟缩缩地走(falter)，大摇大摆地走(swagger)，蹑手蹑脚地走(pad), etc.

In the domain of "jumping", English has several motion verbs expressing specific manners of "jumping", such as *hop* for "jump on one foot", *leap* for "jump with big steps", *skip* for "jump lightly with quick steps", *gambol* for "jump about in play", *spring* for "jump suddenly", and *bounce* for "jump like a ball", etc. In contrast, besides 跳 (jump), Chinese has only three verbs expressing specific manners of "jumping", which are 弹跳(spring), 雀跃(gambol) and 飞跃(leap). What's more, all the motion verbs for "jumping" in English are single words, whereas the three verbs for "jumping" in Chinese are compound words and therefore they are not so much lexicalized as their English counterparts. Moreover, these three verbs are seldom used in motion event descriptions in Chinese. To express specific manners of jumping, Chinese usually resorts to adverbial expressions.

Similarly, in the domain of "climbing", English has several motion verbs expressing specific manners of "climbing", such as *crawl* and *creep* for "climb with body close to the ground", *clamber* and *scramble* for "climb up with difficulty", *shin* for "climb up and down quickly and easily", and *slither* for "climb like snake". In contrast, besides 爬(climb), Chinese has only one verb — 攀(clamber) expressing specific manner of "climbing", but it is seldom used in motion event descriptions. Chinese usually uses the combination of "adverbial expressions + 爬" to express different manners of "climbing".

In the domain of "running", English also has a few motion verbs expressing specific manners of "running", such as *scuttle* and *scurry* for "run with quick short steps", *scamper* for "run quickly taking short steps, usu. playfully or in fright", *sprint* for "run at one's fastest speed, esp. for a short distance", and *skitter* for "run very quickly and lightly". However, except for the general manner verb 跑 (run), Chinese has only 飞奔 and 奔跑 expressing specific manners of "running". To express other specific manners of running, Chinese also resorts to adverbial expressions.

For the convenience of checking and comparison, motion verbs for "jumping, climbing and running" in English and Chinese are presented in the following three tables.

Table 9-4 Manner verbs of "jumping" in English and Chinese

Manners of jumping	English	Chinese
on one foot	*hop*	—
with big steps	*leap*	飞跃
lightly with quick steps	*skip*	—
playfully	*gambol*	雀跃
suddenly	*spring*	弹跳
like a ball	*bounce*	—

Table 9-5 Manner verbs of "climbing" in English and Chinese

Manners of climbing	English	Chinese
with body close to the ground	*crawl, creep*	—
up with difficulty	*clamber, scramble*	攀
up and down quickly and easily	*shin*	—
like a snake	*slither*	—

Table 9-6 Manner verbs of "running" in English and Chinese

Manners of running	English	Chinese
with quick short steps	*scuttle, scurry*	奔跑
quickly taking short steps, usu. playfully or in fright	*scamper*	—

Continued

Manners of running	English	Chinese
quickly and lightly	*skitter*	飞奔
at one's fastest speed, esp. for a short distance	*sprint*	—

Next we turn to the second difference in manner verbs between English and Chinese.

The second difference in the constitution of manner verb lexicon between English and Chinese is that Chinese has no counterparts for manner verbs of certain domains in English. For instance, Chinese has no verbs for expressing the concept of "moving with noise or sound emission", but English has a fair number of such motion verbs, such as *rattle, roar, spatter, splat, splatter, thunder, whiz, whoosh, clatter, click, crunch, plop, rumble, wheeze, whistle,* etc.

To express the concept "moving with noise or sound emission", which are lexicalized as verbs in English, Chinese uses analytic expressions such as "唰的一声飞过""轰隆轰隆驶过"。

Another group of motion verbs which exist in English but are absent in Chinese are those verbs expressing the concept of "moving with a certain attitude", such as *flounce* for "moving violently esp. with anger", *prance* for "moving happily or proudly", *strut* and *swagger* for "moving proudly", and *stamp*, *stomp*, *stump*, *storm* for "moving angrily", etc. To express those concepts, Chinese uses analytic expressions such as "忿忿地走出房间""气急败坏地冲进办公室""昂首阔步地踱出礼堂"。

To sum up, manner verbs in Chinese are not as diverse as those in English, which are reflected in two aspects: first, manner verbs in Chinese do not express as specific distinctions of manner as those in English; second, certain domains of manner verbs existing in English have no counterparts in Chinese. In both cases, Chinese resorts to analytic expressions, that is, [adverbial expressions + motion verb], to express the specific manners that are conveyed by manner verbs in English.

9.4.2 Conflation patterns of path verbs in English and Chinese

The following is a contrastive study of path verbs in English and Chinese, focusing on their different features in the two languages and the implication for conceptualization.

9.4.2.1 Path verbs in English

Although English is a manner language, it does have a collection of path verbs, such as *enter, exit, ascend, descend, cross, pass, circle, advance, proceed, approach, arrive, depart, return, join, separate, part, rise, leave, near, follow*, which express motion along various paths, as described in 31).

31) a. [Move + In/Out]: *enter, exit*
   b. [Move + Up/Down]: *ascend, descend, rise*
   c. [Move + Forward/Backward]: *advance, proceed, approach, near*
   d. [Move + To/Away/From the speaker]: *arrive, depart, leave, return*
   e. [Move + Together/Apart]: *join, separate, part*
   f. [Move + After]: *follow*
   g. [Move + Past]: *pass*
   h. [Move + Around]: *circle*
   i. [Move + Above/Through]: *cross*

However, Talmy (2000, Vol. Ⅱ : 53) states: "these verbs are not the most characteristic type in English, and many are not the most colloquial alternatives available. And significantly, the great majority — here, all but the last four verbs listed (*rise, leave, near, follow*) — are not even original English forms but rather are borrowings from Romance, where they are the native type." What Talmy says has two implications:

First, path verbs in English are not preferred in motion event descriptions, especially in colloquial language. Second, most path verbs in English are not English originals, but borrowings from other languages. Nevertheless, English has a group of particles — prepositions or adverbs expressing path concepts, which are English originals, like *in, out, up, down, back, past, across, through, along, on, over, above, below, off, aside, away, ahead, apart*, and *together*, etc. These particles are more often used to express path in motion event descriptions in English than path verbs are. This fact means that path concepts tend to be lexicalized in English as prepositions or adverbs instead of verbs.

9.4.2.2 Path verbs in Chinese

Chinese also has a collection of path verbs, which express motion along various paths and can correspond to the respective domains of path verbs in English, as listed below in 32):

32) a. [Move + In/Out]: 进，出
b. [Move + Up/Down]: 上，下，起，升，降
c. [Move + Forward/Backward]: 前进，退，撤，后退，撤退
d. [Move + To/Away/From the speaker]: 回，到，离开
e. [Move + Together/Apart]: 凑，围，聚，散
f. [Move + After]: 跟
g. [Move + Past]: 过，经过
h. [Move + Around]: 绕
i. [Move + Above/Through]: 通过，穿过，穿越

In contrast to English path verbs, Chinese path verbs show very different characteristics. The differences are reflected mainly in two aspects which will be elaborated in what follows.

9.4.2.2.1 Path verb as a colloquial lexicalization pattern

Chinese path verbs can stand alone in a sentence to express motion. Distinct from English path verbs of Latin origin, which are not the most characteristic type in English and not the most colloquial alternatives in motion event descriptions, Chinese path verbs are highly colloquial and of frequent use in this function. And it is equally natural for Chinese speakers to use either path-verb-based constructions as in 33)a or manner-verb-based constructions as in 33)b to represent most events of autonomous or self-agentive motion:

33) a. 恰好那时杜学诗又飞跑着来了……（《子夜》）
b. 忽然她转身飞跑到厢房的前半间……（《子夜》）

According to Li Xue (2011: 117), in the novel《平凡的世界》, path verbs are even used with greater frequency than manner verbs, occupying 52.11% of the total motion verbs used. So it can be concluded that path verb is also a colloquial lexicalization or conflation pattern for motion verbs in Chinese, as is true with manner verb.

9.4.2.2.2 Double features of Chinese path verbs

Different from English path verbs, which can only be used as main verbs in motion event descriptions, many Chinese path verbs (the directional and deictic path verbs) can be used not only independently as main verbs in motion event descriptions as in examples 34)a and 34)b, but after a manner verb to serve as the satellite of the manner verb as well, in the way that English verb particles or prepositions serve as the satellite of a manner verb, as in examples 34)c and 34)d (the elements in discussion are underlined).

34) a. 鸿渐正在解释，柔嘉进门。(《围城》)

(cf. Again the bell rang: all formed in file, two and two, and in that order descended the stairs and entered the cold and dimly lit schoolroom. (*Jane Eyre*))

b. 他赶紧上了炕，蹲在坐着的老祖母面前，准备把她从那一堆破烂被褥里扶起来。(《平凡的世界》)

(cf. Oliver, groping his way with one hand, and having the other firmly grasped by his companion, ascended with much difficulty the dark and broken stairs… (*Oliver Twist*))

c. 潘玉龙踉踉跄跄地**走**进一家门脸简陋的小诊所。(《五星饭店》)

(cf. Early on the seventh morning after he had left his native place, Oliver **limped** slowly into the little town of Barnet. (*Oliver Twist*))

d. (鸿渐)这样惘惘不甘地**跳**上电车，看见邻座一对青年男女喁喁情话。(《围城》)

(cf. Mrs. Reed was rather a stout woman; but, on hearing this strange and audacious declaration, she **ran** nimbly up the stair… (*Jane Eyre*))

However, in the second function, Chinese path verbs are grammaticalized[①] into directional complements (or path satellites) rather than serve as full verbs. This means that path verbs and the grammaticalized form of them (path satellites or directional complements) coexist in the contemporary language.

9.4.2.3 Implication for conceptualization

As discussed above, most English path verbs are not originals in English but borrowings from other languages such as Romance and are not preferred

① Grammaticalization is a process whereby a content or lexical word, in the evolvement of language, becomes an empty or function word. For more details of grammaticalization, see 10.8.

in motion event descriptions. However, English has a group of particles — prepositions or adverbs expressing path concepts, which are English originals and are more often used to express path in English motion event descriptions than path verbs are. These facts mean that path concepts tend to be lexicalized in English as prepositions or adverbs instead of verbs. In contrast, Chinese path verbs have double features. They can be used independently as main verbs in motion event descriptions to express path, and can also be used after a manner verb to express path. But, in the second function, they are grammaticalized into directional complements (or path satellites) and are equivalent to English verb particles or prepositions. This means that path concepts are lexicalized as both verbs and prepositions in Chinese.

Different lexicalizations of path concepts may imply different conceptualizations about path. Here Langacker's distinction of two cognitive processes involved in the conceptualizations of complex scenes — "summary scanning" and "sequential scanning" (Langacker, 1987: 141-146, 248-253), offers us a useful line of thinking. As defined by Langacker:

> ***Summary scanning*** *is basically additive, and the processing of conceptual components proceeds roughly in parallel. All facets of the complex scene are simultaneously available, and through their co-activation they constitute a coherent gestalt. This is the mode of processing characteristic of things and atemporal relations, even those for which conceived time is a central domain.* ***Sequential scanning****, on the other hand, involves the successive transformations of one configuration into another. The component states are processed in series rather than in parallel, and though a coherent experience requires a certain amount of continuity from one state to the next, they are construed as neither coexistent nor simultaneously available. This is the mode of processing that characterizes processual predictions and defines what it means to follow the evolution of a situation through time.* (Langacker, 1987: 248)

When sequential scanning is used in the conceptualization of path, path is conceptualized as a process, which leads to its lexicalization as verbs in language expression. When summary scanning is used in the conceptualization of path, path is conceptualized as a static scene, which leads to its lexicalization as prepositions in language expression.

So, it's likely that English speakers mainly use summary scanning in the conceptualization of path, whereas Chinese speakers may use either sequential scanning or summary scanning in the conceptualization of path.

9.5 Predication analysis

Linguists have proposed different ways to analyze the meaning of sentences. They might differ in their framework of analysis, but they share the aim to abstract the meaning of sentences. What we are going to introduce briefly is the **predication analysis** proposed by the British linguist G. Leech. In his framework of analysis, the basic unit is called **predication,** which is the abstraction of the meaning of a sentence. This applies to all forms of sentence, including statements, imperative and interrogative forms. A predication consists of two types of constituents: **argument(s)** and **predicate.** An argument is a logical participant in a predication, which are usually functioned by the nominal element(s) in a sentence. A predicate is something said about an argument or it states the logical relation linking the arguments in a sentence. It is usually functioned by lexical verbs or verb phrases. For example, the predication of the sentence "Tom smokes" is said to consist of the argument "TOM" and the predicate "SMOKE", and the predication can be written as TOM (SMOKE). As the grammatical form of the sentence does not affect the semantic predication of the sentence, all the sentences in example 35) are said to have the same predication:

35) Tom smokes.
Tom is smoking.
Tom has been smoking.
Tom, smoke!
Does Tom smoke?
Tom does not smoke.

They can all be regarded as the various grammatical realizations of the same semantic predication: TOM (SMOKE).

Then some sentences contain more than one argument. For example, the sentence "Kids like apples" has two nominal elements "kids" and "apples", so its predication can be written as KID, APPLE (LIKE). The sentence "He gave me a book" has three arguments, so its predication can be written as HE, ME, BOOK (GIVE). And then in some sentences there is no argument at all, such as those English sentences containing the impersonal "it", e.g. "It is hot". "It" in this sentence can not be considered as an argument, and (BE HOT) is the predicate of the predication. According to the number of arguments contained in a predication, we classify the predications into three-place predication (containing three arguments), two-place predication (containing two arguments), one-place predication (containing one argument), and no-place predication (containing no argument).

Although predicate and argument are the same kind of unit in terms of the componential make-up of a sentence, they have different roles in the predication. The predicate can be regarded as the main element, for it includes tense, modality, etc. and it may also be said to govern the arguments for it determines the number and nature of the arguments.

9.6 Summary

In this chapter we reviewed two ways of analyzing lexical meaning and sentence meaning which are called respectively **componential analysis** and **predication analysis**. The idea behind the two ways is that word is not the smallest unit of meaning but is built up of smaller components of meaning called **semantic components**, **semantic features**, or **semantic primitives**, and the meaning of a sentence in its abstract sense can be decomposed into its own components — **predicate** and **argument(s)**. In our analysis of word meaning, we first gave a detailed description of Katz's semantic theory, then we introduced Leonard Talmy's identification of semantic components associated with verbs of motion and how languages differ in the patterns of conflation of these semantic components in verbs and verb phrases. In our analysis of sentence meaning, we introduced briefly the predication analysis proposed by the British linguist G. Leech. What is new in this chapter is our introduction of a contrastive study of the conflation patterns of motion verbs in English and Chinese, through which the differences and similarities between the conflation patterns of the two languages are revealed.

Chapter 10 *Cognitive semantics*

Cognitive semantics began in the 1970s as a reaction against the **objectivist world-view** assumed by the Anglo-American tradition in philosophy and the related approach, **truth-conditional semantics**, developed within formal linguistics. Cognitive semantics represents an approach to the study of mind and its relationship with embodied experience and culture. It proceeds by employing language as a key methodological tool for uncovering conceptual organization and structure.

Cognitive semantics is part of the larger enterprise of cognitive linguistics. The latter holds that language and language use are based on our bodily experience and the way we conceptualize it. Cognitive linguists often point to a division between **formal** and **functional** approaches to language. Formal approaches, such as **Generative Grammar** (Chomsky, 1988), are often associated with a certain view of language and cognition: that knowledge of linguistic structures and rules forms an autonomous module (or faculty), independent of other mental processes of attention, memory, and reasoning. This external view of an independent linguistic module is often combined with a view of internal modularity: that different levels of linguistic analysis, such as phonology, syntax and semantics, form independent modules. In this view, the difference between modules is one of kind: thus externally, it is good practice to investigate linguistic principles without reference to other faculties; and internally, to investigate, say, syntactic principles without reference to semantic content. This characterization of formal approaches concentrates on its epistemological implications. Formalism also implies the desirability and possibility of stating the autonomous principles in ways that are formally elegant, conceptually simple, and mathematically well-formed.

Functionalism, with which cognitive linguists identify themselves, implies a quite different view of language: that externally, principles of language use embody more general cognitive principles; and internally, that explanation must cross boundaries between levels of analysis. In this view the difference between language and other mental processes is possibly one of degree but is not one of kind. Thus it makes sense to look for principles shared across a range of cognitive domains. Similarly, it is argued that no adequate account of grammatical rules is possible without taking the meaning of elements into account.

This general difference of approach underlies specific positions taken by cognitive linguist on a number of issues: in each case their approach seeks to break down the abstractions and specializations characteristic of formalism. Many of which we have met in earlier chapters. Thus studies in cognitive semantics have tended to blur, if not ignore, the commonly made distinctions between linguistic knowledge and encyclopaedic, real world knowledge — a topic we touched upon earlier; and between literal and figurative language, as we shall see. Similarly cognitive linguists share the functionalist view that distinguishing linguistic levels of analysis, while a useful ploy for practical description, is potentially harmful to our conceptions of language, since, syntax, for example, can never be autonomous from semantics or pragmatics. Ultimately, this view goes, the explanation of grammatical patterns cannot be given in terms of abstract syntactic principles but only in terms of the speaker's intended meaning in particular contexts of language use.

If we turn to meaning, a defining characteristic of cognitive semantics is the rejection of what is termed **objectivist semantics**. George Lakoff (1988:123-124), for example, assigns to objectivism the basic metaphysical belief that categories exist in objective reality, together with their properties and relations, independently of consciousness. Associated with this is the view that the symbols of language are meaningful because they are associated with these objective categories. This gives rise to a particular approach to semantics which Lakoff characterizes under three "doctrines":

(1) The doctrine of truth-conditional meaning: Meaning is based on reference and truth.

(2) The "correspondence theory" of truth: Truth consists in the correspondence between symbols and states of affairs in the world.

(3) The doctrine of objective reference: There is an "objectively correct" way to associate symbols with things in the world.

In rejecting these views, cognitive semanticists place themselves in opposition to the formal semantics approach. Cognitive semanticists take the view that we have no access to a reality independent of human categorization and that therefore the structure of reality as reflected in language is a product of human mind. Consequently they reject the **correspondence theory of truth**, discussed partly in chapter 4. For these writers, linguistic truth and falsity must be relative to the way an observer construes a situation, based on his or her conceptual framework. The real focus of investigation should, in this view, be these conceptual frameworks and how language use reflects them. In the rest of this chapter we examine this line of inquiry; we might begin here by asking of this approach our deceptively simple question: what is meaning?

One answer in the cognitive semantics literature is that meaning is based on conventionalized conceptual structures. Thus semantic structure, along with other cognitive domains, reflects the mental categories which people have formed from their experience of growing up and acting in the world. A number of conceptual structures and processes are identified in this literature but special attention is often given to **metaphor**. In cognitive linguistics metaphor is considered to be an essential element in our categorization of the world and our thinking processes. As we shall see, metaphor is seen as related to other fundamental structures such as **image schemas**, which provide a kind of basic conceptual framework derived from perception and bodily experience, and Fauconnier's (1985, 1994) notion of **mental spaces**, which are mental structures which speakers set up to manipulate reference to entities. Such mental spaces underlie the process of **conceptual blending** (Fauconnier and Turner, 2002), where speakers develop extended analogies which selectively combine existing domains of knowledge to create new scenarios. Cognitive linguists also investigate the conceptual processes which reveal the importance of the speaker's construal of a scene: processes such as **viewpoint shifting**, **figure-ground shifting** and **profiling**. Topics discussed in cognitive semantics also include metonymy, categorization, idealized cognitive models (ICMs), iconicity, grammaticalization, and so on. We look at all these in successive sections in this chapter.

A consequence of the view of language we have briefly outlined is that the study of semantics, and linguistics, must be an interdisciplinary activity. One result is that scholars working within this and related frameworks tend to stray across intra- and inter-disciplinary boundaries more easily than most. The approach to metaphor and metonymy we discuss in the next section has, for example, been applied not only to the study of grammar and semantics, but also to historical linguistics, categories of thought, poetic language, rhetoric, and ethics, amongst other areas. In our discussion, we concentrate on semantic issues and we begin with metaphor and metonymy in section 10.1.

10.1 Metaphor and metonymy

10.1.1 Metaphor

Traditionally, **metaphor** is viewed as a figure of speech in which one thing is compared to another by saying that one is the other, as in "Achilles is a lion". It is a property of words, and is used for some artistic and rhetorical purpose. There are many explanations of how metaphors work but a common idea is that metaphor is somewhat like **simile** in that a comparison is involved between two categories in both metaphor and simile, the difference being the comparison in metaphor is not explicitly marked while that in simile is overtly signaled by the use of *as* or *like*: *Achilles is as brave as a lion*; *Achilles is brave, like a lion.*

There are two traditional positions on the role of metaphor in language. The first, often called the **classical** view since it can be traced back to Aristotle's writings on metaphor, sees metaphor as a kind of decorative addition to ordinary plain language; a rhetorical device to be used at certain times to gain certain effects. This view portrays metaphor as something outside normal language and which requires special forms of interpretation from listeners or readers. A version of this approach is often adopted in the **literal language theory** we described in chapter 1. In this view metaphor is often seen as a departure from literal language (or a deviation from the norm of language use in stylistics terms), detected as anomalous by the hearer, who then has to employ some strategies to construct the speaker's intended meaning. We can take as an example of this general approach Searle(1979: 114) who describes the start of the process thus (where a contextual assumption is that Sam is a person):

> *Suppose he hears the utterance, "Sam is a pig". He knows that cannot be literally true, that the utterance, if he tries to take it literally, is radically defective. And, indeed, such defectiveness is a feature of nearly all the examples that we have considered so far. The defects which cue the hearer may be obvious falsehood, semantic nonsense, violations of the rules of speech acts, or violations of conversational principles of communication. This suggests a strategy that underlies the first step: where the utterance is defective if taken literally, look for an utterance meaning that differs from sentence meaning.*

We won't go into details of the various proposals that have been made for the next steps that the hearer uses to repair the "defective" utterance. It is commonsense in pragmatics that various kinds of contextual knowledge are employed to reach a correct interpretation of the meaning of a literally anomalous utterance.

The second traditional approach to metaphor, often called the **romantic** view since it is associated with eighteenth and nineteenth century romantic views of the imagination, takes a very different view of metaphor. In this view metaphor is integral to language and thought as a way of experiencing the world. In this view metaphor is evidence of the role of the imagination in conceptualizing and reasoning and it follows that all language is metaphorical. In particular, there is no distinction between literal and figurative language.

10.1.1.1 Metaphor in cognitive linguistics

In cognitive linguistics, metaphor is viewed as a property of concepts, not as a property of words, thus metaphor in cognitive linguistics is also called **conceptual metaphor**. Given the classical/romantic opposition we have described, the cognitive linguistics approach to metaphor can be seen as an extension of the romantic view. Cognitive linguists argue that metaphor is a powerful cognitive tool for our conceptualization of abstract categories, a very important mode of thinking and talking about the world, and that metaphor is ubiquitous in ordinary language, though they pull back a little from the strong romantic position that all language is metaphorical.

Cognitive linguists define metaphor as understanding or construing one **conceptual** or **cognitive domain** in terms of another conceptual or cognitive domain. The conceptual domain from which we draw metaphorical expressions to understand another conceptual domain is called **source domain**, while the conceptual domain that is understood this way is called **target domain**. The target domain is the starting point or described concept and the source domain is the comparison concept or the analogy. The target domain is the experience being described by the metaphor and the source domain is the means that we use in order to describe the experience. For example:

1) You're wasting my time.

As described in chapter 1(1.4.4), this sentence is based on the metaphor "TIME IS MONEY" in which the target domain, TIME, is conceptualized in terms of the source domain of MONEY. Very often, abstract concepts or experiences are described in terms of more concrete ones. In cognitive linguistics, metaphors are represented by a simple formula: "X is Y", in which X is the target domain and Y is the source domain.

Although metaphors like *Achilles is a lion* (metaphors called **resemblance metaphors** by Grady (1999) in which the target domain is not a quite abstract concept) have received considerable attention within conceptual metaphor theory, particularly within the approach now known as **Cognitive Poetics**, for the most part, research in the conceptual metaphor tradition has not been primarily concerned with metaphors of this kind. Instead, research in this tradition has focused on the kind of everyday language illustrated in the following examples. These examples represent common ways of referring to particular experiences of relations like marriage. The examples in 2) are from Lakoff and Johnson (1980: 44-45).

2) a. Look *how far we've come*.

b. We're *at a crossroads*.

c. We'll just have to go *our separate ways*.

d. We can't *turn back* now.

e. I don't think this relationship is *going anywhere*.

f. *Where* are we?

g. We're *stuck*.

h. It's been *a long, bumpy road*.

i. This relationship is *a dead-end street*.

j. We're just *spinning our wheels*.

k. Our marriage *is on the rocks*.

l. We've *gotten off the track*.

m. This relationship is *foundering*.

What is striking about these examples is that they represent ordinary everyday ways of talking about relationships: there is nothing stylized or overtly poetic about these expressions. However, these expressions are clearly non-literal: a relationship cannot literally spin its wheels, nor stand at the crossroads. In cognitive linguistics, all the above examples are viewed as linguistic realizations of the same conceptual metaphor "LOVE IS A JOURNEY".

The following is another example of conceptual metaphor, together with its linguistic realizations.

3) IDEAS ARE FOOD

a. There are too many facts here for me to *digest* them all.

b. I just can't *swallow* that claim.

c. That's *food* for thought.

d. He *devoured* the book.

In emphasizing the important role of conceptual metaphor in ordinary language, Lakoff and his colleagues have identified a large number of common metaphors. These conceptual metaphors are classified by Lakoff and Johnson (1980) into three types: **ontological metaphors**, **structural metaphors** and **orientational metaphors**.

Ontological metaphor means that human experiences with physical objects provide the basis for ways of viewing events, activities, emotions, ideas, etc., as entities and substances. Ontological metaphors can serve various purposes. By ontological metaphors we give bounded surfaces to less clearly discrete entities (mountains, hedges, street corners) and categorize events, actions and states as substances. Take the experience of rising prices as an example, which can be metaphorically viewed as an entity via the noun *inflation*. This gives us a way to refer to experiences (Lakoff and Johnson, 1980):

4) INFLATION IS AN ENTITY

a. Inflation is lowering our standard of living.

b. If there's much more inflation, we'll never survive.

c. We need to combat inflation.

d. Inflation is backing us into a corner.

e. Inflation is taking its toll at the checkout counter and the gas pump.

f. Buying land is the best way of dealing with inflation.

g. Inflation makes me sick.

In these cases, regarding inflation as an entity allows human beings to refer to it, quantify it, identify it, treat it as a case, act with respect to it, and even believe that we understand it. Ontological metaphors are necessary for dealing with human experiences.

Ontological metaphors can be further classified into three kinds: **entity and substance metaphor**, which views experience as entity or substance in order to understand the former in terms of the latter and give the former a relevant substantial description (e.g. *There are too many fact here for me to digest them all.*); **container metaphor**, which views event, activity, state, visual field, etc. as a container, thus we can go into or go out of it (e.g. *out of sight, out of mind*; *go into action*; *put into operation*; *come into vision/use/my mind*, etc.); **personification metaphor**, which renders an inanimate thing human properties (e.g. *His theory explains to us that...*; *This fact argues against...*; *Yesterday found me...*; *Life has cheated me.*).

Structural metaphor plays the most important role because it allows us to go beyond orientation and referring and gives us the possibility to structure one concept according to another. This means that structural metaphors are grounded in our experience. Structural metaphors imply how one concept is metaphorically structured in terms of another. For example, ARGUMENT IS WAR leads to an English expression like "He attacked every weak point in my argument".

5) ARGUMENT IS WAR

a. Your claims are *indefensible*.

b. He *attacked every weak point* in my argument.

c. His criticisms were *right on target*.

d. I *demolished* his argument.

e. I've never *won* an argument with him.

f. You disagree? Okay, *shoot*!

g. If you use the *strategy*, he'll *wipe* you *out*.

h. He *shot down* all of my arguments.

It is obvious that we don't just talk about argument in terms of war. We can actually win or lose arguments. We see the person we are arguing with as an opponent. We attack his positions and we defend our own. We gain and lose ground. We plan and use strategies. If we find a position indefensible, we can abandon it and take a new line of attack. Many of the things we do in arguing are partially structured by the concept of war.

Orientational metaphor, also called **spatial metaphor**, gives a concept a spatial orientation. They are characterized not so much by structuring one concept in terms of another, but by a co-occurrence in our experience. The orientational metaphors are grounded in an experiential basis, which link together the two parts of the metaphor. The link verb "is", part of the metaphor, should be seen as the link of two different co-occurring experiences. For example, MORE IS UP. This metaphor is grounded in the co-occurrence of two different kinds of experiences: adding more of a substance and perceiving the level of the substance rise.

Orientational metaphors are based on human physical and cultural experience. For example, in some cultures the future is in front of us, whereas in others it is in back of us. Now let us study some orientational metaphors and give a brief hint about how each metaphorical concept might have arisen from human physical and cultural experience (Lakoff and Johnson, 1980: 14-21):

6) a. HAPPY IS UP; SAD IS DOWN

I'm feeling *up*. That *boosted* my spirits. My spirits *rose*. You're in *high* spirits. Thinking about her always gives me a *lift*. I'm feeling *down*. I'm *depressed*. He's really *low* these days. I *fell* into a depression. My spirits *sank*.

b. CONSCIOUS IS UP; UNCONSCIOUS IS DOWN

Wake *up*. I'm *up* already. He *rises* early in the morning. He *fell* asleep. He *dropped* off to sleep. He's *under* hypnosis. He *sank* into a coma.

c. HEALTH AND LIFE ARE UP; SICKNESS AND DEATH ARE DOWN

He's at the *peak* of health. He's in *top* shape. He *fell* ill. He's *sinking* fast. He came *down* with the flu. His health is *declining*. He *dropped* dead.

d. HAVING CONTROL OR FORCE IS UP; BEING SUBJECT TO CONTROL OR FORCE IS DOWN

I have control *over* her. He's at the *height* of his powers. He's in a *superior* position. He ranks *above* me in strength. He is *under* my control. He *fell* from power. He is my social *inferior*.

e. GOOD IS UP; BAD IS DOWN

Things are looking *up*. We hit a *peak* last year, but it's been *downhill* ever since. Things are at an all-time *low*. He does *high*-quality work.

f. VIRTUE IS UP; DEPRAVITY IS DOWN

He is *high*-minded. She has *high* standards. She is an *upstanding* citizen. That was a *low* trick. Don't be *underhanded*. I wouldn't *stoop* to that. That was a *low-down* thing to do.

As the authors point out, these metaphors seem to be based on our bodily experiences of lying down and getting up and their associations with consciousness, health and power, i.e. of verticality in human experience. For example, the conceptual metaphor "HAPPY IS UP; SAD IS DOWN" obviously derives from our everyday experience in which drooping posture typically goes along with sadness and depression, erect posture with a positive state.

From our elaboration of the three types of metaphor we can see Lakoff and Johnson's point is that when using language as what is shown in the above examples, speakers are not adding rhetorical or poetical flourishes to their language: this is how we conceive of happiness, health, etc. As a result metaphors are conceptual structures which pervade ordinary language.

10.1.1.2 Features of metaphor

Cognitive semanticists argue that, far from being idiosyncratic anomalies, metaphors exhibit characteristic and systematic features. We will look at some of these features under the headings of **pervasiveness**, **conventionality**, **systematicity**, **unidirectionality**, **abstraction**, and **cultural coherence**.

• *Pervasiveness*

In conceptual metaphor theory, metaphor is viewed as a prevalent phenomenon in everyday life, "not just in language but also in thought and action" (Lakoff and Johnson, 1980: 3). Many scholars have recognized the pervasiveness or ubiquity of metaphor in language. For example, Michael J. Reddy asserts that "A conservative estimate would thus be that, of the entire metalingual apparatus of the English language, at least seventy percent is directly, visibly, and graphically based on the conduit metaphor" (Reddy, 1979). "Conduit metaphor" in this statement is related to a class of linguistic expressions used when discussing communication itself. It operates whenever people speak or write as if they "insert" their mental contents (feelings, meanings, thoughts, concepts, etc.) into "containers" (words, phrases, sentences, etc.) whose contents are then "extracted" by listeners and readers. Thus, language is viewed as a "conduit" conveying mental content between people. Examples of conduit metaphor include "Try to pack more thoughts into fewer words" "Insert those ideas elsewhere in the paragraph". In view of the classification of metaphors by Lakoff and Johnson discussed above, we may say Reddy's conduit metaphor is a subtype of ontological metaphor, according to which ideas are objects that can be sent and received.

In further developing Reddy's statement of metaphor's ubiquity in language, Lakoff and Johnson (1980: 4) declare that "most of our conceptual system is metaphorical in nature". As part of their linguistic evidence, Lakoff and Johnson use the conceptual metaphor "ARGUMET IS WAR" and many linguistic metaphors to illustrate that in our ordinary language, we talk about arguments largely metaphorically because "the concepts that govern our thought are not just matters of the intellect. They also govern our everyday functioning, down to the most mundane details. Our concepts structure what we perceive, how we get around in the world, and how we relate to other people. Our conceptual system thus plays a central role in defining our everyday realities" (Lakoff and Johnson, 1980: 3).

• *Conventionality*

This feature raises the issue of novelty of metaphor. In chapter 1, we mentioned some writers would claim that some metaphors have become fossilized or dead metaphors. In the literal language theory this means that they have ceased to be metaphors and have passed into literal language, as suggested by Searle

(1979: 122):

> *Dead metaphor. The original sentence meaning is bypassed and the sentence acquires a new literal meaning identical with the former metaphorical meaning. This is a shift from the metaphorical utterance ... to the literal utterance.*

Cognitive semanticists argue against this approach, pointing out that even familiar metaphors can be given new life, thus showing that they retain their metaphorical status. If we take, for example, the UP-DOWN metaphor, we might consider an instance like *My spirits rose* to be a dead metaphor, yet this general metaphor is continually being extended: it is no accident in this view that stimulant recreational drugs were called *uppers* and tranquilizer, *downers*.

• *Systematicity*

The systematicity of conceptual metaphor is reflected in two aspects: (1) Each conceptual metaphor heads and governs a system of correspondences between the source domain and the target domain; (2) Conceptual metaphors may also be systematically related to each other to form either a hierarchical or a parallel structure. For (1) Lakoff and Turner (1989: 3-4) take as an example the metaphor LIFE IS A JOURNEY, which pervades our ordinary way of talking. They identify a systematicity in the mapping between the two concepts LIFE and JOURNEY:

7) LIFE IS A JOURNEY

The person leading a life is a traveler.
His purposes are destinations.
The means for achieving purposes are routes.
Difficulties in life are impediments to travel.
Counselors are guides.
Progress is the distance travelled.
Things you gauge your progress by are landmarks.
Material resources and talents are provisions.

Their point is that we use this mapping every day in ordinary speech as when we use expressions like: *Giving the children a good start in life*; *He's over the hill*; *He's gone off the rails*; *He got a head start in life*; *He's without direction in his life*; *I'm where I want to be in life*; *I'm at a cross-roads in my life*; *He's gone through a lot in life*; *He's never let anyone get in his way*, etc.

Another example concerning this systematicity of metaphor is related to the three conceptual metaphors of TIME, as shown below (Lakoff and Johnson, 1980: 7-8):

8) a. TIME IS MONEY
How do you spend your time these days?
The flat tire cost me an hour.
b. TMIE IS A LIMITED RESOURCE
You don't use your time profitably.
You are running out of time.
c. TIME IS A VALUABLE COMMODITY
I don't have time to give you.
Thank you for your time.

TIME IS MONEY, TIME IS A LIMITED RESOURCE, and TIME IS A VALUABLE COMMODITY are all metaphorical concepts in that they capture the way we use our everyday experiences with money, limited resources, and valuable commodities to conceptualize time. These three conceptual metaphors form a coherent system based on subcategorization, since in our society money is a limited resource, and a limited resource is a valuable commodity. In other words, TIME IS MONEY entails that TIME IS A LIMITED RESOURCE, which entails that TIME IS A VALUABLE COMMODITY.

• *Unidirectionality*

An important observation made by conceptual metaphor theorists is that conceptual metaphors are **unidirectional**. This means that metaphors map structure from a source domain to a target domain but not vice versa. For example, while we conceptualize LOVE in terms of JOURNEY, we cannot conventionally structure JOURNEY in terms of LOVE. Hence, the terms "target" and "source" encode the unidirectional nature of the mapping.

Lakoff and Turner (1989) observed that unidirectionality holds even when two different metaphors share the same domains. For example, they identified the two metaphors PEOPLE ARE MACHINES and MACHINES ARE PEOPLE, which are illustrated in examples 9) and 10), respectively.

9) PEOPLE ARE MACHINES
a. John always gets the highest scores in maths; he's a human

calculator.

b. He's so efficient; he's just a machine!

c. He's had a nervous breakdown.

10) MACHINES ARE PEOPLE

a. I think my computer hates me; it keeps deleting my data.

b. This car has a will of its own!

c. I don't think my car wants to start this morning.

Although these two metaphors appear to be the mirror image of one another, close inspection reveals that each metaphor involves distinct mappings: in the PEOPLE ARE MACHINES metaphor, the mechanical and functional attributes associated with computers are mapped onto people, such as their speed and efficiency, their part-whole structure and the fact that they break down; in the MACHINES ARE PEOPLE metaphor, it is the notion of desire and volition that is mapped onto the machine. This shows that even when two metaphors share the same two domains, each metaphor is distinct in nature because it relies upon different mappings.

• *Abstraction*

This feature is related to the feature of unidirectionality or asymmetry. It has often been noted that a typical metaphor uses a more concrete source to describe a more abstract target. Again the LIFE IS A JOURNEY metaphor exhibits this feature: the common, everyday experience of physically moving about the earth is used to characterize the mysterious (and unreported) processes of birth and death, and perhaps the equally mysterious processes of aging, organizing a career, etc. This is not a necessary feature of metaphors: the source and target may be equally concrete or abstract, but as we shall see, this typical viewing of the abstract through the concrete is seen in cognitive semantics as allowing metaphor its central role in the categorizing of new concepts, and in the organization of experience.

• *Cultural coherence*

The most fundamental values in a culture will be coherent with the metaphorical structure of the most fundamental concepts in the culture (Lakoff and Johnson, 1980: 22). That is to say, the cultural values of a society are, to a large extent, expressed through metaphorical concepts. For instance, the value of

"Time is precious", deeply rooted in both Chinese culture and English culture, is reflected through the metaphorical concept 时间是金钱 (TIME IS MONEY), which is further illustrated by many metaphorical expressions in everyday life, such as "一寸光阴一寸金 (An inch of time is worth an inch of gold)" "一刻千金 (Every minute is precious)" "花时间 (spend time)" "浪费时间 (waste time)" "节约时间 (save time)", etc. Although TIME is viewed as MONEY in both cultures, the English people and the Chinese people look at it from somewhat different perspectives in that the English people seldom emphasize that the value of time is greater than that of money, while we Chinese often say time is more valuable than money. So in Chinese we have many old sayings about time as shown in 11) and 12).

11) 一寸光阴一寸金，寸金难买寸光阴。
An inch of time is worth an inch of gold, but it is impossible to buy an inch of time with an inch of gold.

12) 百金买骏马，千金买美人，万金买高爵，何处买青春？
With gold you can buy a stout horse, a beautiful girl or a high position of power, but you can not buy youth.

This value of time derives from the life experiences of the Chinese people in the past thousands of years. It has become an integral part of the Chinese culture and is handed down from generation to generation. Therefore, metaphorical conceptual system, as part of culture, is bound to be consistent with the basic cultural value of a society. It can be concluded that the similarities and differences between different cultures determine the similarities and differences between the conceptual metaphors in the cultures.

10.1.1.3 The experiential basis of metaphor

The conceptual system underlying a language contains thousands of conceptual metaphors. The question now is: why do we have the conventional metaphors that we have? Is there any reason why the conceptual system contains one set of metaphorical mappings rather than another? The answer is provided by experiential realism, the philosophy of the cognitive approach to metaphor: cognition is embodied; we have the conventional metaphors we have because of our bodily and physical experience.

Consider an example. MORE IS UP is a conceptual metaphor noted by

Lakoff and Johnson (1980). It underlies expressions like *prices go up*; *his income came down*; *unemployment is up*; *exports are down*, etc. The cognitive theory postulates that this metaphor arises from the common experiences of pouring more fluid into a container and seeing the level go up, or adding more things to a pile and seeing the pile get higher. These are thoroughly pervasive experiences which we encounter every day. Further more, they have a structure, i.e. a set of correspondences between the domain of quantity and the domain of verticality, where MORE corresponds to UP and LESS corresponds to DOWN. These correspondences in real life experiences provide the basis for the correspondences in the metaphorical cases. For example, in *unemployment is up*, there is no real life correspondence between the changes in unemployment rate and vertical movements, nevertheless understanding the former in terms of the latter makes sense because there is a regular correspondence between quantity and verticality in so many other real life experiences.

Take another example. KNOWING IS SEEING is a widespread metaphor underlying a lot of expressions like *I see what you're saying*; *his answer was clear*; *this paragraph is murky*, etc. What forms the experiential basis for this metaphor is the fact that most of what we know comes through vision, and in the overwhelming majority of cases, we believe something is true when we have seen it with our own eyes. The Chinese phrase "眼见为实" (only what is seen with the eye is true) captures the idea nicely.

What is to be emphasized is that experiential bases only motivate metaphors but do not predict them. Therefore, although all human beings experience a correspondence between MORE and UP, we cannot say for certain that every language has come up with the MORE IS UP metaphor (Lakoff, 1993: 241). However, the experiential basis for this particular metaphor does predict that there should be no language which has the opposite metaphor LESS IS UP. It also predicts that it should be much easier for a speaker of a language without the MORE IS UP metaphor to pick it up than to pick up its reverse.

In section 10.2 we will continue to consider the experientialist basis of metaphors with a look at another, more basic cognitive structure: **image schemas**.

10.1.2 Metonymy

Like metaphor, metonymy has traditionally been regarded as a figure of speech, i.e. as a more or less ornamental device used in rhetorical style. According to the classical definition, metonymy is a figure of speech in which one word is substituted for another on the basis of some material, causal, or conceptual relation. Some typical substitutions include author for work, place for a characteristic product of that place, object for possessor, abstract features for concrete entities, etc. Some examples are:

13) Have you ever read *Shakespeare*?

14) Wary wants *Burgundy* (red or white wine from the Burgundy area of France).

15) The *crown* objects to the proposal.

16) I want my *love* to be with me all the time.

However, the rhetorical treatment of metonymy faces an interesting paradox. On the one hand, it captures a lot of phenomena which continue to be productive and widespread in a variety of languages; in addition, these seem to be produced and understood naturally and spontaneously. On the other hand, it regards metonymy as a figure of speech, that is, a departure from the linguistic norm, serving ornamental and literary purposes and demanding suitable training for its successful use and comprehension.

When we turned to a cognitive view of figurative language, we only paid attention to the role of metaphor but not that of metonymy, in the construction of abstract categories. However, metonymy does play a very important part in structuring abstract categories. In recent years, a considerable amount of research has been devoted to metonymy. Indeed, some scholars has begun to suggest that metonymy may be more fundamental to conceptual organization than metaphor, and some has gone so far as to claim that metaphor itself has a metonymic basis, as we will see later in this part.

The earliest approach to conceptual metonymy in cognitive semantics was developed by Lakoff and Johnson (1980). They argued that, like metaphor, metonymy is a conceptual phenomenon, but one that has quite a distinct basis. Consider example 17).

17) The ham sandwich has wandering hands.

Imagine that the sentence in 17) is uttered by one waitress to another in a café. This use of the expression *ham sandwich* represents an instance of metonymy: two entities are associated so that one entity (the item the customer ordered) stands for the other (the customer). As this example demonstrates, linguistic metonymy is **referential** in nature: it relates to the use of expressions to "pin-point" entities in order to talk about them. This shows that metonymy functions differently from metaphor. For example 17) to be metaphorical we would need to understand *ham sandwich* not as an expression referring to the customer who ordered it, but in terms of a food item with human qualities. Imagine a cartoon, for example, in which a ham sandwich sits at a café table. On this interpretation, we would be attributing human qualities to a ham sandwich, motivated by the metaphor AN INANIMATE ENTITY IS AN AGENT. As these two quite distinct interpretations show, while metonymy is the conceptual relation "X stands for Y", metaphor is the conceptual relation "X is understood in terms of Y".

A further defining feature of metonymy pointed out by Lakoff and Johnson is that it is motivated by physical or causal associations. Traditionally, this was expressed in terms of **contiguity**: a close or direct relationship between two entities. This explains why the waitress can use the expression *ham sandwich* to refer to the customer: there is a direct experiential relationship between the ham sandwich and the customer who ordered it.

A related way of viewing metonymy is that metonymy is often **contingent** on a specific context. Within a specific discourse context, a salient vehicle **activates** and thus highlights a particular target. Hence, while correlation-based metaphors (e.g. *The price of shares is going up*), as opposed to resemblance-based metaphors (e.g. *Achilles is a lion*), are pre-conceptual in origin and are therefore in some sense inevitable associations (motivated by the nature of our bodies and our environment), conceptual metonymies are motivated by communicative and referential requirements.

Finally, Lakoff and Turner (1989) added a further component to the cognitive semantic view of metonymy. They pointed out that metonymy, unlike metaphor, is not a cross-domain mapping, but instead allows one entity to stand for another because both concepts coexist within the same domain. This explains why a metonymic relationship is based on contiguity or conceptual "proximity". The reason *ham sandwich* in 17) represents an instance of metonymy is because both the **target** (the customer) and the **vehicle** (the ham sandwich) belong to the same CAFÉ domain. Kövecses and Radden (1998: 39) summarise this view of metonymy as follows:

> *Metonymy is a cognitive process in which one conceptual entity, the vehicle, provides mental access to another conceptual entity, the target, within the same domain, or ICM.*

This is a definition of metonymy in terms of the conceptual access it affords. This idea is based on proposals made by Langacker (1993: 30) who argues that "the entity that is normally designated by a metonymic expression serves as a reference point affording mental access to the desired target (that is, the entity actually being referred to)". In other words, metonymy serves as point of access to a particular aspect of a domain and thus provides access to the target concept. Furthermore, each vehicle provides a different route into the relevant conceptual domain.

Observe that Kövecses and Radden frame the notion of metonymy in terms of **access** rather than mapping. Indeed, other scholars have suggested that metonymy might be usefully considered in terms of a mapping process that **activates** or **highlights** a certain aspect of a domain. From this perspective, metonymy provides a "route" of access for a particular target within a single domain. For example while it is not usual to describe a human in terms of food, from the perspective of a waitress, the food ordered may be more salient than the customer. For this reason, the food ordered "activates" the customer sitting at a particular table in the café.

Metonymies are represented by the formula "B for A", where "B" is the vehicle and "A" is the target, e.g. PLACE FOR INSTITUTION. This contrasts with the "A is B" formula that represents conceptual metaphor.

Metonymy differs from metaphor in a cognitive theory, but they also work together. As a matter of fact, the main claims made by cognitive linguists in the description of metaphor also apply to metonymy: (1) both are regarded as being conceptual in nature; (2) both can be conventionalized (i.e. automatic, unconscious, effortless and generally established as a model of thinking); (3) both are means of extending the resources of a language; and (4) both can be explained as mapping processes. The main difference between them is that metaphor involves a mapping across different conceptual or cognitive domains while metonymy is a mapping within one conceptual domain. In metonymy, one category within a domain is taken as standing for another category in the same domain. The main function of a metonymic expression is to activatc one cognitive category by referring to another category within the same domain, and by doing that, to highlight the first category or the subdomain to which it belongs. Consider the following three examples of part-whole relations (Croft, 1993: 350):

18) We need a couple of strong bodies for our team.

19) There are a lot of good heads in the university.

20) We need some new faces around here.

Obviously, in each of the three sentences above a reference to human beings is being made. What is interesting here about them is that in each case one particular relevant aspect of a human being is highlighted. In the sports context of the first example, the domain PHYSICAL STRENGTH related to the category BODY is highlighted, and in the university context the domain INTELLIGENCE is related to HEAD. The category FACE is particularly appropriate in the context of new people, because this is what we usually perceive first when we meet strangers.

So, given the observations above, we can offer the cognitive linguistic definition of metonymy: Metonymy is a cognitive process in which one cognitive category, the source, provides mental access to another cognitive category, the target, within the same cognitive domain, or idealized cognitive model (ICM). Fig. 10-1 gives a diagrammatic illustration of the distinction between conceptual metaphor and conceptual metonymy.

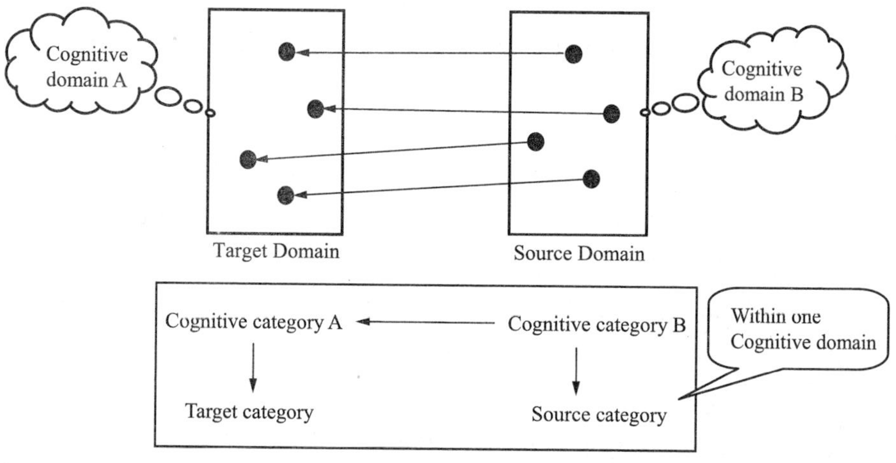

Fig. 10-1 Distinction between metaphor and metonymy

There are a number of distinct kinds of metonymy that have been identified in the cognitive semantics literature. We briefly illustrate some of these below. In each of the following examples, the vehicle is italicized.

21) PRODUCER FOR PRODUCT

a. I've just bought a new *Ford*.

b. Pass me the *Shakespeare* on the top shelf.

c. She likes eating *Burger King*.

22) PLACE FOR EVENT

a. America doesn't want another *Pearl Harbor*.

b. *Watergate* changed American politics.

c. Let's hope that *Beijing* will be as successful an Olympics as *Athens*.

23) PLACE FOR INSTITUTION

a. *Washington* is negotiating with *Beijing*.

b. *Wall Street* is in a panic.

c. *Hollywood* is putting out terrible movies.

24) PART FOR WHOLE

a. My *wheels* are parked out the back.

b. Lend me *a hand*.

c. She's not just a *pretty face*.

25) WHOLE FOR PART

a. *England* beat *Australia* in the 2003 rugby World Cup final.

b. *The European Union* has just passed new human rights legislation.

c. *My car* has developed a mechanical fault.

26) WHOLE SCALE FOR UPPER END OF THE SCALE

Henry is *speeding* again. (= Henry is going too fast.)

27) UPPER END OF THE SCALE FOR WHOLE SCALE

How *old* are you? (= What is your age?)

28) EFFECT FOR CAUSE

a. He has *a long face*.

b. He has *a spring in his step* today.

c. Her *face is beaming*.

29) CONTROLLER FOR CONTROLLED

a. *Nixon* bombed Hanoi.

b. *Ozawa* gave a terrible concert last night.

30) CONTROLLED FOR CONTROLLER

The Mercedes has arrived.

31) OBJECT USED FOR USER

a. The *sax* has the flu today.

b. We need a better *glove* at the third base.

32) AGENT FOR ACTION

a. He *authored* a new book this year.

b. The man *butchered* the cow in the open air.

33) INSTRUMENT FOR ACTION

a. She *shampooed* her hair.

b. He *hammered* the nail into the wood.

34) TIME FOR ACTION

The young couple *summered* in Paris.

35) DESTINATION FOR MOTION

He *porched* the newspaper.

36) THING PERCEIVED FOR PERCEPTION

There goes my *knee*. (= There goes the pain in my knee.)

37) PERCEPTION FOR THING PERCEIVED

The setting sun on the horizon is a magnificent *sight*.

38) INSTRUMENT FOR PRODUCT

Did you hear *the whistle*? (=Did you hear the sound from the whistle?)

39) PRODUCT FOR INSTRUMENT

Turn up *the heat* (= the radiator), please.

40) POSSESSOR FOR POSSESSED

a. That's *me* (= my bus).

b. *I* (= my car) am parked there.

41) POSSESSED FOR POSSESSOR

She married *money* (= a person with money).

42) CONTAINER FOR CONTENTS

The bottle (= the milk in the bottle) is sour.

43) CONTENTS FOR CONTAINER

The milk (= the milk bottle) tipped over.

44) PLACE FOR INHABITANTS

The whole town (= All the people in the town) showed up.

45) INHABITANTS FOR PLACE

The French (= France) hosted the World Cup Soccer Games.

46) TIME OF MOTION FOR AN ENTITY INVOLVED IN THE MOTION

The 8: 40 just arrived.

47) CATEGORY FOR MEMBER OF CATEGORY

She took *a pill* (= a birth control pill) to prevent pregnancy.

48) MEMBER OF CATEGORY FOR CATEGORY

Aspirin for "any pain-relieving tablet"

From the above examples we can see that, metonymies, similar to metaphors, are conceptual in nature, and conceptual metonymies are realized by metonymic linguistic expressions.

While most of the examples of metonymy we have considered so far relate to noun phrases, metonymic vehicles (i.e. source categories) are not restricted to individual lexical items. For instance, Panther and Thornburg (2003) have argued that indirect speech acts represent instances of metonymy. Consider example 49):

49) Can you pass the salt?

Recall from Chapter 8 that a speech act is an utterance that performs a (linguistic) action. The example in 49) is "indirect" because it counts as a conventional way of making a request, but does so "via" a question about the ability of the addressee to carry out the action (signaled by the interrogative form of the clause), rather than making the request directly (by using an imperative clause like *Pass me the salt*). Panther and Thornburg argue that indirect speech acts are metonymic, in that the question stands for the request. In other words, the ability to perform the action is a necessary prerequisite (or "felicity condition") for a request to be carried out (Searle, 1969), and a question about this ability stands for the request itself.

10.1.3 Metaphor-metonymy interaction

While metaphors and metonymies are often distinguished from each other in cognitive linguistics, cognitive linguists have noticed that the two can also work together. What follows is a brief discussion on how metaphor and metonymy interact in structuring the human conceptual system. Let's first look at an example from one of Shakespeare's sonnets.

50) Mine eye and heart are at a mortal war.
How to divide the conquest of thy sight.

Obviously this example involves both metaphor and metonymy at the same time: the word *eye* is used as referring to the whole visual capacity of a person which is contrasted with the field of affections symbolized by the *heart* (both are fairly conventional instances of metonymy); in addition, the visual and the affective domain are treated as persons or parties engaged in a war (a frequent and conventional type of metaphor). The novelty of this example lies largely in the combination of metaphor and metonymy. One field where a co-occurrence of metaphors and metonymies is particularly frequent is the field of emotion categories.

Before concluding our discussion on the interaction of metaphor and metonymy, let us briefly introduce the analysis by Goossens (1990) of the way in which metaphor and metonymy interact. Goossens calls the interactive phenomenon of metaphor and metonymy **metaphtonymy**. He identified a number of logically possible ways in which metaphor and metonymy could potentially interact; however, he found that only two of these logically possible interactions were commonly attested.

The first way in which metaphor and metonymy interact is called **metaphor from metonymy**. In this form of interaction, a metaphor is grounded in a metonymic relationship. For example, the expression *close-lipped* can mean "silent", which follows from metonymy: when one has one's lips closed, one is (usually) silent, therefore to describe someone as *close-lipped* can stand metonymically for silence. However, *close-lipped* can also mean "speaking but giving little away". This interpretation is metaphoric, because we understand the absence of meaningful information in terms of silence. Goossens argues that the metaphoric interpretation has a metonymic basis in that it is only because being closed-lipped can stand for silence that the metaphoric reading is possible: thus metaphor from metonymy.

The second common form of interaction is called **metonymy within metaphor**. Consider the following example adapted from Goossens (1990):

51) She caught the Prime Minister's ear and persuaded him to accept her plan.

This example is licensed by the metaphor ATTENTION IS A MOVING PHYSICAL ENTITY, according to which ATTENTION is understood as a MOVING ENTITY that has to be "caught" (the minister's ear). However, within this metaphor there is also the metonymy EAR FOR ATTENTION, in which EAR is the body part that functions as the vehicle for the concept of ATTENTION in the metaphor. In this example, the metonym is "inside" the metaphor.

According to some cognitive semanticists (e.g. Barcelona, 2003; Taylor, 2003), metonymy is an operation that may be more fundamental to the human conceptual system than metaphor. Barcelona (2003: 31) goes so far as to suggest that "every metaphorical mapping presupposes a prior metonymic mapping". In other words, all metaphor is ultimately motivated by metonymy. One obvious way in which metaphor might have a metonymic basis relates to the idea of experiential correlation that we discussed earlier. As we saw, primary metaphors are argued to be motivated by experiential correlation. Yet, as Radden (2003) and Taylor (2003) have pointed out, correlation is fundamentally metonymic in nature. For example, when height correlates with quantity, as when fluid is poured into a glass, greater height literally corresponds to an increase in quantity. When this correlation is applied to more abstract domains, such as HIGH PRICES, we have a metaphor from metonymy, in the sense of Goossens.

10.2 Image schema

In this section we consider the theory of image schemas developed by Johnson (1987). According to Johnson, image schemas are relatively abstract conceptual representations that arise directly from our everyday interaction with and observation of the world around us. That is, they are concepts arising from embodied experience. Image schemas are an important form of conceptual structure in the cognitive semantics literature. The basic idea is that because of our physical experience of being and acting in the world — of perceiving the environment, moving our bodies, exerting and experiencing force, etc. — we form basic conceptual structures which we then use to organize thought across a range of more abstract domains. In Mark Johnson (1987), image schemas are proposed as a more primitive level of cognitive structure underlying metaphor and which provide a link between bodily experience and higher cognitive domains such as language. Evidence from language shows that semantic structure reflects conceptual structure, and conceptual structure arises from embodied experience.

It is worth noting that although the term "image" is restricted to visual perception in everyday language, it has a broader application when used in "image schemas", where it is not only related to visual experience but also to experiences of touch, hearing, movement and balance, etc. The term "schema" in "image schema" is also very important: it means that image schemas are not rich or detailed concepts, but rather abstract concepts consisting of patterns emerging from repeated instances of embodied experience.

Another point that should be made clear is that image schemas are not the same as mental images.

Close your eyes and imagine the face of your mother or father, child or close friend. This is a mental image, relatively rich in detail. Image schemas are not the same as mental images. Mental images are detailed and result from an effortful and partly conscious cognitive process that involves recalling visual memory. Image schemas are schematic and therefore more abstract in nature, emerging from ongoing embodied experience. This means that you can't close your eyes and "think up" an image schema in the same way that you can "think up" the sight of someone's face or the feeling of a particular object in your hand.

One of the reasons why we are not able to close our eyes and "think up" an image schema is because image schemas derive from experiences across different modalities (different types of sensory experience) and hence are not specific to a particular sense. In other words, image schemas are buried "deeper" within the cognitive system, being abstract patterns arising from a vast range of perceptual experiences and as such are not available to conscious introspection. In contrast, mental images are only visually formed. For instance, blind people have access to image schemas for CONTAINERS, PATHS and so on precisely because the kinds of experiences that give rise to these image schemas rely on a range of sensory-perceptual experiences in addition to vision, including hearing, touch and our experience of movement and balance, to name but a few.

The schemas identified by Mark Johnson include *Containment*, *Path*, *Links*, *Forces*, *Balance*, *Up-Down*, *Front-Back*, *Part-Whole*, *Centre-Periphery*, and some others. But here we only look at the **Containment** schema, the **Path** schema, and the **Force** schema, since these three schemas have been much used in many linguistic studies.

10.2.1 Containment schema

Mark Johnson(1987: 21ff) gives the example of the schema of **Containment**, which derives from our experience of the human body itself as a container; from experience of being physically located ourselves within bounded locations like rooms, beds, etc.; and also of putting objects into containers. The result is an abstract schema, of physical Containment, which can be represented by a very simple image like Fig. 10-2, representing an entity within a bounded location.

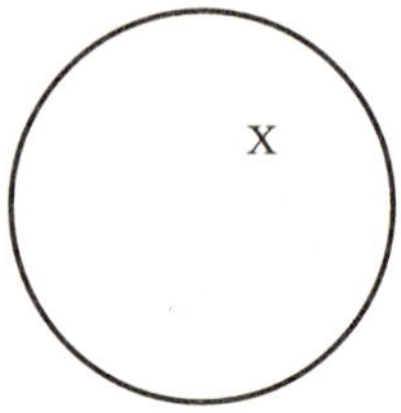

Fig. 10-2 Containment schema (Mark Johnson, 1987: 23)

Such a schema has certain experientially-based characteristics: it has a kind of natural logic, including for example the "rules" below:

(1) Containers are a kind of disjunction: elements are either inside or outside the container.

(2) Containment is typically transitive: if the container is placed in another container the entity is within both, as Johnson says "If I am *in* bed, and my bed is *in* my room, then I am *in* my room".

The schema is also associated with a group of implications, which can be seen as natural inferences about Containment. Johnson calls these "entailments" and gives examples like the following:

(1) Experience of Containment typically involves protection from outside forces.

(2) Containment limits forces, such as movement, within the container.

(3) The contained entity experiences relative fixity of location.

(4) The Containment affects an observer's view of the contained entity, either improving such a view or blocking it (containers may hide or display).

Though we have represented this schema in a static image like Fig. 10-2, it is important to remember that these schemas are in essence neither static nor restricted to images. The schema may be dynamic, as we shall see shortly with the path schema, which involves movement and change.

This schema of Containment can be extended by a process of metaphorical extension into abstract domains. Lakoff and Johnson (1980) identify **container** as one of a group of **ontological** metaphors, where our experience of non-physical phenomena is described in terms of simple physical objects like substances and containers. For example the visual field is often conceived as a container, as in examples like: *The ship is coming into view; He's out of sight now; There's nothing in sight.* Similarly, activities can be viewed as containers: *I put a lot of energy into washing the windows; He's out of the race; She's deep in thought.* States can be viewed in the same way: *He's in love; He's coming out of the coma now; She got into a rage; We stood in silence.* For Lakoff and Johnson these examples are typical and reveal the important role of metaphor in allowing us to conceptualize experience.

Although Fig. 10-2 represents the basic Containment schema, there are a number of other image schemas that are related to this schema which gives rise to distinct concepts related to Containment. Let's consider just two variants of the Containment schema lexicalized by *out*. These image schemas are diagrammed in Fig. 10-3 and 10-4, and are illustrated with linguistic examples.

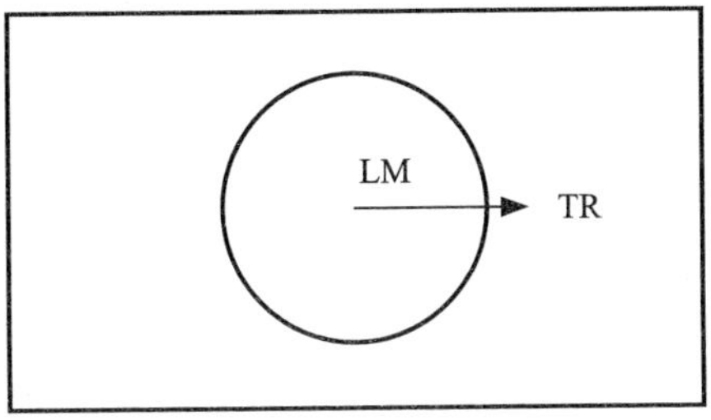

Fig. 10-3 Image schema for OUT1

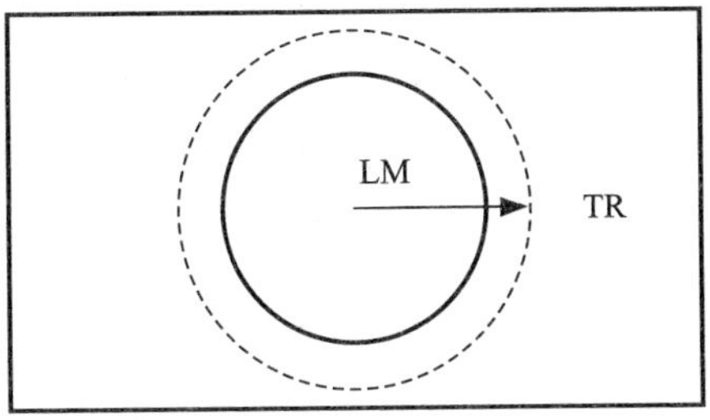

Fig. 10-4 Image schema for OUT2

52) John went out of the room. OUT1

53) The honey spread out. OUT2

The diagram in Fig. 10-3 corresponds to example 52). The **trajector** (TR) *John*, which is the entity that undergoes motion, moves from a position inside the LM to occupy a location outside the LM. The image schema in Fig. 10-4 corresponds to example 53). In this example, the meaning of *out* is "reflexive", which is a technical way of saying that something refers to itself: we could paraphrase example 53), albeit redundantly, as *The honey spreads itself out*. In other words, liquid substances like honey, because of their physical properties, can simultaneously be the LM and the TR. The LM is the original area occupied by the honey, while the honey is also the TR because it spreads beyond the boundary of its original location.

At the end of our discussion of Containment schema, we consider an extract from Johnson's (1987) book, which reveals the fact that image schema of Containment come from our recurrent and ubiquitous experiences with containers.

54) You wake *out* of a deep sleep and peer *out* from beneath the covers *into* your room. You gradually emerge *out* of your stupor, pull yourself *out* from under the covers, climb *into* your robe, stretch *out* your limbs, and walk *in* a daze *out* of the bedroom and *into* the bathroom. You look *in* the mirror and see your face staring *out* at you. You reach *into* the medicine cabinet, take *out* the toothpaste, squeeze *out* some toothpaste, put the toothbrush *into* your mouth, brush your teeth *in* a hurry, and rinse *out* your mouth. At breakfast you perform a host of further *in-out* moves—pouring *out* the coffee, setting *out* the dishes, putting the toast *in* the toaster, spreading *out* the jam on the toast, and on and on. Once you are more awake you might even get lost *in* the newspaper, might enter *into* a conversation, which leads to your speaking *out* on some topic. (Johnson, 1987: 331)

As this example reveals by the recurrent use of the expressions *in* and *out*, a great number of everyday objects and experiences are categorized as specific instances of the schematic concept **container**: not only obvious containers like bathroom, cabinets and toothpaste tubes or less obvious "containers" like bedcovers, clothing and rooms, but also states like sleep, stupor and daze.

10.2.2 Path schema

The **Path** schema is shown in the following Fig.10-5.

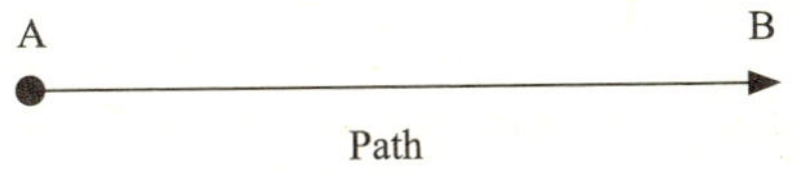

Fig. 10-5 Path schema (Mark Johnson, 1987: 114)

Johnson claims that this schema reflects our everyday experience of moving around the world and experiencing the movements of other entities. Our journeys typically have a beginning and an end, a sequence of places on the way and direction. Other movements may include projected paths, like the flight of a stone thrown through the air. Based on such experiences the path schema contains a starting point (marked A in Fig. 10-5), an end point (marked B), and a sequence of contiguous locations connecting them (marked by the arrow). This schema has a number of associated implications, as listed below:

(1) Since A and B are connected by a series of contiguous locations, getting from A to B implies passing through the intermediate points.

(2) Paths tent to be associated with directional movement along them, say from A to B.

(3) There is an association with time. Since a person traversing a path takes time to do so, points on the path are readily associated with temporal sequence. Thus an implication is that the further along the path an entity is, the more time has elapsed.

These implications are evidenced in the metaphorical extension of this schema into abstract domains: we talk, for example, of achieving purposes as paths, as in 55) below:

55) a. He's writing a PhD thesis and he's nearly there.

b. I meant to finish painting it yesterday, but I got side-tracked.

and the metaphor LIFE IS A JOURNEY discussed in 10.1.1.2 also derives from this schema.

One consequence of the internal SOURCE-PATH-GOAL structure of the Path schema is that different components of the schema can be referred to or foregrounded. This is illustrated in example 56), where the relevant linguistic units are bracketed. In each sentence of this example, different components of the path are profiled by the use of different lexical items.

56) a. SOURCE

John left [England].

b. GOAL

John travelled to [France].

c. SOURCE-GOAL

John travelled [from England] [to France].

d. PATH-GOAL

John travelled [through the Chunnel] [to France].

e. SOURCE-PATH-GOAL

John travelled [from England] [through the Chunnel] [to France].

10.2.3 Force schema

Force schemas arise from our experience of acing upon other entities, or being acted upon by other entities, resulting in the transfer of motion energy. Johnson illustrates the **interactional derivation** of Force schema (in other words, how it arises from experience) as follows:

> *Force is always experienced through interaction. We become aware of force as it affects us or some object in our perceptual field. When you enter an unfamiliar dark room and bump into the edge of the table, you are experiencing the interactional character of force. When you eat too much the ingested food presses outwards on your much stretched stomach. There is no schema for force that does not involve interaction or potential interaction.* (Johnson, 1987: 43)

Force schemas share a number of properties (proposed by Johnson, 1987) which include: Force schemas are always experienced through interaction; Force schemas involve a force vector, i.e. a directionality; Force schemas typically involve a single path of motion; Force schemas have sources for the force and targets that are acted upon; forces involve degrees of intensity; forces involve a chain of causality, a consequence of having a source, target, force vector and path of motion, e.g. a child throwing a ball at a coconut. Johnson identifies no fewer than seven Force schemas that share these properties. These schemas are shown in Fig. 10-6 to 10-12 (Johnson, 1987: 45-48).

Fig. 10-6 The **Compulsion** image schema

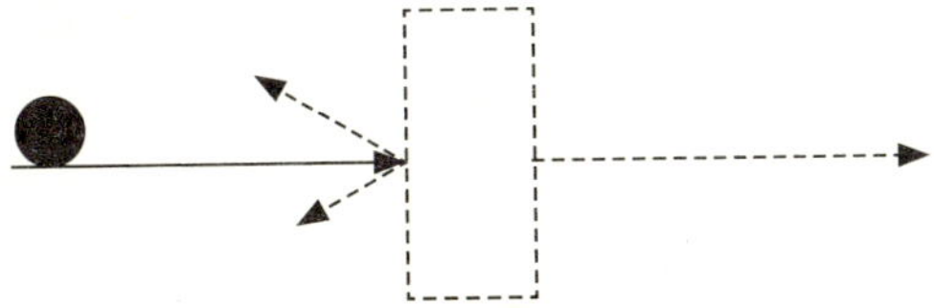

Fig. 10-7 The **Blockage** image schema

Fig. 10-8 The **Counterforce** image schema

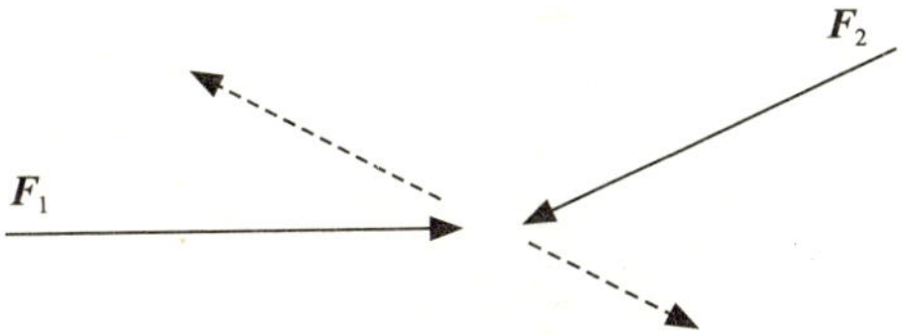

Fig. 10-9 The **Diversion** image schema

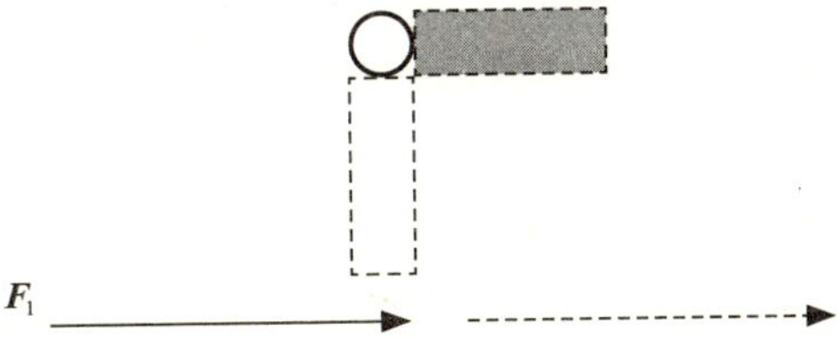

Fig. 10-10 The **Removal of Restraint** image schema

Fig. 10-11 The **Enablement** image schema

Fig. 10-12 The **Attraction** image schema

The small dark circle represents the source of the force, while the square represents an obstruction of some kind. An unbroken arrow represents the force vector (the course taken by the force), while a broken arrow represents a potential force vector.

The first is the basic force schema of **Compulsion** (Fig. 10-6), where a force vector ***F*** acts on an entity □. In this diagram the essential element is movement along a trajectory: the dashed line represents the fact that the force may be blocked or may continue. This schema emerges from the experience of being moved by an external force, for example being pushed along helplessly in a large dense crowd, being blown along in a very strong wind and so on.

The second force-related image schema is the more specific schema of **Blockage** (Fig. 10-7), where a force meets an obstruction and acts in various ways: being diverted, or continuing on by moving the obstacle or passing through it. Obviously, this image schema derives from encounters in which obstacles resist force, for example when a car crashes into an obstacle like a tree.

The third force-related image schema is the **Counterforce** schema (Fig. 10-8). This derives from the experience of two entities meeting with equal force, like when we bump into someone in the street. F_1 and F_2 represent the two counterforces.

The fourth force-related image schema is the **Diversion** schema (Fig. 10-9). This occurs when one entity in motion meets another entity and this results in diversion. Examples include a swimmer swimming against a strong current so that she is gradually pushed along the shoreline, or the ricochet of a bullet.

The fifth force-related schema is the **Removal of Restraint** schema (Fig. 10-10), where the removal (by another cause) of a blockage allows an exertion of force to continue along a trajectory. This describes a situation like leaning on a door that suddenly opens.

The sixth force-related image schema is the **Enablement** schema (Fig. 10-11). This image schema derives from our sense of potential energy, or lack of it, in relation to the performance of a specific task. While most people who are fit and well feel able to pick up a bag of grocery shopping, for example, few people feel able to lift up a car. It is important to observe that while this image schema does not involve an actual force vector, it does involve a potential force vector. According to Johnson, it is this property that marks the **Enablement** schema as a distinct image schema.

Finally, the **Attraction** schema (Fig. 10-12) derives from experiences in which one entity is drawn towards another entity due to the force exerted upon it. Examples include magnets, vacuum cleaners and gravity.

These force schemas, like other image schemas, are held to be pre-linguistic and to shape the form of our linguistic categories. In other words, image schemas which relate to and derive ultimately from pre-conceptual embodied experience can serve to structure more abstract linguistic categories. In the next section we discuss an important application of image schema: to describe polysemy.

10.3 Polysemy

Image schemas and their extension by metaphor have been used to describe a number of areas of language which display polysemy: the phenomenon discussed in chapter 3 where we find a group of related but distinct meanings attached to a word. G. Lakoff (1987) uses the term **radial category** for the characteristic pattern produced by the metaphorical extension of meanings from a central origin. We can look at two examples of this phenomenon from English: prepositions and modal verbs.

10.3.1 Prepositions

The schema of Containment has been used to investigate the semantics of spatial prepositions in a number of languages. These studies use schemas to explore the typical polysemy of prepositions: the fact that we can for example use the English preposition *in* in a number of related but distinct ways, as in the examples below given by Herkovits (1986):

57) a. the water in the vase
 b. the crack in the vase
 c. the crack in the surface
 d. the bird in the tree
 e. the chair in the corner
 f. the nail in the box
 g. the muscles in his leg
 h. the pear in the bowl
 i. the block in the box
 j. the block in the rectangular area
 k. the gap in the border
 l. the bird in the field

It is easy to see the different relationships between the entity and the container in these examples. The water is likely to be entirely contained in the vase in 57)a but the pear in 57)h could easily be sitting on top of a pile of fruit and thus protrude beyond the top edge of the bowl. Similarly the bird in 57)d might be inside a hole in the tree-trunk but equally, might be sitting on a branch which if "inside" anything is inside our projection of the tree's shape. Meanwhile in 57)l the bird might be flying or hovering several feet above the field. Herkovits's point is that such extended uses are typical and regular, i.e. not idiomatic. This seems to be supported by the fact that the studies of other languages come up with similar examples. Herkovits claims that these uses are most satisfactorily described by viewing them as extensions from a central, ideal Containment schema which she describes in words as "the inclusion of a geometric construct in a one-, two-, or three-dimensional geometric construct".

There are two important points to make about this polysemy from a cognitive semantics perspective: the first is that the various and varying real world situations are described in language in a way that is essentially metaphorical in nature, relating them all to an underlying schema of Containment. The second is that the relationship between the various senses is not arbitrary but systematic and natural. We can see the latter point if we look briefly at Brugman and Lakoff's (1988) description of the preposition *over*. They argue that the polysemous nature of this and other prepositions cannot be accurately described using semantic features or definitions but instead requires an essentially topographical approach, i.e. a description employing spatial models. They claim (1988: 479):

> *Topographical concepts are needed in order to account for how prepositions can be used to characterize an infinity of visual scenes.*

The polysemous nature of *over* can be shown, as we did for *in* earlier, by a set of examples (Brugman and Lakoff, 1988):

58) a. The plane is flying over the hill.
b. Sam walked over the hill.
c. The bird flew over the yard.
d. The bird flew over the wall.
e. Sam lives over the hill.
f. The painting is over the mantel.
g. The board is over the hole.
h. She spread the tablecloth over the table.
i. The city clouded over.

j. The guards were posted all over the hill.

k. Harry still hasn't gotten over his divorce.

Brugman and Lakoff propose a complex structure for the meaning of *over*: the preposition has a number of related senses, of which we can select three, termed the **above-across** sense, the **above** sense, and the **covering** sense. Each of these senses is then structured as a radial category with extensions from a central prototype. Let us take the **above-across** sense first. This sense of *over* is described in terms of a **Path** image schema: using the terms **trajector** (TR) for a moving entity and **landmark** (LM) for the background against which movement occurs. Brugman and Lakoff represent this in a schema like Fig. 10-13. This schema would fit for example 58)a, *The plane is flying over the hill*. In this approach several other senses of *over* can be systematically related to this central schema by a number of basic processes, for example by adding information to the schema or by metaphor. In the first type of process the central schema may alter along a number of parameters: for example there may be contact between the trajector and landmark as in 58)b *Sam walked over the hill*, shown schematically in Fig. 10-14. Other information may be added about the landmark, which may be viewed as different geometric shapes: as an extended area as in 58)c; or as a vertical form as in 58)d. Alternatively the focus may be on the endpoint of the path as in 58)e. In the second type of process the preposition can be used metaphorically, where it interacts with the metaphorical structures available to the language users. Thus in 58)k we see a version of the LIFE IS A JOURNEY metaphor we discussed earlier, where problems are seen as obstacles.

A second major sense of *over* is the **above** sense, as in 58)f above: *The painting is over the mantel*. This sense is stative and has no path element. It can be represented by the schema in Fig. 10-15. Since this schema does not include a path element it has no meaning of **across**. It also differs from the first sense in that there are no restrictions on the shape of the landmark, nor can there be contact between trajector and landmark. If there is contact we are more likely to use another preposition, such as *on* as in *The painting is on the mantel*.

Our third sense, or group of senses, of *over* is the **covering** sense which can be represented in Fig. 10-16. The schema in this figure corresponds to sentence 58)g above: *The board is over the hole*. This schema may have a path element depicting the motion of the trajector into its position over the landmark as in 58)h

She spread the tablecloth over the table or 58)i *The city clouded over*. In this schema the use of a quantifier like *all* changes the nature of the trajector, as for example in sentence 58)j: *The guards were posted all over the hill*. Here the trajector is what Brugman and Lakoff call a **multiplex** trajector, made up of many individual elements. This is schematically represented as in Fig. 10-17.

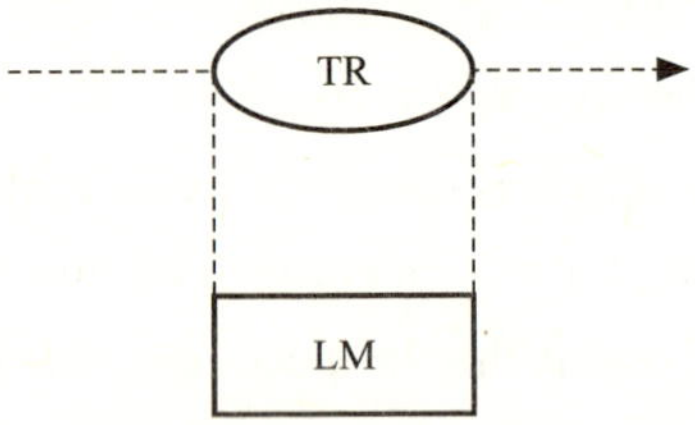

Fig. 10-13 Prototypical **above-across** sense of *over*

(Brugman and Lakoff, 1988: 482)

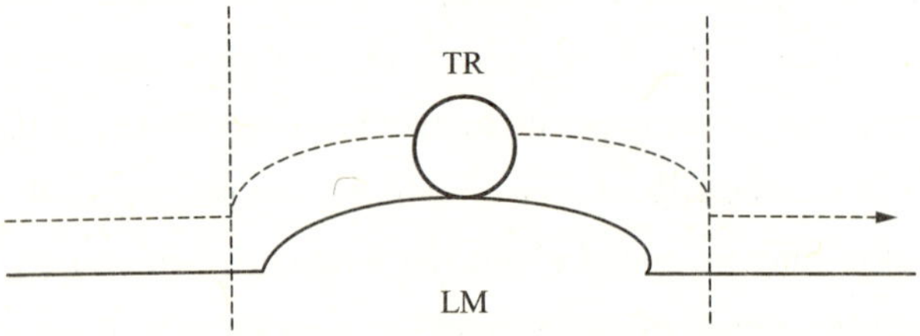

Fig. 10-14 Sam walked over the hill

(Brugman and Lakoff, 1988: 483)

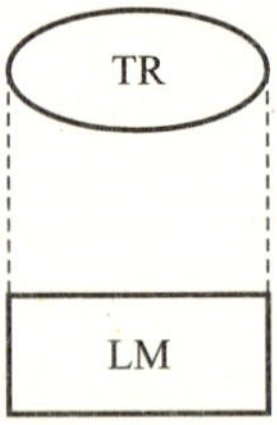

Fig. 10-15 The **above** sense of *over*

(Brugman and Lakoff, 1988: 487)

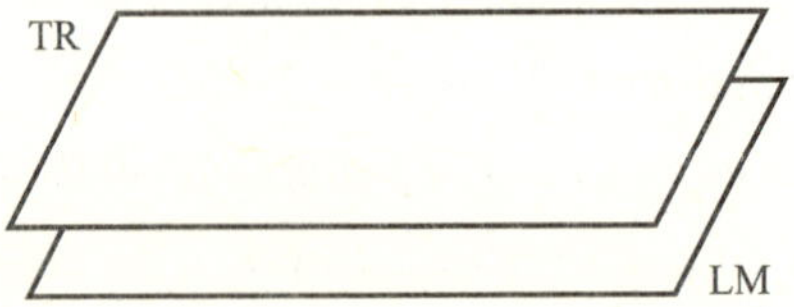

Fig. 10-16 The **covering** sense of *over*

(Brugman and Lakoff, 1988: 489)

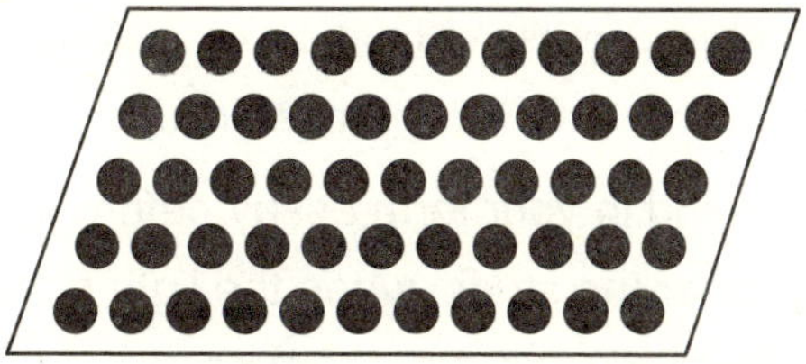

Fig. 10-17 Multiplex version of the **covering** sense of *over*
(Brugman and Lakoff, 1988: 490)

We have looked at three of the major sense groups of *over* identified in this analysis. In each sense group there is a prototypical schema which is related to a number of extended senses, thus exhibiting the radial category structure we mentioned earlier. This prototypicality also extends to the relationship between the sense groups: our first sense group, the **above-across** sense, is the prototypical group for *over*.

An important element of this analysis is the claim that the processes which extend senses from a central prototype to form a radial category are systematic and widespread. Brugman and Lakoff (1988) claim, for example, that any path schema will allow a focus on the end point, as we saw for *over* in 58)e. We can see this with the prepositions in 59)-61) below:

59) a. He walked across the road.
    b. He works across the road.
60) a. You go around the corner.
    b. She lives around the corner.
61) a. Walk through the atrium and turn to the left.
    b. His office is through the atrium and to the left.

Each of the prepositions in 59)-61) shows this ability to support a motion variant in the a sentence and a stative variant in the b sentence, where the latter identifies the end point or destination of the path.

10.3.2 Modal verbs

Force schemas have been used to describe polysemy in modal verbs. As we saw in chapter 5, modal verbs like English *may* and *can* typically have both **deontic** and **epistemic** senses. Talmy (1985, 1988), for example, uses Force schemas to analyze modal verbs like *must*, *may*, and *can* in their deontic uses:

for example *must* used to express obligation as in 62)a below, *may* used for permission as in 62)b and *can* used for ability as in 62)c.

62) a. You *must* hand in your term essay before the end of this week.
b. You *may* enter the studio when the light goes out.
c. She *can* swim much better than me.

Talmy analyzes these deontic uses in terms of forces and barriers. He proposes, for example, that a typical use of *may* as permission is an example of removing a barrier or keeping back a potential but absent barrier. Thus in 62)b some potential barrier to entering the studio is identified as being negated.

Sweetser (1990) adopts and extends this analysis of *may*. She observes that the normal use of *may* is when the barrier is a social one (deriving from authority). The verb *let* is used in a similar way, as in 63)a below, but as Sweetser notes, with this verb there are physical analogues to this removal of a potential barrier as in 63)b:

63) a. I'll *let* you smoke in the car, but just for today.
b. The hole in the roof *let* the rain in.

In this approach, the other deontic modals can also be given a force schema analysis: for example, the use of *must* for obligation is an example of the Compulsion Force schema. In 62)a above the force is the teacher's authority but it can also be a moral or religious force as in *You must respect your parents* or *You must pray five times a day*. The idea seems to be that there is a conceptual link between someone physically pushing you in a direction and a moral force impelling you to act in a certain way. Both are forces which can be resisted or acceded to; in this approach a common conceptual schema unites the characterization of the two situations.

Besides Talmy and Sweetser, Johnson (1987) also examines the relationship between the Force schemas and the deontic sense of English modal verbs. He suggests that certain Force schemas underlie the basic or **root** meanings of these verbs: these meanings relate to socio-physical experience, as illustrated in the following sentences:

64) a. You **must** move your foot or the car will crush it.
[physical necessity]
b. You **may** now kiss the bride.

[no parental, social or institutional barrier now prevents the bride from being kissed by the groom]

c. John **can** throw a javelin over 20 metres.

[he is physically capable of doing this]

Johnson argues that the root meaning of *must* (physical necessity) derives from the Compulsion schema, while the root meaning of *may* (permission) to relates to the Removal of Restraint schema and the root meaning of *can* (physical capacity) derives from the Enablement schema. Thus his claim is that the meanings associated with the modal verbs have an image-schematic basis which arises from embodied experience.

Sweetser (1990) analyzes the epistemic use of modals as a metaphorical extension of these deontic uses. We can take the examples of *must* and *may*. In its epistemic use *must* can express a reasonable conclusion as in 65)a and b:

65) a. It's dead. The battery *must* have run down.

b. You've travelled all day. You *must* be tired.

The epistemic use of *may* expresses possibility as in 66):

66) a. You *may* feel a bit sick when we take off.

b. He *may not* last out the whole game.

Sweetser argues that such uses of modals for rational argument and judgment are derived from their uses for the real world of social obligation and permission. This derivation follows the usual metaphorical extension from the external concrete world to the internal world of cognition emotion. Thus to take the example of *may*, the epistemic use is again taken to represent a lack of barrier. Here though the barrier is to the line of reasoning leading to the conclusion expressed. Thus a sentence like 67)a below can be paraphrased as 67)b:

67) a. You may be right.

b. There is no evidence preventing the conclusion that you are right.

Thus an overt parallel is drawn in this account between barriers in social action and barriers in mental reasoning.

In a similar way epistemic *must* is interpreted as the Compulsion Force schema extended to the domain of reasoning. So 68)a below is paraphrased as 68)b:

68) a. You must have driven too fast.

b. The evidence forces my conclusion that you drove too fast.

Thus Sweetser is arguing that evidence is conceptualized as a force analogous to social pressure and laws, moving a person's judgment in a certain direction.

This type of analysis is extended to other modals but we need not follow the analysis further: we can identify from these few examples her claim that the relationship between the deontic and epistemic use of each modal is not accidental but a further example of polysemy, i.e. the different uses are semantically related. What relates them, in this view, is the metaphorical extension of the force and barriers schemas from the social world to our inner reasoning.

So to conclude this section, we have seen that image schemas are proposed as experientially-based conceptual constructs by which we characterize, for example, spatial relations, and which can be metaphorically extended across a range of domains, typically shifting from the external and concrete to the internal and abstract. Such schemas are seen as the building blocks of metaphor, allowing us to conceive of emotional states as containers (*She's in love*), evidence as compulsion (*He must be guilty*), or purposes as paths (A: *Have you finished the book?* B: *I'm getting there*). Polysemy is the result of this extension of schemas to form radial categories and is seen as a natural and ubiquitous phenomenon in language.

10.4 Categorization and idealized cognitive models

10.4.1 Categorization

Categorization refers to the mental process of classifying entities in the world into different groups based on perceived similarities. The results or products of categorization are categories.

Categorization occurs everywhere around us, without which a lot of information would be in disorder. In fact, people are able to divide the world into categories, and they can learn to distinguish between different categories such as CAR and BUS. For example, as a student, you may be classified as a FRESHMAN, SOPHOMORE, JUNIOR or SENIOR; you may also be classified by your major. As to the color system, we have color categories, such as RED, WHITE, BLACK, YELLOW and BLUE. Movies in America have already been categorized as G (General Audiences: used to mean that a film is suitable for anyone to watch), PG (Parental Guidance: used to describe a film containing scenes, subjects, or language considered unsuitable for children unless they have a parent with them), R (Restricted: used to mean that the people under the age of 17 cannot go to a particular film unless they go with an adult), or X (used to mean that a film is not suitable for people under the age of 18). The list of categorization examples is practically endless.

But what principles do people use when they do categorizing? Generally speaking, there are two major theories which deal with this problem. One is the **classical theory**, and the other is the **prototype theory**.

10.4.1.1 The classical theory

The classical theory of categorization can be traced back to Aristotle, and it is carried forward by structuralist and transformationalist linguists.

According to this theory, in the BIRD category, for example, if a creature has two wings, two legs, a beak, feathers, lays eggs and can fly (these are the necessary conditions), then it is a bird; on the other hand, if a creature has all these features, it is sufficient to classify it as a bird (these features are now called sufficient conditions). This seems to tell us that categories are defined by a limited set of necessary and sufficient conditions (these conditions are regarded as defining features). An entity must exhibit all the defining features to be member of the category BIRD. In other words, if any of the defining features is not exhibited by the entity, then the entity is not a member of the category. This is the first assumption of the classical theory.

In the definition of a category, one of the two values, either [+] or [−], can be used. For example, the BIRD category has the feature [+two legs], but [−four legs]. This means that a feature is either in the definition of a category, or it is not; an entity either has this feature, or it does not. That is, features are binary. There are no fuzzy cases where it can be said that from one perspective an entity has a certain feature while from another perspective it does not. This is the second assumption.

Once a category has been established, it divides the universe into two sets of entities. In this case, some entities are the members of the category, while the others are not. There are no ambiguous or borderline cases, no entities which "in a way" or "to some extent" belong to the category, but which in another way do not. For instance, after the BIRD category is formed, some creatures such as the sparrow, the robin, and the swallow are the members of BIRD, but others such as lions, tigers, and bears are not, because the latter are the members of the BEAST category. The view can be demonstrated in Fig. 10-18.

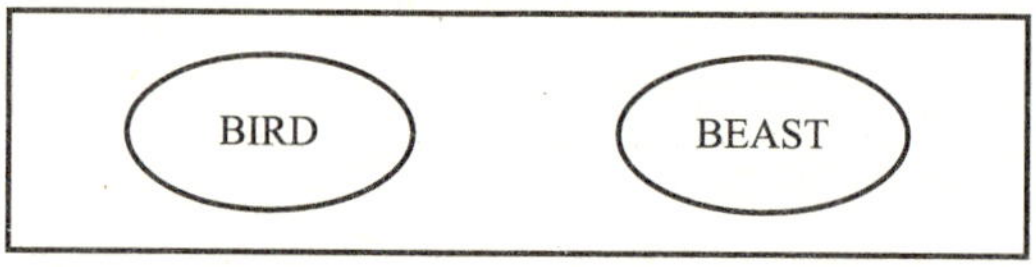

Fig. 10-18 Boundary between two categories

This shows that the two categories BIRD and BEAST have clear boundaries. In general, categories have clear boundaries. This is the third assumption.

The fourth assumption is that all members of a category have equal status. This means that a member that has all the features of a category is a full member of the category; a member that does not have all the features is not a member. There is no such case in which one member is better than others in the same category. Therefore, according to this view, we cannot say that the sparrow is a better member than the ostrich in the BIRD category.

The classical theory has dominated for a long time, but it has also suffered from criticisms. Such a view of categorization is bound to run into difficulties when it is used to describe categories which have good and bad members and fuzzy boundaries. Things in the world are much too complex for a theory as neat as the classical theory. Linguists, both formal and cognitive, have reached a consensus that there are a number of problems with the classical theory. We discuss here three of the most serious problems with this theory.

The first problem concerns the necessary and sufficient condition approach to categorization. As discussed above, the classical theory holds that categories are defined in terms of a limited set of necessary and sufficient conditions. This requires the identification of all those features that are shared by all members of a category (necessary features) and that together are sufficient to define that category (no more features are required). But in practice it has proved remarkably difficult to identify a precise set of conditions that are necessary and sufficient to define a category. Let us take as a simple example the category CAT. We might define this category as follows: "is a mammal" "has four legs" "is furry" "has a long tail" "has pointy ears". What happens if your cat gets into a fight and loses an ear, or gets ill and loses its fur? Does it then stop being a member of the category CAT? The necessary and sufficient condition approach therefore suffers from the problem that definitions which are based on necessary and sufficient conditions (or semantic features) are, in reality, subject to exceptions. A three-legged one-eared hairless cat is still a cat. It seems hard to determine which, except the first one, of the defining features is necessary, and correspondingly how many of them are sufficient. Thus it might be possible to say that a category need not have set of conditions shared by all members in order to "count" as a meaningful category in the human mind.

The second problem with the classical theory concerns the assumption that categories have definite and distinct boundaries which means an entity either will or will not possess the "right" features for category membership. Indeed, this appears to be the case for many categories. Consider the category ODD NUMBER. As we learn at school, members of this category are all those numbers that cannot be divided by 2 without leaving a remainder: 1, 3, 5, 7, 9 and so on. This category has clearly defined boundaries, because number is either odd or even: there is no point in between. However, many categories are not so clearly defined but instead have "fuzzy" boundaries. Consider the category FURNITURE. While *table* and *chair* are clearly instances of this category, it is less clear whether *carpet* should be considered a member. Consider the category BIRD. While it is obvious that birds like *robin* and *sparrow* belong to this category, it is less obvious that animals like penguins and ostriches do, neither of which can fly. The difficulty in deciding to set the boundary for certain categories is the problem of conceptual "fuzziness". If the classical theory of categorization is correct, this problem should not arise.

The third problem with the classical view of categories is related to the second problem, but while the second problem concerns what happens at the **boundaries** of a category, this third problem concerns what happens at the **centre** of a category. As we will see in the next section, findings from experimental cognitive psychology reveal that categories give rise to **prototype** or **typicality effects**. For example, while people judge table or chair as "good examples", or "typical examples" of the category FURNITURE, carpet is judged as a less good example. These asymmetries between category members are called typicality effects. While we might expect this to happen in the case of categories that have fuzzy boundaries, experiments have revealed that categories with distinct boundaries also show typicality effects. For example, Armstrong et al. (1983) found that the category EVEN NUMBER exhibits typicality effects: participants in their experiments consistently rated certain members of the category including 2, 4, 6 and 8 as "better" examples of the category than, say, 98 or 10 002. Categories that exhibit typicality effects are called graded categories. Typicality effects represent a serious challenge for the classical theory, because if each member of a category shares the same definitional structure, then each member should be equally "typical".

10.4.1.2 The prototype theory

Because of the problems with the classical view of categories, several more sophisticated theories of categories have been proposed. One influential proposal is due to Eleanor Rosch and her co-workers (e.g. Rosch, 1973, 1975; Rosch and Mervis, 1975; Rosch et al., 1976) who have suggested the notion of **prototypes**. This is a model of categories which views them as structured so that there are central or typical members of a category, such as BIRD or FURNITURE, but then a shading off into less typical or peripheral members. So *orange* is a more central member of the category FRUIT than *papaya* or *tomato*, for example. Or *sparrow* a more typical member of the category BIRD than *penguin* or *ostrich*. Category members like *orange* or *sparrow* are called prototypes as they are considered to be the best examples of the FRUIT category and the BIRD category. This approach seems to have been supported by Rosch's experimental evidence: speakers tend to agree more readily on typical members than on less typical members; they come to mind more quickly, etc. Another result of this and similar work (e.g. Labov, 1973) is that the boundaries between categories can seem to speakers uncertain, or "fuzzy", rather than clearly defined. It follows that this approach allows for borderline uncertainty: an entity in the world might bear some resemblance to two different prototypes. This permits the seeming contradiction between the two sentences a and b in 69):

69) a. Strictly speaking, a whale is not a fish but a mammal since it is viviparous.

b. Loosely speaking, a whale is a fish, in that it lives in the oceans, can swim, and has fins.

There are a number of interpretations of these typicality effects in the psychology literature: some researchers for example have argued that the central prototype is an abstraction. This abstraction might be a set of **characteristic features**, to which we compare real items. These characteristic features of BIRD might describe a kind of average bird, small, perhaps, with wings, feathers, the ability to fly, etc. but of no particular species. Other researchers have proposed that we organize our categories by **exemplars**, memories of actual typical birds, say sparrows, pigeons and hawks, and we compute the likelihood of something we meet being a bird on the basis of comparison with these memories of real birds. Langacker supports the second understanding of prototypes. He (1987: 371) says, "A prototype is a typical instance of a category, and other elements are assimilated to the category on the basis of their perceived resemblance to the prototype; there are degrees of membership based on degrees of similarity."

Thus, we have two basic ways of categorization: categorization by exemplars or categorization by an abstraction which is composed of a set of characteristic features. Both ways are possible in the process of categorization. In the former case, an entity happens to be fully compatible with an abstract representation; in the latter case, it is only partially compatible. It follows that categorization by exemplars and categorization by abstraction give rise to different predictions concerning degree of membership judgments, i.e. with categorization by abstraction membership is not a matter of degree. We have seen above, however, that for very many categories, membership clearly is a matter of degree. In contrast, categorization by exemplars fully reflects the different degrees of membership of entities in a category. Besides, from the perspective of developmental psychology categorization by exemplars occurs prior to categorization by abstraction.

At the end of this point, we present an opposing view about categorization by abstraction, which holds that this way of categorization also shows degrees of membership: the more category-relevant features a particular entity has, the more representative it is, that is, the number of relevant features possessed by a particular category member correlates with how representative that member is judged to be.

Before concluding our discussion of typicality effects, let us stop for a while to summarize the main assumptions of the prototype theory.

(1) Not all categories are organized by means of a set of necessary and sufficient conditions. An overwhelming majority of categories are organized around prototypes.

(2) Members of a category are not equal in status. That is, members of a category differ in their prototypicality, or degree to which they are prototypical. For example, a robin and a sparrow are very prototypical birds, while ostriches and penguins are very low in prototypicality. In fact, ostriches and penguins can be called non-prototypes because they are far away from being the prototype of a bird. Fig. 10-19 shows the categorial status of some birds in the BIRD category.

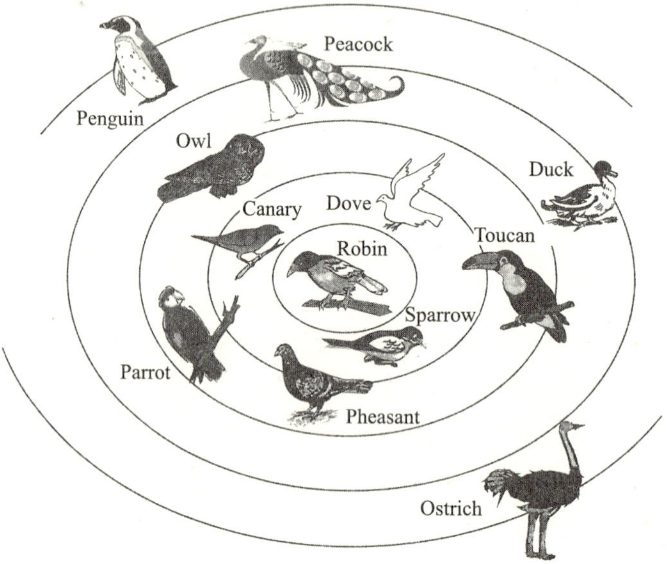

Fig. 10-19 The BIRD category

(3) Not all categories have clear-cut boundaries. The boundaries between many categories are fuzzy and undeterminate.

(4) Not all defining features are binary. For example, for a bisexual person, the feature [male] or [female] is not a matter of yes or no, or either [+] or [−]. Biologically, such a person can be seen as located in the overlapping area of the two categories MAN and WOMAN, or BOY and GIRL, an atypical member standing across two categories.

Having summarized the main assumptions of the prototype theory, we now turn to another approach to typicality effects from within linguistics, which is interesting because of the light it sheds on the relationship between linguistic knowledge and encyclopedic knowledge, a topic we discussed in chapter 1. Charles Fillmore (1982b) and George Lakoff (1987) both make similar claims that speakers have folk theories about the world, based on their experience and rooted in their culture. These theories are called **frames** by Fillmore and **idealized cognitive models** (ICMs) by Lakoff. They are not scientific theories or logically consistent definitions, but collections of cultural views. Fillmore gives an example of how these folk theories might work by using the word *bachelor*. It is clear that some bachelors are more prototypical than others, with the Pope, for example, being far from prototypical. Fillmore, and Lakoff in his discussion of the same point (1987: 68-71), suggests that there is a division of our knowledge about the word *bachelor*: part is a **dictionary**-type definition (perhaps simply "an unmarried man") and part is a **encyclopedia**-type entry of cultural knowledge about bachelorhood and marriage — the frame or ICM. The first we can call linguistic or semantic knowledge and the second real world or general knowledge. Their point is we only apply the word *bachelor* within a typical marriage ICM: a monogamous union between eligible people, typically involving romantic love, etc. It is this idealized model, a form of general knowledge, which governs our use of the word *bachelor* and restrains us from applying it to celibate priests, or people living in isolation like Robinson Crusoe on his island or Tarzan living among apes in the jungle. In this view then using a word involves combining semantic knowledge and encyclopedic knowledge, and this interaction may result in typicality effects. We will discuss typicality effects from ICMs in more detail in the next section.

10.4.1.3 Levels of categorization

Proponents of prototype theory, for example Rosch et al. (1976), have also investigated categorial hierarchies and have found that there are three levels of generality in categories: a **superordinate** level, a **basic** level, and a **subordinate** level. The idea is that the levels differ in their balance between informativeness and usefulness. If we take one of Rosch et al.'s (1976) examples, that of furniture, the superordinate level category is FURNITURE, which is informationally more general and has relatively few characteristic features; the basic level categories would include CHAIR, DESK, SOFA, etc., which are informationally more specific (but not too specific) and have more features; and the subordinate level categories would include ARMCHAIR, DINING CHAIR, DESK CHAIR, etc., which have still more features and are thus more specific again. Basic level categories have a special status. They are identified as cognitively important. Notice that there are differences between the terms **prototype** and **basic-level category**. A prototype is the best example of a category, whether the category level is superordinate, basic-level, or subordinate. It has been found that children learn basic-level words first, for the simple reason that they are not too general nor too specific and they are most useful. Basic-level categories are basic in three respects:

(1) Perception: overall perceived shape; single mental image; fast identification (in experiments it is the level at which adults spontaneously name objects and such objects are recognized more quickly).

(2) Communication: shortest, most commonly used in everyday life and contextually neutral words, first acquired by children and first to enter the lexicon.

(3) Knowledge organization: most features of category members are stored at this level.

It is not hard to see that basic-level categories take primacy over categories at other levels. This is mostly because it is at this level that we perceive the evident differences between objects and organisms of the world. Most of the time, we understand superordinate categories with the aid of basic-level categories. For instance, the comprehension of FURNITURE comes from the understanding of its typical members like *chairs*, *tables*, *desks*, and *beds*, each of which forms a basic-level category. Similarly, by the time a child can understand *animal*, he must have learnt *cat*, *dog*, *lion*, *tiger*, *cow*, and many others.

10.4.2 Idealized cognitive models

The theory of **idealized cognitive models** was developed by George Lakoff in his book *Women, Fire and Dangerous Things* published in 1987. It is a theory of category structure at the cognitive level that could account for the empirical findings presented by Rosch and her colleagues. According to Lakoff (1987: 68), the ideas about cognitive models come from four sources: Fillmore's frame semantics (Fillmore, 1982b), Lakoff and Johnson's theory of metaphor and metonymy (Lakoff and Johnson, 1980), Langacker's cognitive grammar (Langacker, 1987), and Fauconnier's theory of mental spaces (Fauconnier, 1985).

Lakoff argued that categories relate to idealized cognitive models. These are relatively stable mental representations that represent theories about the world. In this respect, ICMs are similar to Fillmore's notion of frames, since both relate to relatively complex knowledge structures. In Lakoff's theory, ICMs guide cognitive processes like categorization and reasoning. Our knowledge is organized by means of idealized cognitive models, and that category structures and prototype effects are by-products of that organization. Lakoff (1987: 68) also states that each ICM is a complex structured whole, a gestalt, which uses four kinds of structuring principles: propositional structure, image-schematic structure, metaphoric mappings, and metonymic mappings. If a definition of ICM is required, it may be defined as an abstract, unified and idealized structure of organization and representation about the experience and knowledge of a certain field formed by human beings in the process of interacting with the outside world.

10.4.2.1 Characteristics of ICMs

As complex conceptual structures created by human beings, ICMs have the characteristics of idealization, bodily experience, complexity, prototypicality structure, and cultural coherence.

Firstly, ICMs are idealized. They are complex structures of knowledge representation created by human beings. ICMs do not exist objectively in the outside world, "they may be defined relative to idealized circumstances rather than circumstances as they are known to exist" (Lakoff, 1987b: 65). Lakoff fully illustrates this characteristic with an example concerning the understanding of the English word *Tuesday*.

> *Tuesday can be defined only relative to an idealized model that includes the natural cycle defined by the movement of the sun, the standard means of characterizing the end of one day and the beginning of the next, and a larger seven-day calendric cycle — the week. In the idealized model, the week is a whole with seven parts organized in a linear sequence; each part is called a day, and the third is Tuesday. Similarly, the concept weekend requires a notion of a work week of five days followed by a break of two days, superimposed on the seven-day calendar.*

> *Our model of a week is idealized. Seven-day weeks do not exist objectively in nature. They are created by human beings. In fact, not all cultures have the same kinds of weeks.* (Lakoff, 1987: 68–69)

Secondly, ICMs come from bodily experience. They are the result of human's interaction with the world. Once they are created on the basis of human bodily experience, ICMs are promoted to folk theory through conceptualization. ICMs have become one of the main topics in contemporary embodied philosophy, indicating, to some extent, an abandonment of the traditional objectivist philosophy.

Thirdly, it commonly happens that an ICM is not a simple model but a complex structured whole, a gestalt, which is composed of a number of cognitive models. ICMs like this are referred to as **cluster models**. A typical example is Lakoff's (1987: 74) analysis of the concept MOTHER. This category is based on a cluster model which consists of a number of individual cognitive models, including the birth model, the genetic model, the nurturance model, the marital model, and the genealogical model. The five cognitive models converge to form the ICM or prototype of the MOTHER category. Stepmother, birth mother, adoptive mother, foster mother, surrogate mother, etc. only foreground one of the five cognitive models of an idealized mother.

Fourthly, ICMs are characterized by prototypicality structure, or center-periphery schema. The individual CMs of an ICM are not equal in status. Only the typical or central CM can stand for an ICM and the other CMs derive from metaphorical or metonymic extension.

Finally, ICMs are characterized by cultural coherence. Lakoff argues that, given the embodied nature of human cognition, different cultures present both similar and different culturally related bodily experience. Ungerer and Schmid (1996: 50) also point out that the formation of cognitive models depend on the culture in which a person grows up and lives and the culture provides the background for all the situations that we have to experience in order to be able to form a cognitive model. Therefore, cognitive models for particular domains are ultimately restrained by cultural models.

10.4.2.2 Typicality effects from ICMs

Lakoff argues that typicality effects can arise in a range of ways from a number of different sources. In this section, we present some of the ICMs proposed by Lakoff, and show how these are argued to give rise to typicality effects.

10.4.2.2.1 Gradience

Typicality effects can arise due to mismatches between the background conditions of an ICM and our knowledge about the world. The worse the fit between the background conditions of an ICM and the world as we know it, the less appropriate it is for us to apply a certain concept related to the ICM. The result is a gradience — a simple kind of prototype effect.

Lakoff takes Fillmore's (1982a) classic analysis of the category defined by the English word *bachelor* as an example to illustrate this simple kind of prototype effect. The following is a quotation from Fillmore:

> *The noun bachelor can be defined as an unmarried adult man, but the noun clearly exists as a motivated device for categorizing people only in the context of a human society in which certain expectations about marriage and marriageable age obtain. Male participants in long-term unmarried couplings would not ordinarily be described as bachelors; a boy abandoned in the jungle and grown to maturity away from contact with human society would not be called a bachelor; John Paul II is not properly thought of as a bachelor.*

Lakoff concludes from this quotation that the concept or category BACHELOR must be defined or understood with respect to an ICM in which there is a human society with (typically monogamous) marriage, and a typical marriageable age. The idealized model says nothing about the existence of priests, "long-term unmarried coupling", homosexuality, Moslems who are permitted four wives and only have three, etc. Only with respect to this idealized cognitive model, can BACHELOR be understood as an unmarried adult man.

However, since this model is idealized, it naturally does not fit the world very precisely, and this is what gives rise to typicality effects. There are some segments of society where the idealized model fits reasonably well, and where an unmarried adult man might well be called a bachelor. But the ICM does not fit the case of the Pope or people abandoned in the jungle, like Tarzan. In such cases, unmarried adult males are certainly not representative members of the category of bachelors. In other words, the category BACHELOR has a prototypical structure. Its prototypes are those unmarried adult males with whom the ICM of bachelorhood makes a perfect fit. The unmarried adult males such as the monks, the priests, the homosexuals, etc., with whom the ICM of bachelorhood does not fit in one way or another, are considered to be the peripheral members of the category. The categorial status of the non-typical members is determined on how far they deviate from the prototypes.

10.4.2.2.2 Typicality effects due to cluster models

It commonly happens that a number of cognitive models combine to form a complex cluster that is psychologically more basic than the models taken individually. Lakoff (1987: 74) refers to these models as **cluster models**. Wang Yin (2007: 223) argues that cluster models are ICMs. Lakoff takes the category MOTHER as an example to show how some concepts or categories are structured by a cluster model and how typicality effects arise from cluster models.

According to the classical theory, it should be possible to give clear necessary and sufficient conditions for MOTHER that will fit all the cases and apply equally to all of them. Such a definition might be something like: *a woman who has given birth to a child*. But as we will see, no such definition will cover the full range of cases. MOTHER is a concept that is based on a complex model in which a number of individual cognitive models combine, forming a cluster model. The models in the cluster are:

a. THE BIRTH MODEL: a mother is the person who gives birth to the child.

The birth model is usually accompanied by a genetic model, although since the development of egg and embryo implants, they do not always coincide.

b. THE GENETIC MODEL: a mother is the person who provides the genetic material for the child.

c. THE NURTURANCE MODEL: a mother is the person who brings up and looks after the child.

d. THE MARITAL MODEL: a mother is the person who is married to the child's father.

e. THE GENEALOGICAL MODEL: a mother is the closest female ancestor of the child.

In reality, if a female plays all the roles that the five models characterize, then she is a "good" or "ideal" mother, and thus a central or prototypical member of the category MOTHER. It embodies the ICM of the concept MOTHER. The mothers who deviate from the cluster model or ICM, or in other words, whose characterization does not include all the five models are non-prototypical members of the category. This is what gives rise to typicality effects.

In actual use of the word mother, we quite often take a certain model from the cluster model as the most important and view it as the criterion for judgment and decision. That is why we sometimes hear people say "This cannot be counted as a 'real mother' " or "This can be counted as a 'real mother' ". But different people may choose a different cognitive model as a criterion for a "real mother", and even the same person, under different circumstances, may use different models to make his judgment. The following example reveals how different models are employed for MOTHER in stipulating what counts as a "real mother".

70) a. I was adopted and I don't know who my real mother is. (BIRTH MODEL)

b. I am not a nurturant person, so I don't think I could ever be a real mother to my child. (NURTURANCE MODEL)

c. My real mother died when I was an embryo, and I was later frozen and implanted in the womb of the woman who gave birth to me. (GENETIC MODEL)

d. I had a genetic mother who contributed the egg that was planted in the womb of my real mother, who gave birth to me and raised me. (BIRTH MODEL and NURTURANCE MODEL)

e. By genetic engineering, the genes in the egg my father's sperm fertilized were spliced together from genes in the eggs of twenty different women. I wouldn't call any of them my real mother. My real mother is the woman who bore me and raised me, even though I don't have any single genetic mother. (BIRTH MODEL and NURTURANCE MODEL)

Every sentence in 70) profiles one or two cognitive models. The five models form a MOTHERHOOD-ICM, which is encyclopedic knowledge about the concept MOTHER. As said before, if and only if a female involves all the five models she is counted as a typical mother.

There is another sense of typicality effects from cluster models. Lakoff argues that cluster models give rise to typicality effects when one of the CMs that contributes to the cluster is viewed as primary. This results in the other subcategories being ranked as less important: "When the cluster of models that jointly characterize a concept diverge, there is still a strong pull to view one as the most important." (Lakoff, 1987: 75) This is reflected in dictionary definitions, for example, which often privilege one of the MOTHER sub-models over the others. Although many dictionaries treat the BIRTH MODEL as primary, Lakoff found that *Funk and Wagnall's Standard Dictionary* selected the NURTURANCE MODEL while the *American College Dictionary* chose the GENEALOGICAL MODEL.

10.4.2.2.3 Typicality effects due to metonymy

Lakoff argues the third source of typicality effects is metonymy — a situation in which some subcategory or member or submodel is used to stand for the category as a whole. He (1987: 78) holds that there are some general principles guiding the formation of metonymy. The principles take the following form: Given an ICM with some background condition (e.g. institutions are located in places), there is a "stand for" relation that may hold between two elements A and B, such that one element of the ICM, B, may stand for another element A. In this case, B = place and A = the institution. Lakoff (1987: 78) refers to such ICMs containing stands-for relations as **metonymic models**.

There are many metonymic models in a rich conceptual system, and they are used for a wide variety of purposes. The kind related to our present discussion of typicality effects are those in which a member or subcategory can stand metonymically for the whole category for the purpose of making inferences or judgments. The member or subcategory, which stands for the whole category, serves as a **cognitive reference point**, setting up norms and expectations against which other members of the category are evaluated and assessed. It follows that metonymic models give rise to typicality effects, as other members of the category are judged as atypical relative to the member or subcategory that is used to comprehend the category as a whole.

Lakoff proposes a number of different kinds of metonymic models, any of which can in principle serve as a cognitive reference point and can thus give rise to typicality effects. We briefly outline some of these below.

• *Social stereotypes*

Social stereotypes are cases of metonymy — where a subcategory has a socially recognized status as standing for the category as a whole, usually for the purpose of making quick judgments about people. One example of social stereotype is the cultural stereotype HOUSEWIFE-MOTHER, which involves a married woman who does not have paid work but stays at home and looks after the house and family. The HOUSEWIFE-MOTHER stereotype can give rise to typicality effects when it stands for, or represents, the category MOTHER as a whole. Typicality effects arise from cultural expectations associated with members of the category MOTHER. According to the HOUSEWIFE-MOTHER stereotype, mothers nurture their children, and in order to do this they stay at home and take care of them. A WORKING MOTHER, by contrast, is not simply a mother who has a job, but also one who does not stay at home to look after her children. Hence the HOUSEWIFE-MOTHER model, by metonymically representing the category MOTHER as a whole, serves in part to define other instances of the category such as WORKING MOTHER, which thus emerges as a non-prototypical member of the category.

Obviously, this typicality effect is not due to the clustering of cognitive models for MOTHER as we have seen in our discussion on typicality effects due to cluster models, but rather to the case of a metonymic model in which one subcategory, the housewife-mother, stands for the whole category in defining cultural expectations of mothers.

Another example of social stereotype is related to the category BACHELOR. The BACHELOR stereotype provides a second level of prototype effects addition to those that are a consequence of the BACHELOR ICM not fitting certain situations. The stereotypical bachelor in contemporary American culture is a womanizer who lacks domestic skills. Typicality effects can arise if a particular bachelor contrasts with this stereotype. For instance, an unmarried man with one sexual partner who enjoys staying at home cooking and takes pride in his housework may be judged atypical with respect to the social stereotype for bachelors. This shows how the social stereotype BACHELOR, which represents one element in the category BACHELOR, can stand for the category as a whole thus giving rise to typicality effects.

• *Typical examples*

Typicality effects can also arise in relation to **typical examples** of a particular category. For instance, in some cultures robin and sparrow are typical members of the category BIRD. This is because in some parts of the world these birds are very common. In this respect, our environment has consequences for what we judge as good examples of a category. Furthermore, Lakoff argues that we may evaluate a member of the category BIRD with respect to a typical example. In this way, typicality effects arise when the typical example stands for the entire category.

• *Ideals*

Lakoff suggests that some categories are understood in terms of **ideals**, which may contrast with typical or stereotypical instances. For example, we might have an ideal for the category POLITICIAN: someone who is public-spirited, altruistic, hardworking, and so on. This may contrast with our stereotype of politicians as egotistical, power-hungry and obsessed with "spin". Once more, typicality effects occur when the ideal stands metonymically for the entire category. For instance, with respect to our ideal the utterance *He's a great politician* might be interpreted as a positive evaluation. However, with respect to our social stereotype, the same utterance would be interpreted as a negative evaluation.

• *Paragons*

Individual category members that represent an ideal or its opposite are **paragons**. For instance, David Beckham, arguably the world's best-known soccer star, is good-looking, a committed father, glamorous, married to a pop star and captain of the England team, as well as being one of the world's most successful footballers. For many people around the world, Beckham represents a FOOTBALL paragon. Similarly, Rolls-Royce represents a paragon in terms of LUXURY CARS, Nelson Mandela in terms of POLITICAL LEADERS, Winston Churchill in terms of WAR LEADERS, Noam Chomsky in terms of GENERATIVE LINGUISTS, and so on. Because paragons stand for an entire category, they set up norms and expectations against which other members of the category may be evaluated. For instance, the comment, "He's no Nelson Mandela" about a particular political leader may represent a negative assessment as to the leader's altruism and so forth. In this way, paragons give rise to typicality effects.

• *Generators*

According to Lakoff, members of some categories are "generated" by a core subset of category members called **generators**. These generators are judged to be more prototypical than the other category members that they generate. For example, the natural numbers are represented by the set of integers between zero and nine, which are combined in various ways in order to produce higher natural numbers. For instance, the number 10 combines the integers 1 and 0. Thus the entire category NUTURAL NUMBERS is generated from a small set of single-digit integers. Lakoff argues that this is why the numbers 1 to 9 are judged as prototypical members of the category NATURAL NUMBERS than much larger numbers.

• *Salient examples*

It is common for people to use familiar, memorable, or otherwise salient examples to comprehend categories. For example, if your best friend is a vegetarian and you don't know any others well, you will tend to generalize from your friend to other vegetarians. After a widely publicized DC-10 crash in Chicago, many people refused to fly DC-10s, choosing other types of planes despite the fact that they had overall worse safety records than DC-10s. Such people used the salient example of the DC-10 that crashed to stand metonymically for the entire category of DC-10s with respect to safety judgments. In other words, salient examples, like prototypes in general, provide cognitive reference points that not only structure a category metonymically, but can influence the decisions or judgments we make.

Table 10-1 provides a summary of some of the types of metonymic models proposed by Lakoff. They have a cognitive status, that is, they are used in reasoning. And they all yield prototype effects of some sort.

Table 10-1 Summary of some metonymic models

Metonymic models	Summary
Social stereotypes	represent cultural norms and expectations regarding instances of the category
Typical examples	represent the most frequent or commonly encountered instances of the category

Continued

Metonymic models	Summary
Ideals	combine the ideal properties of the category
Paragons	represent actual instances of an ideal
Generators	members of a category are "generated" by a core subset of members
Salient examples	represent memorable or well-known actual instances of a category

10.4.2.2.4 Typicality effects due to radial categories

Lakoff proposes that the cluster model for MOTHER and the metonymic HOUSEWIFE-MOTHER stereotype taken together contribute to a **composite prototype** for MOTHER: a prototype derived from two models. This prototype provides **representative structure** for the category. For example, the composite prototype for the category MOTHER includes a female who gave birth to the child, was supplier of 50 per cent of the genetic material, stayed at home in order to nurture the child, is married to the child's father, is one generation older than the child and is also the child's legal guardian. In other words, the composite prototype draws upon information from the BIRTH MODEL, the GENETIC MODEL, the NURTURANCE MODEL, the MARITAL MODEL, the GENEALOGICAL MODEL and the HOUSEWIFE MODEL, which is a social stereotype. This type of prototype is an idealization which provides schematic information. Importantly, further models can be derived from this composite prototype. These models include ADOPTIVE MOTHER, FOSTER MOTHER, BIRTH MOTHER and SURROGATE MOTHER, etc. As Lakoff points out:

> *These variants are not generated from the central model by general rules; instead, they are extended by convention and must be learned one by one. But the extensions are by no means random. The central model determines the possibilities for extensions, together with the possible relations between the central model and the extension models.* (*Lakoff, 1987: 91*)

A composite prototype and extensions of this kind are modeled in terms of a radiating lattice structure. The composite prototype is positioned centrally with other subcategories represented as extending from the **central case** (see Fig. 10-20).

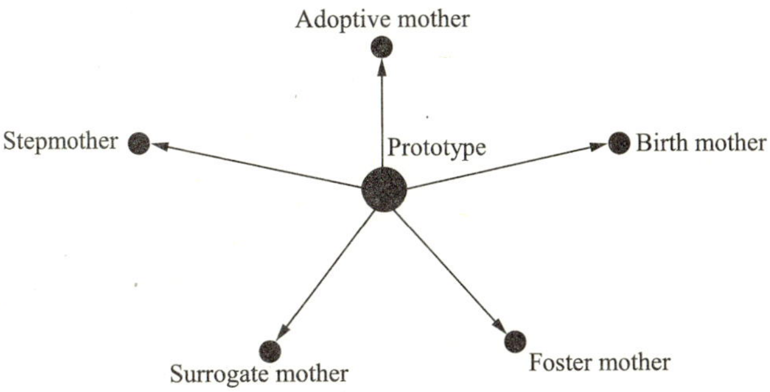

Fig. 10-20 Radial network for the category MOTHER

Crucially, the non-central cases in such **radial categories** are not strictly predictable from the central case but are cultural products. For instance, the subcategories of MOTHER listed below are all understood in terms of how they diverge from the central case.

(1) STEPMOTHER — married to the father but didn't supply genetic material or give birth.

(2) ADOPTIVE MOTHER — provides nurturance and is the legal guardian.

(3) BIRTH MOTHER — gave birth and supplied genetic material but put the child up for adoption hence does not nurture the child and has no legal responsibilities.

(4) FOSTER MOTHER — paid by the state to nurture the child but is not the child's legal guardian.

(5) SURROGATE MOTHER — gives birth to the child, typically does not supply the genetic material and has no other obligations to the child.

Thus radial categories of this kind provide a fourth way in which typicality effects can arise. These effects occur when the subcategories are seen to deviate from the composite prototype. Moreover, as particular categories can become more conventionalized than others, different subcategories in a radial category can develop different degrees of prototypicality.

Importantly, radial categories are not "generators". The central case does not productively generate new subcategories of the MOTHER category. While the subcategories are **motivated** in the sense that they are licensed by the prototype, this is a consequence of our cultural experience. For instance, the subcategory SURROGATE MOTHER is a consequence of recent achievements in medicine and cultural trends and has appeared in the second half of the twentieth century.

In sum, radial categories are motivated, but knowing a prototype does not predict what subcategories will become conventionally adopted in the culture.

To summarize this part, we have seen that there are four ways in which Lakoff accounts for typicality effects. The first kind of typicality effect arises from mismatches between an ICM and real situations. The second kind of typicality effect arises from more complex cognitive models which Lakoff calls cluster models. These consist of a number of distinct subcategory models. Typicality effects occur when one subcategory is deemed to be more salient than the others, or when there is a central case (which forms the ICM of a category) where all the subcategory models converge. The third kind of typicality effect relates to metonymic models. These are essentially exemplar-based cognitive models in which a particular member of a given category stands for the category as a whole. Assessed with respect to the metonymic models, other members of a category may be evaluated as being atypical. The fourth kind of typicality effect arises from radial categories, in which members of a radial category exhibit degrees of typicality depending on how close to the composite prototype they are.

10.5 Iconicity

The idea that language is fundamentally arbitrary, and that there is no intrinsic or logical connection between the signs of language and the thoughts they stand for, is one of the oldest commonly held views in linguistic thought. The first significant challenge to this dogma in the respectable philological tradition is Roman Jakobson's famous article "Quest for the Essence of Language" (1965). Recent studies in cognitive linguistics are also against this traditional view. Instead, they claim that while arbitrariness does exist in language, there is also an iconic correspondence between the structure of language and the cognitive or experiential structure of human beings. They call this corresponding relation between language and cognition or experience **iconicity**.

There are various wordings on the definition of iconicity. What come after are some of them.

"The intuition behind iconicity is quite simple: the structure of language reflects in some way the structure of experience, that is to say, the structure of the world, including (in most functionalists' view) the perspective imposed on the world by the speaker. The structure of language is therefore motivated or explained by the structure of experience to the extent that the two match." (Croft, 1990: 164)

"(Iconicity refers to) the principle by which semantic relations are reflected in the formal patterns by which they are realized." (Matthews, 1997)

"(Iconicity refers to the) concept of text interpretations developed within the framework of semiotics that is based on the correspondence between the characteristics of a particular representation and the characteristics of that which it represents. Thus, under certain stylistic conditions, a report addressed to a hearer or a reader is as complex as the events being described in the report. Similarly, the linear structure of a report can be deduced from the natural sequence of the events." (Bussmann, 1996)

"Linguistic structure reflects to some extent the world structure people have experienced." (严辰松 , 1997)

"Iconicity refers to the correspondence between linguistic structure and people's experiential or conceptual structure."(文旭 , 2001)

The above are some typical concepts of iconicity. We find that the statements about iconicity are made either in terms of linguistic structure (Croft, 1990; Matthews, 1997; 严辰松, 1997; 文旭, 2001) or in terms of textual structure (Bussmann, 1996). At present most linguists tend to study iconicity in syntactic structures. John Haiman (1985a, 1985b) is the first scholar who has investigated systematically the various aspects of iconicity in syntactic structures, and the two books he wrote on iconicity are titled *Natural Syntax* and *Iconicity in Syntax*.

The major types of iconicity in language which have frequently been proposed are those of order, distance, and quantity or complexity.

10.5.1 Iconicity of order

Iconicity of order refers to the similarity between temporal events and the linear arrangement of elements in a linguistic construction. Or the linear order of syntactic elements mirrors the order of actions or events described. The much cited example of this is Caesar's famous *Veni, vidi, vici* (I came, I saw, I conquered) in which order of mention matches order of action stated. The order of linguistic signs also mirrors the order of thoughts and cultural view.

It is generally accepted that cause precedes result and condition precedes action. Therefore in complex sentences the subordinate clauses of cause or condition precede in most cases the main clauses (although they usually follow the main clauses in English, research on native language acquisition has shown that at the early stage of their English acquisition, children do put the subordinate clauses before the main clauses). Givon (1990) believes that sentences in particular word order (such as those with contrastive, interrogative or emphatic elements at the initial position) also follow the iconicity principle of order — the principle to express first the information that a speaker is most anxious to convey but which has a lower degree of predictability for the hearer.

10.5.1.1 Temporal order

What this means is that the relative order of two syntactic units is determined by the temporal sequence of the states, events, or actions described by them. Let us consider the following two pairs of sentences:

71) a. He opened the bottle and poured himself a glass of wine.
    b. *He poured himself a glass of wine and opened the bottle.
72) a. He jumped onto his horse and rode out into the sunset.
    b. *He rode out into the sunset and jumped onto his horse.

It is obvious that in 71)a and 72)a, the sequence of the two clauses corresponds to the natural temporal order of events. In contrast, 71)b and 72)b are odd, to say the least, because they do not comply with this natural sequence. As far as the rules of syntax proper are concerned, nothing is wrong with 71)b and 72)b. However, the sentences are unacceptable because the order in which the clauses are arranged violates the principle of order iconicity.

10.5.1.2 Spatial order

Spatial order is related to what is called the **speaker-centered principle**. By speaker-centered principle is meant that what is closest (literally or metaphorically) to the speaker is mentioned first, especially in paratactic structures without conjunction or in frozen expressions. This principle can be approached from three perspectives.

• *spatial-temporal adjacency*

Literally speaking, the speaker-centered phenomenon is quite common and mainly exists in some frozen expressions. This is illustrated in phrases like *here and there*, *this and that*, *these and those*, *now and then*, *sooner and later*, in which words such as *here*, *this*, *now*, etc. come earlier than *there*, *that*, *then*, etc., but not the other way around. This word order is obviously determined by the speaker's visual point, that is, what is mentioned first is more adjacent to the speaker in terms of space and time, and thus is easier to be perceived first.

Speaker-centered principle also exhibits itself in sentences. Let us look at the following example:

73) Struggle and submission are before the colonial people: *this* leads to slavery, *that* to freedom.

This example shows that, in English, when referring back to two words said earlier in a sentence, we use *this* for the word that comes later and *that* for the word that comes earlier. This phenomenon can be explained from a metaphorical angle with the "principle of speaker adjacency" (文旭, 2001). By the "principle of speaker adjacency" is meant that, without the interference of other factors, an entity that is nearer to the speaker (either literally or metaphorically) tend to be mentioned earlier, and vice versa. Considering metaphorically, the speaking of a person has a start point and an end point, just as the journey of a traveler has a start point and a destination. When looking back at the words he has said, what is said later is nearer to the speaker and thus will be first mentioned, and will be referred to with *this*; in contrast, what is said earlier is farther from him and naturally will be mentioned secondly, and will be referred to with *that*. We may say that word order of this kind of sentence follows a spatial sequence with the speaker as the point of reference. Of course, when this sentence is translated into Chinese, we should convert the spatial order into temporal order so as to cater to the psychological expectation of Chinese readers. Thus the translation "殖民地人民面临着两条道路：斗争和屈服。*前者*导向自由，*后者*导向奴役" is better than "殖民地人民面临着两条道路：斗争和屈服。*后者*导向奴役，*前者*导向自由". The following are two more examples.

74) "High" and "tall" are synonymous: *this* may be used in speaking of what grows—a tree; *that* in speaking of what does not grow—a mountain.
(High 和 tall 是同义词：*前者*用来指不生长的东西，如山；*后者*用来指生长的东西，如树。)

75) The two units used most frequently in electricity are ampere and volt: *this* is the unit of voltage and *that* of current flow.
(电学上最常用的两个单位是安培和伏特：*前者*是电流单位，*后者*是电压单位。)

• *prototypical speaker adjacency*

This concerns adjacency in its metaphorical sense. The concept of prototypical speaker was first put forward by Mayerthaler (1980), by which he refers to an ideal speaker with typical psychological, physiological and especially perceptual faculties. Lexical items that are semantically closer to the prototypical speaker tend to be put on the left-hand side of a frozen construction. Naturally, a linguistic element with the semantic feature [+HUMAN] is closest to the prototypical speaker. So we can only say "a man or a mouse" but not "a mouse or a man" in English, and "人与自然" or "人与社会" but rarely "自然与人" or "社会与人" in Chinese. This principle can also explain why the indirect object without a preceding preposition in example 76) must be put before the direct object. It is because the indirect object has the feature of [+HUMAN] while the direct object does not.

76) They gave me a book. (*They gave a book me.)

In the "me-first" principle (Cooper and Ross, 1975: 67) and the "egocentric" principle (John Lyons, 1977: 638), "I", the ideal speaker, is an adult man with the three main features of [+HUMAN][+ADULT][+MALE]. The set of features of "I" is taken as a reference when considering the word order of frozen expressions, that is, what is semantically closer to the ideal speaker comes earlier in a frozen expression. Out of this we set up the following semantic rules related to word order.

77) a. The animate precedes the inanimate: *man-machine*; *person, place or thing*; *life or death*; *live or die*; 人与社会；人类与文化
b. Human precedes animal: *man or beast*; 人与动物
c. The masculine precedes the feminine: *Mr. and Mrs.*; *father and mother*; *papa and mama*; *brother and sister*; *men, women and children*; *husband and wife*; *boys and girls*; *king and queen*; *Adam and Eve*; 男男女女；男女老少；男女不分
d. The adult precedes the under age: *man and boy*; *father and son*

In certain contexts, we also say "mum and dad" "bride and groom" "aunts and uncles" "ladies and gentlemen" "horse and rider", etc. This is either the result of the so-called "politeness convention" (Cooper and Ross, 1975: 105) or because of the regulation of phonological rules. Of course, some cultural elements also play a role in this respect — the ordering of these expressions shows respect to women, while that of the expressions in 77)c and d shows inequality between men and women. As to the regulation of phonological rules, they require that a high vowel should come earlier than a front vowel, a short vowel than a long vowel, a front vowel than a back vowel, and a spreading vowel than a rounded vowel. Moreover, a word with more initial consonants precedes that with fewer initial consonants, and a word with fewer syllables precedes that with more syllables. The ordering of the phrase "horse and rider" is obviously related to the regulation of the phonological rule — a word with fewer syllables precedes that with more syllables.

• *levels of internal adjacency*

Different levels can be distinguished in adjacency to a speaker. Generally speaking, the lexical items in a frozen expression tend be arranged in such a linear order — from the concrete to the less concrete, then to the less abstract and finally to the abstract (e.g. *body and soul*). Therefore, being more abstract means being more marked or further away from the prototype. To put it another way, temporal adjacency is more abstract than spatial adjacency and adjacency to the prototypical speaker in its metaphorical sense is more abstract than that in its literal sense. For example, a word of place should come before a word of time in an English coordinate phrase such as *there and then*, *here and now*, etc.

Although iconicity of order exists both in English and Chinese, it has been found that word order in Chinese follows to a greater extent the iconicity of temporal sequence while word order in English more often adheres to the iconicity of spatial sequence and at the same time is regulated by some abstract syntactic rules. Consider the following examples:

78) a. 他坐公共汽车到这儿。(He came by bus.)

b. 他到这儿坐公共汽车。(He came here to ride in a bus.)

79) a. 他在马背上跳。(He was jumping on the horse's back.)

b. 他跳在马背上。(He jumped onto the horse.)

In 78) and 79) one can easily see that the word order of the Chinese sentences corresponds with the occurring orders of the actions described, while the word order of their English equivalents does not match the occurring sequence of events all the time as it is governed by some abstract syntactic rules (e.g. a prepositional phrase must be put after a verb). Some contrastive studies of word order in Chinese and English have proved that the surface structure of Chinese sentences approximates more the logical structure underlying them than that of English sentences. In the process of projection from semantic or conceptual structure to surface structure, Chinese projects the former to the latter directly while English does this less directly because Chinese has much fewer inflectional devices to employ than English. No wonder Haiman claims that the grammatical structure of Chinese is much like that of child language. The following are two more examples. Note how the actions in the English sentences are rearranged according to temporal order of their occurrence in the Chinese translation.

80) I had spent a long day on a hired mule before the mail carrier who had been my guide pointed to a cabin on the far side of a stream, mutely refused the money I offered, and rode on.
(我雇了一头骡子,邮差权充向导,骑了一整天,然后他遥指着河那边的一幢木屋。我给他钱,他默然拒绝,径自骑骡走了。)

81) We had been dismayed at home while reading of the natural calamities that followed one another for three years after we left China in 1959.
(我们于 1959 年离开了中国。此后,中国连续三年遭遇自然灾害。当我们在国内读到这方面的消息时,心情颇为低落。)

10.5.1.3 Culture-motivated order

This kind of iconicity means that there is a corresponding relationship between word orders and cultural conventions. The corresponding relationship is best illustrated in frozen expressions. For instance, in English we say "right and left", but in Chinese we say" 左右 "(left and right). This phenomenon can only be explained in terms of cultural conventions. "Right" precedes "left" in the linear order of the English phrase "right and left". Some people attribute this to people's habitual use of the right hand when doing things, but we can offer a better explanation in terms of the culture-related notion which signifies that the right side is related to goodness while the left side to badness. In Japan, Polynesia and all the American and European countries, there is a strong belief that the right hand is sacred while the left hand is inauspicious (杨琳, 1996: 92). Some East Africans also believe that the left half of the body is inauspicious — a left-handed person has no right to join the army, and if someone stumbles over something against the toes of the left foot while walking, it is considered a warning of bad luck, so you had better return and stay at home (Robert Loewi, 1986: 220). In many languages of the world, "right" usually has a positive meaning whereas "left" a negative meaning. The English commendatory word "dexterous" originated from a Latin word which means "on the right side" while the derogatory word "sinister" from a Latin word with the meaning "on the left side". We can cite many other English examples to illustrate the opposing connotations of "right" and "left". For instance, *the Right Honorable* (a respectful form of address to high officials, similar to the Chinese "右座"), *Mr./Miss Right* (a very suitable husband/wife), *have two left hands* (quite awkward, clumsy), *a left-hand marriage* (a marriage that is not well-matched in social and economic status), *left-handed wife* (a concubine, similar to the Chinese "左媵"). When talking about things, people usually put the good before the bad. Examples include *good or bad*, *good and evil* in English, and 好坏不分, 好赖不知 in Chinese. Since "right" is related to "goodness" and "left" to "badness", it is no wonder that "right" is put before "left" in the English phrase "right and left".

Another explanation to the phenomenon that "right" precedes "left" is related to the two bearings of "east" and "west". In English, the two directions of "left" and "right" are determined when one faces north (*Concise Oxford English-Chinese Dictionary*, 2003: 1156, 1759). The result is that "east" corresponds with "right" and "west" with "left". The east is where the sun rises, so it often reminds us of sunshine, brightness, warmness, prosperity, life and vitality, etc. In contrast with this, the west is where the sun sets, thus it gives us a feeling of being near one's end in life, a feeling of darkness, coldness, and a feeling of death and fright. In their symbolic sense, "east" is positive (unmarked), while "west" is negative (marked). Since everyday the sun rises from the east and then sets in the west, facing such a fixed natural phenomenon it is reasonable to say that among the four directions (north, south, east and west) the first two concepts of direction that came to the mind of most of the primitive people are "east" and "west", and what determines “east” and “west” is the rise and set of the sun. In addition, in their daily life, people always first see the rise of the sun, then the set of it, so the fact that “east” precedes “west” is the result of imitating the order of natural events. This explains why in Chinese we have such expressions as 东南西北，东张西望，东涂西抹，东征西讨, etc., and in English we have “east and west” “East or west, home is best” “East is east and west is west and never the twain shall meet”. Just because of what is discussed above, in English “right” comes before “left”.

As to the fact that Chinese people say “ 左右 ” (left and right) but English people say “right and left”, the answer to it can only be sought for in the special Chinese culture.

In the long history of the Chinese people, there once appeared two kinds of traditions — one took the right side as honorable and the left side humble, the other held the opposite view, that is, it took the left side as honorable and the right side as humble. Between the two kinds of cultural customs in China honoring the right or the left side respectively, why we now only say “ 左右 ”(left and right) but not “ 右左 ”(right and left)? Obviously, it is not easy to find a sound explanation from the aforementioned traditions. It is necessary to turn elsewhere in the Chinese culture for an answer. After some research, it has been found that the linear order of“ 左右 ” is closely related to the Chinese quadrangle culture. In Chinese culture, the four directions of left, right, front and back correspond respectively to east, west, south and north. This correspondence undoubtedly comes from the inhabiting custom that leaves the front door of a house face the south. With the layout of a house like this, the due front of it is the south, and the back of it is the north. Accordingly, the left side is naturally the east and the right side the west since people take the south as the front (杨琳, 1996: 65). Because of the influence of the quadrangle culture, “left” and “right” in Chinese are determined when one faces the south (现代汉语词典，2002: 1683). Since “east” precedes “west”, and “left” and “right” correspond with “east” and “west”, it is natural that “left” comes before “right”. Besides “ 左右 ”, we also have other supporting expressions such as 左右逢源，左右开弓，左支右绌，左说右说，左思右想, and so on. In view of the above, we can conclude that frozen expressions such as the Chinese “ 左右 ” and the English “right and left” are characterized by the culture-motivated iconicity.

10.5.1.4 Word order related to asymmetry in cognition

Studies in the field of cognitive psychology have shown that human's cognition is asymmetric. And this asymmetry has its physiological basis. Firstly, the structure of the human body is asymmetric — when one stands, the main sense organs are located in the upper part of his body. For example, as the eyes are at the top of the body and face forward, what is located in a high or front position will be first perceived by them. Following the sequential principle by which the first perceived is to be first expressed, "above" usually comes before "below", "up" before "down", "high" before "low", "front" before "back" in some linguistic constructions. Supporting examples include *high and low*, *mountains and seas*, *heaven and earth*, *ups and downs*; *in front and behind*, *before and after*, *front and back*, *forwards and backwards*, etc. As for the word order in which "inside" comes before "outside", it is also possible to give an explanation if the asymmetrical physiological structure of the human body is taken into consideration. Human beings get to know the outside world by first knowing their own bodies. Human body is a container. Air, water, food etc. first enter the body, and then come out of it. So what enters the body is felt earlier than what comes out of it. Because of this physical experience, it is natural for people to put "inside" before "outside" in their speaking. This is illustrated in expressions like *inside and outside*, *the ins and outs*, *in and out(of)*, *face opposition within and without*, etc.

10.5.2 Iconicity of distance

Iconicity of distance accounts for the fact that things which belong together conceptually tend to be put together linguistically, and things that do not belong together are put at a distance. That is, elements which have a close relationship must be placed close together. This entails that iconicity of distance means conceptual distance corresponds to linguistic (i.e. structural) distance.

In this subsection, we are going to demonstrate with examples the existence of distance iconicity in causation, coordination, possession, negation, internal structure of word, multi-modifier construction, attributive clause, and subjunctive mood.

10.5.2.1 Causation

In almost all languages which distinguish direct versus indirect causation, the semantic difference between the two constructions in 82) corresponds with the formal difference between them. In English, the formal distance between "causing" and "dying", i.e. between cause and result, is apparently smaller in 82)a than that in 82)b:

82) a. I killed the dog.
    b. I caused the dog to die.

The same relation holds between conceptual distances reflected respectively by 82)a and 82)b: typically, in 82)a, causing and dying occurred at the same time and in the same place, and obviously there is an indication of physical contact or there is an implication that the agent himself did the killing. In 82)b, it seems that there is no physical contact between the killer and the killed, and that the action is in some sense magical. Thus, we can say that a single word (e.g. "kill") tends to convey a more direct causation than a phrase (e.g. "cause to die"). The magical association of the action will be much stronger when the patient is inanimate. Compare the following two pairs of sentence:

83) a. Tom felled the willow tree.
    b. Tom caused the willow tree to fall.

84) a. David raised the rock.
    b. David caused the rock to rise.

We can see that the agents in 83)b and 84)b seem to have some magical power.

10.5.2.2 Coordination

Iconicity of distance also exists in coordinate constructions. It has been discovered that in a coordinate construction the distance between one constituent and another corresponds with the distance between the concepts signified by the two constituents, and the meaning of the complex form of a coordinate construction is often different from that of its reduced form.

85) a. X a Y and X b Y
    b. X a and b Y

Quite obviously, the conceptual distance between the coordinate items *a* and *b* in 85)a is not the same as that in 85)b. In 85)a, *a* and *b* are separated by Y and X and form a conceptual contrast. While in 85)b, *a* and *b* are much closer to each other both in formal and conceptual distance. Consequently, 85)a and 85)b are different from each other semantically. It is easier to understand this by means of some examples from natural language.

86) a. black sweaters and green sweaters
    b. black and green sweaters

The only interpretation for 86)a is that there are two kinds of sweaters in terms of colour, one is black, the other is green. While 86)b is more possibly to refer to the same kind of sweaters in black alternating with green, though it may also have the interpretation of 86)a (cf. black and white TV). The following is another similar example:

87) a. John Smith and Mary Smith are employees of the same company.
    b. John and Mary Smith are employees of the same company.

The formal distance between the two words *John* and *Mary* is greater in 87)a than in 87)b. So the interpersonal relation between the two persons named respectively by *John* and *Mary* is less close in the first sentence than in the second sentence. In 87)b *John* and *Mary* can be understood to be members of the same family, while in 87)a *John* and *Mary* do not have such a relation.

10.5.2.3 Possession

Possession can be divided into two kinds: inalienable and alienable. The former refers to a permanent relationship between two entities (the possessor and the possessed). The most conspicuous examples are concerned with body parts (e.g. *my head*, *my nose*, *my hand*, etc.) and kinship relations (e.g. *my mother*, *my son*, etc). The latter refers to a relationship that can be temporary, such as personal belongings (e.g. *my hat*, *my book*, etc.). It is intuitively clear that inalienable possession is a conceptually closer relation than alienable relation, and the investigation of a large number of languages by Haiman has proved that the linguistic expression of inalienable possession is lower on the scale of linguistic distance than the expression of alienable possession. In other words, the distance between the elements in a linguistic form expressing inalienable possession is smaller than that between the elements in a linguistic form expressing alienable possession. For instance, we may either say "my hat" or "a hat of mine", but we can only say "my nose (or father)", never "a nose (or father) of mine". This is because the closer conceptual distance in inalienable possession is closely connected with the closer distance between elements in it. In Chinese, it is grammatically quite appropriate to say 我的父亲 or 我父亲 , but one can only say 我的书桌 , not 我书桌 . As stated just now, the possessive relation between the concepts of 我 and 父亲 is inalienable, so the two signs used for them are structurally closer in distance, and consequently the possessive marker 的 can be deleted. Whereas the possessive relation between 我 and 书桌 is alienable, so we may say that they are conceptually more discrete from each other. Because of this, the possessive marker 的 cannot be removed from between them. This phenomenon shows that the closer the relation between two concepts, the shorter the distance between the two linguistic expressions for them.

10.5.2.4 Negation

Iconicity of distance presents itself in negation shift. Jespersen (1949) pointed out long before that there is a strong tendency in many languages in which the negative "not" logically belonging to the subordinate clause of a complex sentence is "attracted" to the position immediately before the verb of the main clause. For example, in English people usually say "I don't believe he has come" to express the meaning of the sentence "I believe he has not come". Poutsma (1928) is the first to declare that when the former is used to express the meaning of the latter the force of negation is to some extent weakened. To put it more clearly, the latter is the direct negation of the subordinate clause "he has come" while the former is the indirect negation of it. The same is true with some other languages. Here we just take a group of Chinese sentences as examples.

88) a. 我觉得我当时发现没有人在仓库里。
   b. 我觉得我当时没发现有人在仓库里。
   c. 我不觉得我当时发现有人在仓库里。

Obviously, when used as a testimony to deny 有人在仓库里,88)a is the most powerful, 88)b is the second, and 88)c is the least. The more a speaker is uncertain of his negative judgment on a proposition, the more does he tend to move the negative word to a further position from the part to be negated. We may say that there exists such a rule:

The farther is a negative word from the negated constituent, the lower is the degree of semantic negation; the nearer is a negative word from the negated constituent, the higher is the degree of semantic negation.

This rule again reveals distance iconicity: the closeness between two linguistic constituents corresponds with that between the two concepts expressed by them.

In most cases, negation shift is used out of a pragmatic consideration: by enlarging the distance between a negative and the negated constituent, a speaker can weaken the power of negation either to save the "face" of the hearer or to keep his judgement from being arbitrary.

10.5.2.5 Internal structure of word

Iconicity of distance exists, too, in the ordering of affixes within verb complexes. Bybee (1985: 24-25) argues that linguistic distance inside a verb corresponds iconically to the degree to which the semantics of its affixes affects the meaning of the word. For example, in an English verb, if both the derivation and inflection follow the root, the derivation is always between the root and the inflection. We may take the verb form "modernizes" to illustrate this point. The ordering of its morphemes is: root (modern) + derivation (-nize) + inflection (-s). The interpretation for this ordering is that a derivational morpheme alters the lexical meaning of the root, sometimes drastically, whereas an inflectional morpheme does not.

10.5.2.6 Multi-modifier construction

When the head or governor of a phrase has several modifiers, the modifiers usually have three positions: all of them precede the head; all of them follow the head; some of them precede, others follow the head. When either of the first two cases appears, we will come across another kind of distance iconicity, i.e. relative adjacency. It has two features: one is that the modifier which is semantically closest to the head is usually placed nearest to it; the other is that similar elements are put together. Let us take 89) as an example to see how iconicity of distance can give a satisfactory explanation to the sequence of multi-adjectives before a noun.

89) the famous delicious Italian pepperoni pizza

There is a general rule: when several adjectives modify a noun, the adjective which is conceptually closest to it and which most presents its essential feature will be located nearest to it. The usual order is: subjective adjective + objective adjective. In 89), since *pepperoni* refers to the material used to prepare the kind of baked pie called *pizza* and the material is essential for the preparation of this kind of food, it must be put before the noun directly; *Italian*, which denotes the place of origin, deserves the second closest position; the adjectives *delicious* and *famous* give a subjective evaluation of the food *pizza*, thus they are conceptually farther from the head, and accordingly they are structurally more alienated from it. Whereas, compared with *famous*, *delicious* is less subjective since all of us have similar senses and similar senses give us similar taste of the same food. So *delicious* is formally closer to the head noun than *famous*.

If the multi-modifier construction is a verb phrase, the verb modifier which indicates the type of an action is conceptually closer to the verb than that which indicates the time in which the action takes place. 秦洪武(2001) claims that manners of action, such as speed, degree, extent, etc., reflect the nature of an action, thus they are conceptually more closely related to the action than the time and the environment in which the action occurs. In syntactic structure, this psychological and conceptual closeness between modifiers and their head exhibits itself in such a rule: the constituents indicating the manner of an action are nearer to the predicate verb than those indicating the environment or time of an action in terms of linear order. Consider the two examples below:

90) a. The economic structure of our country has changed greatly in the past ten years.

b. The economic structure of our country has changed in the past ten years greatly.

91) a. He was chewing absent-mindedly at the fireplace.

b. He was chewing at the fireplace absent-mindedly.

Sentences 90)a and 91)a are typical structures in English because they accord with people's habit of perception. Sentences 90)b and 91)b are acceptable, but it takes more time and effort to understand them because the ordering of the verb's modifiers goes against people's mental expectation.

10.5.2.7 Attributive clause

Iconicity of distance can explain the difference between restrictive attributive clause and non-restrictive attributive clause. Restrictive attributive clause stands close to the noun it modifies and is in the same intonation contour with the noun, thus it is conceptually closer to the head noun. On the contrary, non-restrictive attributive clause is separated by a comma from the noun it modifies and it has its own intonation contour, thus it is conceptually farther from the head noun. This can be clearly exemplified in the following pairs of sentences.

92) a. I want to buy the house which has a garden.
    b. I want to buy the house, which has a garden.

The pause between attributive clause and the noun it modifies in 92)b is longer than that in 92)a. Moreover, the semantic relationship between the main clause and the attributive clause in 92)a is much closer than that in 92)b. If the attributive clause in 92)a is removed, the meaning of the whole complex sentence will become incomplete; whereas in 92)b, even the non-restrictive attributive clause is deleted, the sentence as a whole still has a complete meaning.

10.5.2.8 Subjunctive mood

The situation that is characterized by subjunctive mood is farther away from reality than the corresponding real situation characterized by present tense. Therefore, past tense is used in order to realize the correspondence between situational distance and time distance. In example 93), sentence a is a conditional of reality which does not characterize an imagined situation, so it employs a present tense structure. While sentence b presents an imagination of the present reality, so it uses past tense to enlarge the distance between the imagined situation and reality. Sentence c presents a supposition of a past reality, thus indicating a further distance between the imagined situation and the present reality, so past perfect tense is used.

93) a. If he writes to her, he will stop her from doing that.
    b. If he wrote to her, he would stop her from doing that.
    c. If he had written to her, he would have stopped her from doing that.

10.5.3 Iconicity of quantity

Iconicity of quantity is also called iconicity of complexity. It means the quantity of linguistic expressions corresponds to the amount of information conveyed by these expressions or to the importance and predictability of the concepts represented by them. Information that is greater in amount, more important to the speaker, or more difficult to predict for the hearer, is expressed as bigger and syntactically more complex grammatical units.

10.5.3.1 Word form

At the lexical level, it is found that a simple concept is universally expressed by a single morpheme, and a complex concept is universally expressed by two or more morphemes. That is why the plural form of a noun has more morphemes than its singular form (e.g. book vs. books), and the number of morphemes in a compound is bigger than that in a simple word (e.g. boy vs. playboy). William Croft (1990: 183) discusses the relation between generic-level and specific-level terms and reveals the iconic motivation for their expression. The specific-level terms are very commonly compounds of the generic-level terms and some modifiers. This pattern is universal in almost all languages. The following are some examples from English.

94) Generic: *oak*; *cedar*

Specific: *tan oak*; *blue oak*; *incense cedar; red cedar*

It is obvious that, interpreted iconically, this pattern proves again the proposition mentioned above — the complexity of concepts is closely related to the complexity of linguistic forms.

Besides, in various Indo-European languages, the positive, comparative, and superlative degrees of adjectives show a gradual increase in the number of phonemes, such as *long*, *longer* and *longest* in English.

10.5.3.2 Emphatic sentence

Let us compare the declarative sentence in 95) with the three corresponding emphatic forms of it, which are respectively marked as a, b, and c.

95) Tom solved the problem yesterday.

a. It was Tom who/that solved the problem yesterday.

b. It was the problem that Tom solved yesterday.

c. It was yesterday that Tom solved the problem.

Apparently, there are more linguistic signs in the three emphatic sentences (as the structure "It was… that/who" is used in them) than there are in the declarative sentence. This is because the three emphatic forms each emphasize a certain part of the declarative sentence. The intention for emphasis results in the increase of the information. Accordingly, more information needs to be expressed with more linguistic signs. In example 96) below, 96)b adds the word "does" for emphasis, which also embodies the principle of quantity iconicity.

96) a. He likes novels written by Mark Twain.
    b. He does like novels written by Mark Twain.

10.5.3.3 Exclamatory sentence

Iconicity of quantity can be used to explain the motivation of exclamatory sentences. Compared with a declarative sentence, an exclamatory sentence is usually used to express the speaker's strong emotion of a certain kind such as praise, surprise, joy, pity, and so on. That is to say, it conveys more information. In the following example, sentence a is a general declarative sentence; sentence b and c are exclamatory sentences. Compared with sentence a, there is one more word in sentences b and c, that is, "what" in b and "how" in c. Therefore, these two sentences convey more information to the readers, that is, they express the additional meaning of admiration and adoration to the girl. This additional meaning can only be conveyed in sentence a when "beautiful" is pronounced with stress.

97) a. She is a beautiful girl.
    b. What a beautiful girl she is!
    c. How beautiful a girl she is!

10.5.3.4 Sentence of politeness

Sometimes in order to achieve the effect of politeness, people do not express their ideas or intentions directly but rather in a roundabout way. Consequently, more complex linguistic forms are required and the hearer needs more effort to understand the speaker. This is because linguistic forms for politeness perform two functions simultaneously — on the one hand they express literal meanings and on the other hand they imply a speaker's intention of avoiding conflict with or shock to other people, or of avoiding unpleasant associations. The following sentences a, b, c, and d all perform the same function of requesting others to do something, but in different length, thus showing different degrees of politeness.

Sentence d has more linguistic signs than a, b, and c, so the degree of politeness expressed by it is the highest.

98) a. Open that window.
    b. Please open that window.
    c. Will you please open that window?
    d. I wonder if you could open that window.

The length of utterance not only reflects different degrees of politeness but also different social distances or extents of intimacy between the interlocutors. Generally speaking, the closer the social distance or the more intimate the relation between two speakers, the more straightforward the speakers are when expressing their intentions, and the shorter the linguistic forms employed; conversely, when intentions are expressed euphemistically and implicitly the longer linguistic forms are required.

In grammar, sentences of politeness are often presented as structures of time distance: compared with a structure of present tense, the structure of past tense indicates a requirement that is farther away from the time of speaking, so it is not that direct and hence gives the hearer leeway to react accordingly. In this case, a past tense structure appears more polite. If the same intention can be expressed with different grammatical structures, generally the longer the grammatical structure, that is, the more the linguistic signs in it, the more euphemistic the intention expressed, and the more the leeway given to the hearer. All the sentences in example 99) below are sentences of politeness, but except for b which is related to iconicity of distance, a is shorter than c, c shorter than d, and d shorter than e. Accordingly, a is less euphemistic than c, c less euphemistic than d, and d less euphemistic than e.

99) a. Can you close the window?
    b. Could you close the window?
    c. Do you mind closing the window?
    d. I wonder if you could close the window.
    e. I was wondering if you could close the window.

Of course, the degree of politeness in these sentences is not only related to the number of linguistic signs but also to the past tense in the predicate.

10.5.3.5 Other structures

Besides the syntactic structures discussed above, some other structures in the realm of syntax also reveal the fact that conceptual and structural complexity tends to go hand in hand. Any modification or elaboration of one meaning-bearing grammatical element by another leads to the increase of both types of complexity. Let us look at the following examples (Ungerer and Schmid, 1996: 254):

100) a. On the Brighten train from Victoria I met *her*.
  b. On the Brighten train from Victoria I met *the girl from next door*.
  c. Just imagine! Last night on the Brighten train from Victoria I met *this fair-haired, fragile, just unbelievably beautiful creature*.

Obviously, the pronoun "her" in 100)a is only justified if the person referred to is both unimportant and known, and the reference is expected. "The girl from next door" in 100)b shows a larger degree of conceptual importance and unexpectedness. And 100)c conveys more information than both 100)a and 100)b.

Iconicity of complexity accounts for our tendency to associate more linguistic signs with more meaning and, conversely, fewer linguistic signs with less meaning. This idea has long been an important aspect of markedness theory. Marked forms and structures are typically both structurally more complex (or at least longer) and semantically more complex than unmarked ones. As mentioned at the beginning of this subsection, some scholars even suggest that the amount of linguistic material corresponds to the importance and the degree of predictability of the information processed.

Iconicity of quantity is also reflected in the correspondence between stress and meaning. We know that a sound is either stressed or unstressed, and a meaning is either full or empty. As discussed earlier, greater amount of information or more important information tends to be conveyed by longer forms. Full meaning is heavier than empty meaning in terms of semantic structure, so the former is conveyed with a stressed sound form which has a higher pitch and a longer duration of time while the latter with an unstressed one which has a lower pitch and a shorter duration of time. This iconic relation can be illustrated as what follows (沈家煊, 1999: 321):

101) **meaning** **(sound) form**

full	=	stressed
empty	=	unstressed

Thus it can be seen that the combination of sound form with meaning is not arbitrary but motivated. Sound form is the result of the "mapping" or "projecting" of meaning. For example, full (or content, notional, lexical) words in English such as nouns, main verbs, adjectives, many adverbs are usually stressed (in the absence of special emphasis) in the context of phrases or sentences, but empty (or function, form) words are usually unstressed, because the meaning of the former are heavier than those of the latter. The following is an example for this point in Chinese.

102) 要走了。

In this sentence, 要 can be either stressed or unstressed. When it is unstressed, it is used as an auxiliary verb, and the whole sentence means 想走了. When it is stressed, it is used as a main verb, and the whole sentence means 索取并拿走了.

At the end of this subsection, let us have a glance of iconicity of quantity in text or discourse which means that a predictable topic is often omitted if it does not present new information in what comes next in the text.

103) A: Bears and squirrels are marvelous.

B: Marvelous and beautiful.

The subject and topic of A's statement (*bears and squirrels*) is predictable and does not convey any new information in B's answer, so it is omitted there.

10.5.4 Philosophical interpretation of iconicity

Philosophers who have a pluralistic concept of language believe that the four essential elements in human society — reality, thought, language and culture — are closely related to and interact with each other. This point of view is actually the philosophical basis for iconicity of linguistic signs. On the one hand, reality determines thought and thought determines language; on the other hand, language reflects thought and thought reflects reality. It is believed that iconic phenomena in language partly come from these "determining" and "reflecting" processes. To state it more exactly, iconicity of linguistic signs is mainly the result of the "reflecting" process. However, in the first reflection going from thought to reality and in the second one going from language to thought exists a "filtering" phenomenon which means that thought cannot reflect everything in reality nor can language reflect everything in thought. In other words, there are always discrepancies between thought and reality, and between language and thought. In addition, there is always a certain degree of deflection or distortion occurring in the two reflecting processes. Just because of the effect of "filtering" and "deflecting", the iconic degree of linguistic signs is lowered. Therefore, it can be concluded that in some respects linguistic signs have iconic features but in other respects they do not. To put it another way, iconicity of linguistic signs has its inevitability as well as its limitations.

We just now mentioned the "filtering" and "deflecting" phenomena existing in the reflection of reality by thought and in that of thought by language, and said that there are always discrepancies between thought and reality, and between language and thought. Why does this happen? It is universally acknowledged that things and phenomena in the real world are infinite in number, but compared with the boundless and rather complex real world, man's thought is still not powerful enough to reflect everything and every phenomenon in the world even though it is evolving all the time. This means that there are always some inadequacies in the reflection of the real world by the thought, that is, something is "filtered out" or missed in the first reflection of the real world by thought. That is why in our brain the modules of knowledge about the real world are dynamic, always ready to be adjusted and complemented because of our new understanding of the world. Moreover, the real world is three-dimensional and the image of it in man's mind should be three-dimensional too, or at least approximately three-dimensional. Whereas language, because of the linear nature of it, is always one-dimensional. When the one-dimensional language is used to represent the three-dimensional thought, distortion or lack of fidelity will inevitably occur. In other words, language can never give adequate expression of thought. For example, it often happens that English people make statements like "I don't know how to express my ideas with words". And sometimes we Chinese also say "只可意会，难以言传". In a word, the horizontal reflection between reality, thought, and language tends to be weakened gradually at each stage, that is, reality > thought > language. So it is natural to conclude from this formula that the degree of iconicity also tends to be lowered gradually when looked from the left to the right. Of course, we must look at this issue dialectically, that is, we must acknowledge the influence and reaction of language on thought and reality. In fact, it has already been made clear that psychological and especially philosophical models of the world and experience are very strongly influenced by the structure of language. Yet it should be noted that here we only mean that language influences or facilitates thought, not that language determines thought. "Linguistic determinism" in the Sapir-Whorf Hypothesis is now widely acknowledged to be too absolute. If language really determined one's thought about and one's outlook of the world, people speaking different languages would have different kinds of thought and world views. The outcome would be that people were not able to communicate with each other, and translation between languages would become absolutely impossible. As a matter of fact, the thought of all human beings, though differs slightly from each other, is roughly the same as all people are facing the same real world.

Since the horizontal reflection between reality, thought and language tends to be weakened gradually, iconicity between them is certainly not absolute, that is, in some respects there is iconicity but in others there is not. Even if iconic devices were employed in all languages, the iconic phenomena in different languages would still vary greatly in degrees and have their own characteristics as the realities of nature and society to be reflected by different languages are not identical. In his *Mind, Code and Context* (1989), Givón holds the same idea about iconicity by saying that human language is a code system which only to some extent has the feature of non-arbitrariness, that is, of iconicity. P. H. Matthews (1991: 223) also points out that iconicity is not a law but only a tendency. Obviously, these views on iconicity are objective and convincing.

10.5.5 Iconicity and other competing principles

Syntax is not only governed by the principle of iconicity but also by other principles such as that of economy, of pragmatics, of abstract syntactic conventions, and so on. The following is a discussion on the relations between iconicity and other competing principles.

10.5.5.1 Iconicity and economy

Iconicity requires that for every distinct concept there should be a distinct word so that the processing of information can be most facilitated. As Givón (1989: 189) puts it, "All other things being equal, a coded experience is easier to store, retrieve, and communicate if the code is maximally isomorphic to the experience". However, one's life is short and his memory is finite. This limitation makes it impossible for us to follow all the time the iconic principle of "one concept, one form". So simplification and ellipsis are necessary in actual linguistic communication. The principle of economy is closely related to the "least-effort" principle proposed by Zipf in his *Psychology of Language* published in 1935 (so it is sometimes called "Zipf's law"). This principle claims that linguistic elements used in high frequency tend to be shortened in form. To quote Zipf's words, "High frequency is the cause of small magnitude" (Zipf, 1935: 29). The shortening of linguistic expressions means the weakening of iconicity. So we may say that the principle of economy means using the smallest number of linguistic forms to convey the largest amount of information. It can explain why in the patterns of markedness unmarked elements are shorter and simpler (some even in zero form) while marked elements are longer and more complex.

Linguistic structures are partly the results of competition between the principle of iconicity and that of economy. Speaking specifically, there are three kinds of result from the competition: iconicity triumphs over economy and thus the phenomenon of "one concept, one form" occurs; economy triumphs over iconicity, which gives rise to homophone; neither of them win, so they work together to restrain the structures of language and in this case polysemy comes into being as a solution to the conflict between them (沈家煊, 1993). However, the results of their competition exclude the possibility that linguistic structures are neither economic nor iconic. For example, there should be three logical possibilities that the marked category is different from the unmarked one in terms of the number of morphemes by which each of them is represented, but in reality there are only two — either the marked category is represented by more morphemes than the unmarked category, which signals the predominance of economy, or both categories are represented by the same number of morphemes, which signals the predominance of iconicity (every distinct concept has a different form). The third possibility, i.e. the marked category is to be represented by fewer morphemes than the unmarked category, will never occur as it violates both the principle of economy and that of iconicity. As far as the syntax of language is concerned, at the synchronic level some structures tend to follow first the principle of iconicity, some the principle of economy, and the others tend to follow simultaneously both of them; at the diachronic level certain structures with particular meanings tend to follow the principle of iconicity during one period of time but that of economy during another period, that is, the solution to the competition between these two principles may vary with time. Scholars in the field of functional typology hold similar views (William Croft, 1990: 253). They believe that linguistic structures can be explained by the concept of "functional adaptation", which indicates that language structure has evolved as an adaptation to language function just as living organisms have evolved as an adaptation to their environment. The concept of "functional adaptation" can be further divided into two parts. The first part is related to the function of **successful** communication of information through language; the second part is related to the **efficient** performance of this function. In a word, both economy and iconicity are basically different manifestations of efficient adaptation, and linguistic structures, whether motivated by the principle of economy or by that of iconicity, all aim to increase the efficiency of information processing. "Functional adaptation" is reflected at synchronic as well as diachronic levels.

10.5.5.2 Iconicity and pragmatic principles

Linguists have proposed a set of universal pragmatic principles for word order. The principles have a long history in functionalism. Here we only list the three most important ones presented by Haiman (1985: 237-238).

(1) What is old information comes first, what is new information comes later, in an utterance.

(2) Ideas that closely connected tend to be placed together.

(3) What is at the moment uppermost in the speaker's mind tends to be first expressed.

Principle (1) is iconic: the temporal order of elements in the utterance reflects the temporal order of the introduction of information into the discourse. Principle (2) is also iconic: elements in a clause that go together semantically tend to occur close together structurally. Principle (3) appears to be iconic too, though in a metaphorical rather than in a direct fashion: the order of elements in the utterance reflects the order of importance in the speaker's mind. By principle (1), new information should follow old information. By principle (3), new information should precede old information. So principles (1) and (3) seem to compete with each other concerning the order of information distribution in the utterance. A resolution to this conflict can be arrived at by resorting to the theory of contexts in pragmatics. In the following examples, the same sentence "John met Mary" may follow, in different contexts, either principle (1) or principle (3).

104) (Who did John meet?)

John (Old information) met Mary (New information).

105) (Who met Mary?)

John (New information) met Mary (Old information).

It is obvious that information structure is closely related to contexts. Both principle (1) and principle (3) are iconic, yet they are in conflict with each other in terms of the order of old and new information. Without the introduction of contexts, this competing phenomenon cannot be understood fully.

Principle (3) is in conflict with principle (2) as well. Fronting of uppermost information often splits up otherwise conceptually close constituents. Since principle (2) tends to place certain constituents together while principle (3) tends to separate them, it is natural that the two principles also form a competing pair. Of course, this conflict occurs only in one word-order phenomenon: WH movement in information questions and relative clauses. In other words, principle (3) applies to information questions only: the questioned element is the focus of a sentence, is generally "new" information, and will therefore move to the focus position (i.e. the initial position of a sentence). Under other circumstances, the two principles do not compete in terms of word order. We can say that both principle (1) and principle (3) are required by the different functions to be performed, that is, they are the results of functional adaptation.

10.5.5.3 Iconicity and abstract syntactic conventions

About the relations between iconicity and the abstract syntactic conventions of language, Peirce (1940) believes that syntactic structure is the result of the joint regulation of iconicity and syntactic conventions. Iconicity can be interpreted from the perspective of philosophy, cognition or historical change of language. But the syntactic conventions are to a great extent arbitrary. It is therefore generally believed that iconicity and syntactic conventions conflict and compete with each other as well. However, according to Givón (1990), iconicity differs from arbitrariness only in degree of abstractness, and grammatical conventions also have iconic features, only at a more abstract level. For example, the grammatical hierarchy that is universal in all languages — agent > dative > patient > location > instrument —is a type of grammatical convention. Many syntactic phenomena (e.g. whether a noun phrase can function as subject or topic; whether the subject of a clause is present or not and what form it has when the clause functions as object) are governed by it. However, this grammatical hierarchy is not wholly arbitrary. In terms of cognitive psychology, it reflects a hierarchy of salience of the things perceived. An action or a behavior is usually first started by the agent and then its force extends to the patient, so the "agent-action-patient" sequence is "natural", and the sentences whose word order follows this sequence are normal, unmarked. In this sense, the abstract syntactic convention discussed here also accords with the principle of iconicity. 许国璋 (1988), after looking at this point from the perspective of social conventions, suggests that the conventional features of linguistic signs exclude to a great extent the possibility that language is created arbitrarily. This view and that of Givón's seem to coincide. At present, there is still disagreement on the applying scope of iconicity and on the relations between iconicity and the conventionalized syntactic rules of language. Generally speaking, iconicity in Haiman's study is narrower in scope and more specific in content, while Givón tends to take as iconic all the phenomena in which there are corresponding relations between form and meaning. So compared with Haiman's study, Givón's understanding of iconicity is wider in scope and more abstract in content.

10.6 Mental spaces

Mental spaces are conceptual structures, originally proposed by Gilles Fauconnier (1985, 1994), to describe how language users assign and manipulate reference, including the use of names, definite descriptions, and pronouns. Fauconnier's structures are set up in the light of a particular view of meaning: that when we study linguistic meaning we are studying the way that language provides a patchy and partial trigger for a series of complex cognitive procedures. In this view meaning is not "in" language; rather, language is like a recipe for constructing meaning, a recipe which relies on a lot of independent cognitive activity. Moreover this process of meaning construction is a discourse-based process, implying that typically a single sentence is only a step in the recipe and cannot be clearly analyzed without recognizing its relationship to and dependency on earlier sentences. This view of meaning can be put another way: language guides meaning construction directly in context, and accordingly sentences cannot be analyzed in isolation from ongoing discourse, and from this it can be further concluded that semantics (traditionally, the context-independent meaning of a sentence) cannot be meaningfully separated from pragmatics (traditionally, the context-dependent meaning of sentences), since meaning construction is guided by context and is therefore subject to situation-specific information.

According to Fauconnier, meaning construction involves two processes: (1) the building of mental spaces; and (2) the establishment of mappings between those mental spaces. Moreover, the mapping relations are guided by the local discourse context, which means that meaning construction is always situated or context-bound. Fauconnier defines mental spaces as "partial structures that proliferate when we think and talk, allowing a fine-grained partitioning of our discourse and knowledge structures" (Fauconnier, 1997: 11).

The fundamental insight the theory of mental spaces provides is that mental spaces partition meaning into distinct conceptual regions or "packets". Mental spaces are regions of conceptual space that contain specific kinds of information. They are constructed on the basis of generalized linguistic, pragmatic and cultural strategies for recruiting information. However, because mental spaces are constructed "on-line", they result in unique and temporary "packets" of conceptual structure, constructed for purposes specific to the ongoing discourse. The principles of mental space formation and the relations or mappings established between mental spaces have the potential to yield unlimited meanings. Let us consider the following utterance:

106) If I were your father I would smack you.

This utterance gives rise to a counterfactual conceptualization. That is, it sets up a scenario that runs counter to a presupposed reality. This scenario represents a mental space. Intuitively, you can think of a mental space as a "thought bubble", rather like the strategy cartoonists use to reveal the inner thoughts of their characters. Crucially, Mental Spaces Theory holds that you can have many "thought bubbles" working simultaneously.

Depending on the context, the utterance in 106) can give rise to different counterfactual scenarios. This is because the context guides mapping operations between the state of affairs that holds in reality and the states of affairs that are set up in different versions of the counterfactual scenario. Imagine that a childminder, Mary, utters the sentence in 106) after the child in her care, James, is particularly unruly. We consider here three distinct possible interpretations of 106) and see how Mental Spaces Theory accounts for them.

• *The lenient father interpretation* ("your father should be stricter")

In this interpretation, the childminder Mary thinks that the unruly child's father should demonstrate more authority and punish the child by smacking him. In terms of mapping operations between reality and the counterfactual scenario, this interpretation is derived by Mary with her stricter disposition "replacing" the father with his more lenient disposition. This mapping is partial in the sense that the child's father remains the same in all other respects: he has a beard, rides a bike, gets home at the same time in the evening and so on. What changes in this counterfactual scenario is that the father is now less tolerant of the child's unruly behavior and smacks the child. A consequence of this interpretation is that in the reality scenario, which is presupposed by the counterfactual scenario, the father is being critically compared to the speaker Mary. Because the childminder would smack the child, by implication the failure of the father to smack the child is interpreted as a fault on his part. In this way, the counterfactual scenario entails consequences for how we view the father and his approach to parenting in reality.

• *The stern father interpretation* ("you're lucky I'm not as strict as your father")

In this interpretation, it is the father, who has a stricter disposition, who is replacing the childminder Mary. In other words, Mary is advising the child that he is lucky that she is looking after him rather than his father, because otherwise the child would have been smacked. In this interpretation, it is the father who is strict and Mary who is lenient in reality, and it is the father who assumes Mary's place in the counterfactual scenario. The implication of this counterfactual scenario for reality might be that where the father would smack the child, Mary exhibits greater restraint. This interpretation might therefore imply a positive assessment of Mary in her role as childminder.

• *The role interpretation* ("the only reason I'm not smacking you is because I'm not allowed to")

In this interpretation, Mary is saying that if she could assume the role of the child's father then she would smack the child. This interpretation assumes nothing about the child's father who may (or may not) smack the child in reality. Instead, this counterfactual scenario replaces the father role with Mary. In this counterfactual scenario, Mary-as-father would smack the child. The implication of this interpretation for reality is that it comments on Mary's role and the limitations that it entails: in her role as childminder, she is legally prohibited from smacking the child.

Several important points emerge from the discussion of example 106). Firstly, the same utterance can prompt for a number of different interpretations, each of which arises from different mappings between reality and the counterfactual scenario that is constructed. Secondly, each of these mappings brings with it different implications for how we view the participants in reality (for example, criticism versus a positive assessment and so on). Finally, this example illustrates that meaning is not "there in the words" but relies on the conceptual processes that make connections between real and hypothetical situations. These processes result in representations that are consistent with, but only partially specified by, the prompts in the linguistic utterance. Of course, the precise interpretation constructed will depend upon the precise details of the context in which it is uttered, upon the speaker's intentions and upon how these intentions are interpreted by the hearer. For example, if James has a father who is far stricter than his childminder in reality, he might be most likely to construct the second of these possible interpretations.

Fauconnier's focus is on the cognitive processes triggered during discourse by linguistic structures. Within this, a particular topic of investigation has been the management of reference: the issue of how speakers and hearers keep track of the entities referred to in the language. The central idea is that when we are involved in using language, for example in conversation, we are continually constructing domains, so that if we talk about, say, Shakespeare's play *Julius Caesar*, we might maintain several relevant domains, or mental spaces. One domain is the world of the play, while another might be the real world, where *Julius Caesar* is a historical figure. Our referential practices make use of such divisions into domains so that we can use the name *Julius Caesar* to talk about the historical person and the character in the play. Between our different uses of the name there are nevertheless links: we might want to say for example that Shakespeare's character is meant to describe the historical figure. Such processes can be quite complicated: we might go to see a performance of the play and afterwards say *Julius Caesar is too young*, referring now to the actor playing the part. Or if we saw some children running of with the foyer's life-size figure of the actor in costume, we might say *Hey, they're stealing Julius Caesar*. So we can use the same name to refer to a historical person, a role in a play written about him, an actor playing that role and a figure of that actor playing the role. Fauconnier's point is that such flexibility is inherent in our use of referring expressions: his mental spaces are an attempt to explain such behavior.

Mental spaces can be seen as a cognitive parallel to the notion of possible worlds in formal semantics, since it is assumed that speakers can partition off and hold separate domains of reference. Some of these might be very complex: we might for example be talking of the world of Charles Dickens's *A Tale of Two Cities* and refer to individuals in that novel, like *Charles Dornay* and *Sydney Carton*. Or the domain might be very sparely furnished, provoked just by a counterfactual as in *If I were you, I'd go on a diet*, where once the shift from the real to the non-real domain is made in the first clause, the *I* in the second clause identifies not the speaker but the addressee. Here, however, any further implications of this domain, or mental space, are not explored and it remains a local, minimal space.

10.6.1 Connections between spaces

Mental spaces are temporary conceptual domains constructed during ongoing discourse. One important issue is how different mental spaces are linked to one another. What, for example, allows us to use the name *Julius Caesar* as we did, for a historical person, a role in a play, an actor, etc.? Fauconnier (1994) discusses the way that speakers can make reference to entities by a number of indirect strategies. We can for example refer to a representation of someone by their name:

so that looking at a photograph of a friend I might say *Graham looks really young*, where *Graham* refers to the picture of Graham (who in reality might look far from young). Fauconnier uses the terms **trigger** and **target** here: the name of the real Graham is the trigger and the target (what I want to describe) is the image. Clearly photographs and the people in them are related by the viewer's recognition of resemblance, but similar strategies are widespread. We can refer, for example, to a book or books by the author's name and say sentences like *Shakespeare's on the top shelf.* Similarly, a nurse might say *The gall bladder in the end bed is awake*; or in a favorite type of example in this literature, a waiter might say *The ham omelette wants his bill*. In chapter 7.2 we called this phenomenon **metonymy**. Fauconnier employs an **identification principle** which allows speakers to use such referential shifts; one version is in 107) below (1994: 3):

107) If two objects (in the most general sense), *a* and *b*, are linked by a pragmatic function *F* (*b* = *F*(*a*)), a description of *a*, d_a, may be used to identify its counterpart *b*.

So since in our photograph example real Graham (*a*) and photo Graham (*b*) are linked by the pragmatic function IMAGE, a description of real Graham (his name, d_a) can be used to identify his photographic image (*b*). It is assumed that there might be a number of such pragmatic functions, as we shall see.

We can look at some more complicated examples of this referential shifting by looking at Fauconnier's account of Jackendoff's (1975) example in 108) below:

108) In Len's painting, the girl with blue eyes has green eyes.

Let us take as an interpretation of this sentence the situation where the speaker knows the identity of the artist's model, knows that she has blue eyes and is pointing out that the painter has decided to give her green eyes in the picture. The proposal is that here two mental spaces are set up: one is the real world (as the speaker knows it) which has in it a girl with blue eyes; the other the space of the painting which has a girl with green eyes. The sentence 108) explicitly connects these two girls, saying in effect they are in the image-person relationship we discussed for our hypothetical friend Graham earlier. This can be represented in Fig. 10-21, which shows the connection (our image relationship) as an arrow.

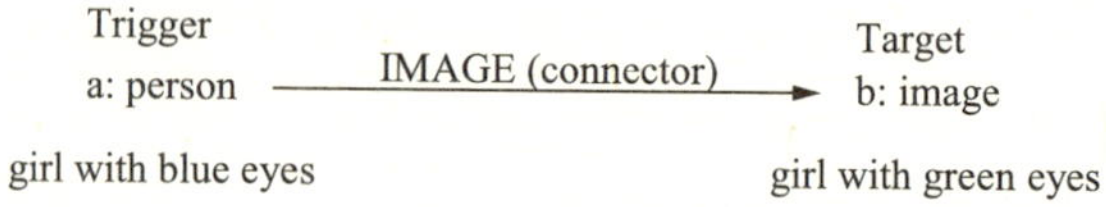

Fig. 10-21 Person-image connector (Fauconnier, 1994)

Fauconnier, following Jackendoff (1975), makes the point that this can be likened to the relationship between beliefs and reality: thus, paralleling 108) above we can say 109) and 110) below:

109) Len believes that the girl with blue eyes has green eyes.

110) Len wants the girl with blue eyes to have green eyes.

Here Len's belief and wish are at odds with reality as known by the speaker. In the semantic literature such examples are often described as instances of **belief contexts**. In this theory they are viewed as a mental parallel to the image relation, and are represented by similar diagrams, using a belief or MIND connector, as in Fig. 10-22. As Fauconnier points out, the speaker can work such relationships in the other direction. Taking the image relationship as an example, a speaker might say, looking at a picture: *In reality, the girl with brown eyes has blue eyes*. Here the trigger is the image and the target is the real girl, as shown in Fig. 10-23.

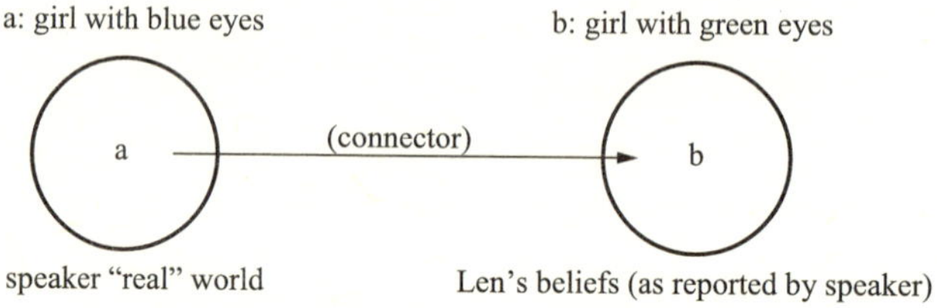

Fig. 10-22 World-mind connector (Fauconnier, 1994)

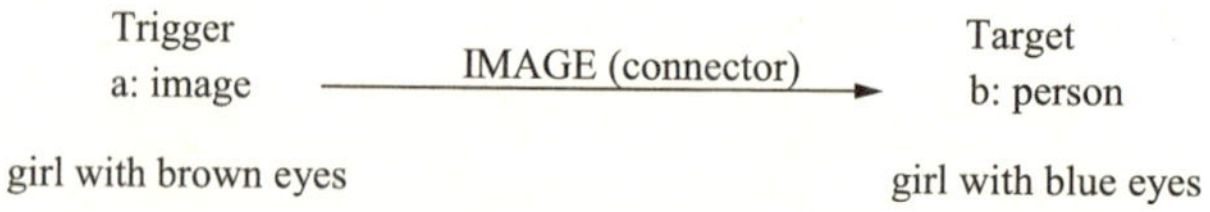

Fig. 10-23 Image-person connector (Fauconnier, 1994)

These examples are of mental spaces created by talking of paintings and a person's beliefs and wishes. There are in fact a whole range of linguistic elements which serve as triggers for setting up mental spaces, which Fauconnier calls **spacebuilders**. These include adverbials of location and time like *in Joan's novel*, *in Peter's painting*, *in Fred's mind's eye*, *from their point of view*, *in 1966*, *when she was a child*, *after we find the crash site*, etc. They also include adverbs like *really, probably*, *possibly* and *theoretically*; connectives like *if ... then, either ... or*; and certain verbs like *believe*, *hope*, *imagine* and *state*. What is "special" about space builders is that they require the hearer to "set up" a scenario beyond the "here and now", whether this scenario reflects past or future reality, reality in some other location, hypothetical situations, situations that reflect ideas and beliefs, and so on. The context in which a sentence is uttered will provide the anchoring or background mental space. Where spaces are stacked inside one another, the including space is referred to as the **parent** space or **base** space, or simply the **base**. Often of course the default (unmarked) highest parent space will be reality, or more accurately the current speaker's assessment of reality. Take for example, a speaker uttering the sentences in 111) below:

111) Barry's in the pub. His wife thinks he's in the office.

Here the initial space is the speaker's reality (R) where Barry is in the pub, then the phrase *his wife thinks* sets up a new mental space (M) in which his counterpart $Barry_2$ is in the office. The speaker can then develop either space, talking about what $Barry_1$, is doing in R or what $Barry_2$ is (supposedly) doing in M.

10.6.2 Referential opacity

One important advantage to this idea of mental spaces and links between them is that it can be used to explain the phenomenon of **referential opacity**. This is the traditionally problematic area where knowledge interacts with reference. Let's take, for example, sentence 112) below to be true of a policeman called Jones:

112) Jones believes that the leader of the Black Gulch Gang is a sociopath.

If Jones does not know that his wife is the leader of the Black Gulch Gang we can also take the sentence 113) below to be true at the same time:

113) Jones doesn't believe his wife is a sociopath.

Because of what Jones knows, we are not ascribing contradictory beliefs to him, even though the nominals *his wife* and *the leader of the Black Gulch Gang* denote the same individual. This is a typical effect of belief contexts and such examples have been used to argue that there must be more to meaning than simply denotation.

Sentences like 112) are described as **opaque contexts**. In this type of example the opacity is associated with embedded clauses under the verbs of propositional attitudes like *believe*, *want*, *suspect*, *hope*, etc. To give another example, a sentence like 114) below can have two distinct interpretations:

114) The Captain suspects that a detective in the squad is taking bribes.

If we take 114) to mean that the Captain suspects a particular detective, this is called the **specific** or **transparent** reading. If on the other hand we take 114) to mean that the Captain suspects that one of the detectives is involved but doesn't know which one, this is called the **non-specific** or **opaque** reading. In another terminology used in logic, the transparent reading (the Captain knows which individual) is given the Latin label the *de re* interpretation (meaning roughly "of the thing") while the opaque reading is called the *de dicto* interpretation (roughly "of what is said").

In the mental spaces approach these two interpretations do not arise from any ambiguity in the sentence but from two different space-connecting strategies that hearers may use. Nor are opaque contexts restricted to verbs of propositional attitudes: they are a regular consequence of referential strategies. To show this, we might go back to an example of identifying actors and parts. Suppose for example a speaker says 115) below:

115) In the film, Michelle is a witch.

This sentence sets up two spaces which we can identify as speaker's reality (R) and the film (F). The name *Michelle* can be used to refer in two ways. In the first there is the kind of referential shifting we described earlier: *Michelle* is the name of a person in R, but the speaker uses her name to describe the film images of her acting the role of a witch (here of course the film images may or may not resemble real-life Michelle). We could call this connector ACTOR. We can represent this interpretation in Fig. 10-24. We can roughly describe this as: real-life Michelle plays the film part of a witch. In the second interpretation there is no referential shifting between the two mental spaces: *Michelle* is the name of a character in the film space and we predicate of this character that she is a witch. This interpretation can be represented in Fig. 10-25. We can roughly describe this as: in the film the character Michelle is a witch.

Fig. 10-24 First interpretation of *In the film, Michelle is a witch*

Fig. 10-25 Second interpretation of *In the film, Michelle is a witch*

These two interpretations are predicted to be regular options whenever two spaces are set up like this and this same behavior is used to explain the examples of referential opacity we have been looking at. If we go back to example 112) *Jones believes that the leader of the Black Gulch Gang is a sociopath*, the verb *believe* is a spacebuilder which adds the space of Jones's belief (call it space B) to the parent space, which we can take to be the speaker's reality (call this space R), although of course our sentence could easily be embedded in a story or someone else's belief. The transparent reading of this sentence will be where Jones knows the identity of the gangleader in reality and sets up a belief space where he describes the gangleader as a sociopath. There is therefore a referential link between the gangleader in reality and the gangleader in Jones's belief, shown by the connector arrow in Fig. 10-26. We can roughly describe this as: Jones knows the identity of the gangleader in R and in his belief space B the gangleader is a sociopath.

The opaque reading of this sentence will be where Jones doesn't know the identity of the gangleader in R but has a belief about this person in B: here there is no referential link between the reality space and the belief space, as we show in Fig. 10-27. We can roughly describe this as: Jones doesn't know the identity of the gangleader in reality but in his belief the gangleader is a sociopath.

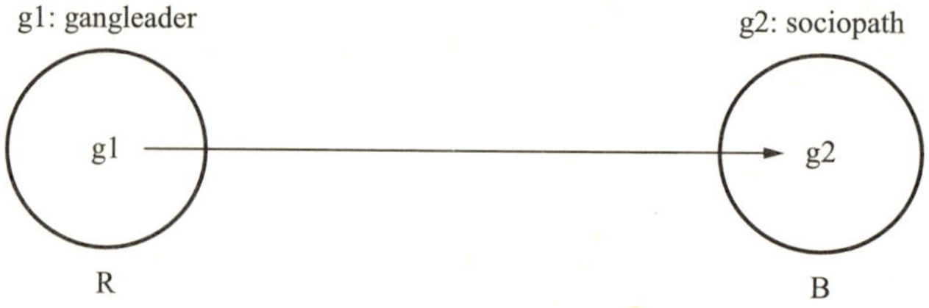

Fig. 10-26 Transparent reading of example 112)

Fig. 10-27 Opaque reading of example 112)

In this approach any spacebuilder can trigger such ambiguities of interpretation so that a time adverbial like *in 1966* can trigger two readings for the sentence 116) below:

116) In 1966 my wife was very young.

Here two time spaces are established: the "now" of the speaker and the time 1966. The reference to the nominal *my wife* can be interpreted in two ways. The first simply identifies a wife in the 1966 time space and is consistent with the speaker either having the same wife in the "now" space or not. The second interpretation is that the person who is the speaker's wife now was not his wife in 1966, but is referred to as *my wife* by a shift linking the mental spaces. On this type of reading there is nothing odd about the sentence *In 1966 my wife was a baby*. As Fauconnier points out, this ability to connect or not connect spaces allows the transparent non-contradictory readings for his examples in 117) and 118) below:

117) In Canadian football, the 50-yard line is 55 yards away.

118) In this new Californian religion, the devil is an angel.

In this approach then the regular system of establishing mental spaces predicts these types of referential flexibility and the prediction naturally includes referential opacity. The advantage over traditional accounts, perhaps, is that this approach moves the phenomenon centre stage, so to speak, in the study of reference and predicts that such ambiguities are very widespread and regular.

10.6.3 Presupposition

One further advantage of the mental spaces approach is that it unifies the account of referential opacity with an analysis of **presupposition**. In our discussion of presupposition in chapter 4 we saw that one of the problematic features is the defeasibility or cancellability of presuppositions. Thus, for example, sentence 119)a below has the presupposition 119)b, but this is cancelled in 119)c by the added clause:

119) a. John hasn't stopped beating his wife.
b. John used to beat his wife.
c. John hasn't stopped beating his wife, because he never beat her.

We saw that presuppositions can be cancelled by various kinds of contextual information, including general background knowledge. We used examples like 120) and 121) below, where the presupposition trigger *before* in 120)a produces the presupposition in 120)b, while in 121) no such presupposition is produced because of what we know about death:

120) a. Aunt Lola drank the whole bottle of wine before she finished the meal.
b. Aunt Lola finished the meal.

121) Aunt Lola dropped dead before she finished the meal.

We won't go into very much detail of the analysis here but the mental spaces approach explains the cancellation phenomenon by viewing presuppositions as moving ("floating" in Fauconnier's term) from space to space unless blocked by contradiction with the entities and relations (essentially the facts) identified in a space.

We can take the well-worn example of *the king of France* as an example. Fauconnier (1994: 101) discusses the example in 122) below:

122) Luke believes that it is probable that the king of France is bald, even though in fact there is no king of France.

Here we have three mental spaces: we begin with the first parent space of the speaker's realty R; then *believe* sets up a space of Luke's belief B; and *probable* sets up another space P. The presupposition *There is a king of France* originates in P from the sentence *The king of France is bald* and is thus a presupposition of *It is probable that the king of France is bald*. It then "floats" up to the encompassing parent space B and thus becomes a presupposition of *Luke believes that it is probable that the king of France is bald*. However the presupposition is blocked from floating into the space R by the explicit clause *in fact there is no king of France*. The advantage of this analysis is that though the presupposition is blocked in R and therefore for the sentence as a whole, the analysis shows how it remains associated with parts of the sentence which relate to other spaces.

The floating or sharing of presuppositions between spaces is possible because of a general similarity principle, or laziness principle, of space creation, which Fauconnier calls optimization, as defined below:

> *Optimization* (Fauconnier, 1994: 91)
>
> *When a daughter space M is set up within a parent space R, structure M implicitly so as to maximize similarity with R. In particular, in the absence of explicit contrary stipulation, assume that*
>
> a. *elements in R have counterparts in M,*
>
> b. *the relations holding in R hold for the counterparts in M, and*
>
> c. *background assumptions in R hold in M.*

Though this is only an initial stab at such a principle, we can see that it must operate in all space building and thus not only explains the sharing of presuppositions across mental spaces but also explains why in counterfactuals like 123) below:

123) If I were rich, I'd move from Ireland to a Caribbean island.

we assume in the hypothetical space that the world is pretty much the same as in reality except for the speaker's increased wealth. We don't assume for example that Caribbean islands change to acquire Ireland's climate.

Given such a principle and the mechanism of presupposition floating, it is a straightforward prediction of this approach that all kinds of knowledge about a parent space, say reality, can cancel an incompatible presupposition.

10.7 Conceptual blending

The subject of this section is the theory known either as **Conceptual**

Integration or **Conceptual Blending Theory**. This approach, which we will call **Blending Theory**, derives from two traditions within cognitive semantics: Conceptual Metaphor Theory and Mental Spaces Theory. In terms of its architecture and in terms of its central concerns, Blending Theory is most closely related to Mental Spaces Theory, and some cognitive semanticists explicitly refer to it as an extension of this approach. This is due to its central concern with **dynamic** aspects of meaning construction and its dependence upon mental spaces and mental space construction as part of its architecture. However, Blending Theory is a distinct theory that has been developed to account for phenomena that Mental Spaces Theory and Conceptual Metaphor Theory cannot adequately account for. Moreover, Blending Theory adds significant theoretical sophistication of its own. The crucial insight of Blending Theory is that meaning construction typically involves integration of structure that gives rise to more than the sum of its parts. Blending theorists argue that this process of **conceptual integration** or **blending** is a general and basic cognitive operation which is central to the way we think. For example, the category PET FISH is not simply the intersection of the categories PET and FISH. If a prototypical PET is fluffy and affectionate and a prototypical FISH is grey in color and medium-sized (like a mackerel), this does not predict that a prototypical PET FISH is small and orange rather than medium, grey, fluffy and affectionate. The category PET FISH selectively integrates aspects of each of the source categories in order to produce a new category with its own distinct internal structure. This is achieved by conceptual blending.

One of the key claims of cognitive semantics, particularly as developed by conceptual metaphor theorists, is that human imagination plays a crucial role in cognitive processes and in what it is to be human. This theme is further developed by Gilles Fauconnier and Mark Turner, the pioneers of Blending Theory. Blending Theory was originally developed in order to account for linguistic structure and for the role of language in meaning construction, particularly "creative" aspects of meaning construction like novel metaphors, counterfactuals and so on. However, recent research carried out by scholars with an interest in Blending Theory has given rise to the view that conceptual blending is central to human thought and imagination, and that evidence for this can be found not only in human language, but also in a wide range of other areas of human activity.

10.7.1 The origins of Blending Theory

The origins of Blending Theory lie in the research programs of Gilles Fauconnier and Mark Turner. While Fauconnier had developed Mental Spaces Theory in order to account for a number of traditional problems in meaning construction, Turner approached meaning construction from the perspective of his studies of metaphor in literary language. Fauconnier and Turner's research programs converged on a range of linguistic phenomena that appeared to share striking similarities and that resisted straightforward explanation by either of the frameworks they had developed. Fauconnier and Turner both observed that in many cases meaning construction appears to derive from structure that is apparently unavailable in the linguistic or conceptual structure that functions as the input to the meaning construction process. Blending Theory emerged from their attempts to account for this observation.

We begin our overview of Blending Theory with an example of the kind of linguistic phenomenon that motivated the development of this approach. The following example is metaphorical in nature, and yet cannot be straightforwardly accounted for by Conceptual Metaphor Theory:

124) That surgeon is a butcher.

Within the conceptual metaphor tradition, examples like 124) have been explained on the basis of a mapping from a source domain onto a target so that the target is understood in terms of the metaphorically projected structure. Applying this explanation to the example in 124), the target domain SURGEON is understood in terms of the source domain BUTCHER. In the source domain we have a butcher, a cleaver and an animal's carcass that the butcher dismembers. In the target domain we have a surgeon, a scalpel and a live but unconscious patient on whom the surgeon operates. The mappings are given in Table 10-2.

Table 10-2 Mappings for SURGEON IS A BUTCHER

Source: BUTCHER	mappings	Target: SURGEON
BUTCHER	⟶	SURGEON
CLEAVER	⟶	SCALPEL
ANIMAL CARCASSES	⟶	HUMAN PATIENTS
DISMEMBERING	⟶	OPERATING

The difficulty that this example poses for Conceptual Metaphor Theory is that the sentence in 124) actually implies a negative assessment. Although butchery is a highly skilled profession, by conceptualizing a surgeon as a butcher we are evaluating the surgeon as incompetent. This poses a difficulty for Conceptual Metaphor Theory because this negative assessment does not appear to derive from the source domain BUTCHER. While the butcher carries out work on dead animals, there is considerable expertise and skill involved, including detailed knowledge of the anatomy of particular animals, knowledge of different cuts of meat and so on. Given that butchery is recognized as a skilled profession, questions arise concerning the conceptual origin of the negative assessment arising from this example. Clearly, if metaphor rests on the mapping between pre-existing knowledge structures, the emergence of new meaning as a consequence of this mapping operation is not explained by Conceptual Metaphor Theory: how does the negative assessment of incompetence arise from conceptualizing one highly skilled professional in terms of another?

This example points to powerful aspects of human cognition. Language and thought are not strictly compositional in the sense that they are **additive**. In other words, meaning construction cannot rely solely upon "simple" conceptual projection processes like structuring one conceptual region in terms of another, as in the case of conceptual metaphors, or establishing connectors between counterparts in mental spaces. In example 124), the negative assessment is obvious and appears to be the driving force behind describing a surgeon as a butcher, yet this negative evaluation seems to be contained in neither of the input domains associated with the metaphor. Blending Theory accounts for the emergence of meanings like these by adopting the view that meaning construction involves **emergent structure**: meaning that is more than the sum of its component parts.

10.7.2 Towards a theory of conceptual integration

In attempting to account for examples like the SURGEON AS BUTCHER metaphor, Fauconnier and Turner took aspects of the two frameworks they had developed and produced a theory of **integration networks**. An integration network is a mechanism for modeling how emergent meaning might come about. Fauconnier and Turner suggest that an integration network consists of **inputs** in which elements in each input are linked by mappings (Fig. 10-28). In this respect, Blending Theory draws upon Conceptual Metaphor Theory. Recall that Conceptual Metaphor Theory represents a two-domain model in which domains are linked by conventional mappings relating comparable elements.

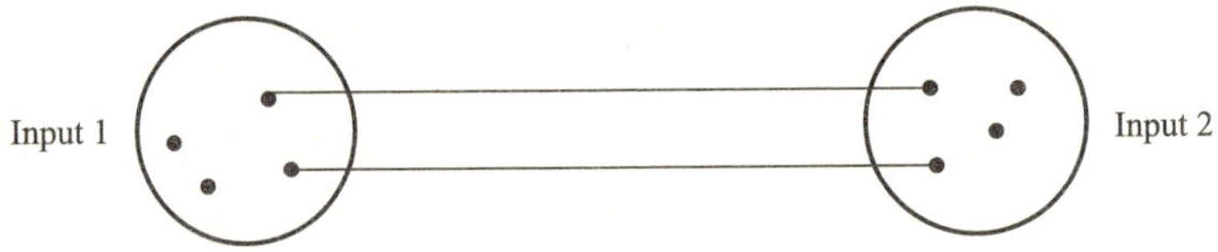

Fig. 10-28 Mappings of elements across inputs

From Mental Spaces Theory, Fauconnier and Turner took the idea that the conceptual units that populate an integration network should be mental spaces rather than domains of knowledge, as in conceptual Metaphor Theory. As we have seen in previous sections, the difference between the two is that domains of knowledge are relatively stable pre-existing knowledge structures, while mental spaces are temporary structures created during the on-line process of meaning construction. Therefore, the initial focus in Blending Theory was to account for local and dynamic meaning construction, a focus that is inherited from Mental Spaces Theory.

Moreover, integration networks in Blending Theory are not simply two-space entities. Because these networks represent an attempt to account for the dynamic aspects of meaning construction, they are multiple-space entities, just like mental space lattices. One of the ways in which this model gives rise to complex networks is by linking two (or more) **input spaces** by means of a **generic space**. The generic space provides information that is abstract enough to be common to both (or all) the inputs. Indeed, Fauconnier and Turner hypothesize that integration networks are in part licensed by interlocutors identifying the structure common to both inputs that licenses integration. Elements in the generic space are mapped onto counterparts in each of the input spaces, which motivates the identification of cross-space counterparts in the input spaces. This is illustrated in Fig. 10-29.

A further distinguishing feature of an integration network is that it consists of a fourth **blended space** or **blend**. This is the space that contains new or **emergent structure**: information that is not contained in either of the inputs. This is represented by the blended space in Fig. 10-30. The blend takes elements from both inputs, as indicated by the broken lines, but goes further in providing additional structure that distinguishes the blend from either of its inputs. In other words, the blend **derives** structure that is contained in neither input. In Fig. 10-30, this emergent structure or "novel" meaning is represented by the elements in the blended space that are not connected to either of the inputs.

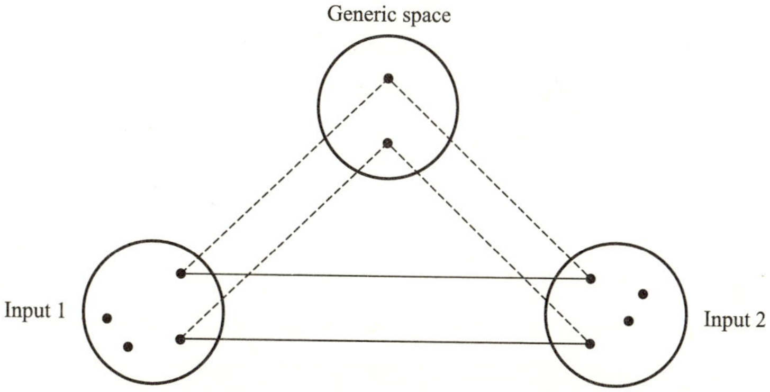

Fig. 10-29 Addition of a generic space

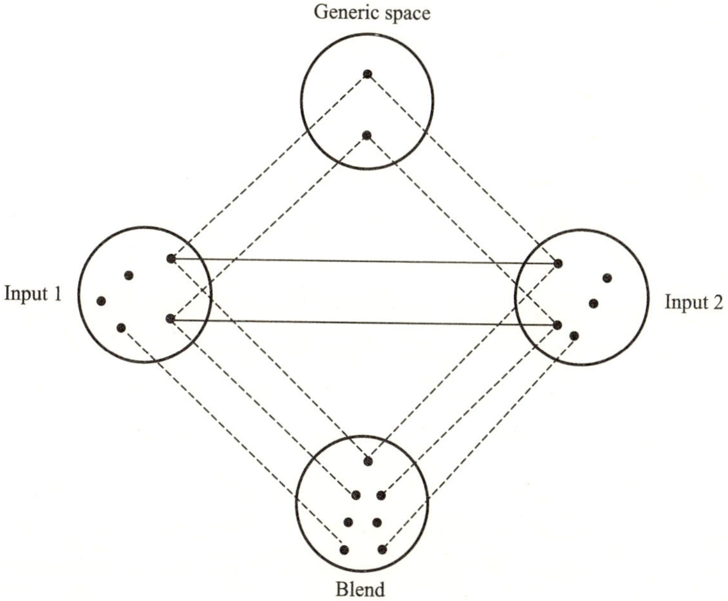

Fig. 10-30 A basic integration network (Fauconnier and Turner, 2002: 46)

• *That surgeon is a butcher: the blending theory account*

Having set out the basic architecture of the Blending Theory model, we outline an analysis of the SURGEON AS BUTCHER metaphor from a Blending

Theory perspective. As noted by Grady, Oakley and Coulson (1999), Blending Theory is able to account for the negative assessment associated with this utterance by allowing for emergent structure. This follows from the fact that, while a blend contains structure projected from both inputs, it also contains additional structure projected from neither. In the input space for BUTCHER, we have a highly skilled professional. However, in the blend, these skills are inappropriate for performing surgery on human patients. While surgeons attempt to save lives, butchers perform their work on dead animals. While the activity performed by butchers is dismembering, the activity performed by surgeons typically involves repair and reconstruction, and so on. The consequence of these contrasts is that in the blend a surgeon who is assessed as a butcher brings inappropriate skills and indeed goals to the task at hand and is therefore incompetent. This emergent meaning of incompetence represents the additional structure provided by the blend.

The emergent structure provided by the blend includes the structure copied from the input spaces, together with the emergent structure relating to a surgeon who performs an operation using the skills of butchery and is therefore incompetent. This individual does not exist in either of the input spaces. The structure in the blend is "emergent" because it emerges from "adding together" structure from the inputs to produce an entity unique to the blend. Furthermore, it is precisely by virtue of the mismatch between goal (healing) and means (butchery), which exists only in the blend, that the inference of incompetence arises. This means that all the structure in the blend can be described as emergent, even though its "ingredients" are provided by the input spaces. Finally, we address the role of the generic space in this integration network. As we noted earlier, the generic space contains highly schematic information which serves as a basis for establishing cross-space mappings between the two input spaces. In other words, the generic space facilitates the identification of counterparts in the input spaces by serving as a "template" for shared structure. It is these counterparts that can then be projected to the blend. The integration network for this blend is illustrated in Fig. 10-31.

While metaphors of this kind originally motivated Fauconnier and Turner's development of Blending Theory, this approach applies equally to non-metaphorical instances of meaning construction. Consider the counterfactual example 125).

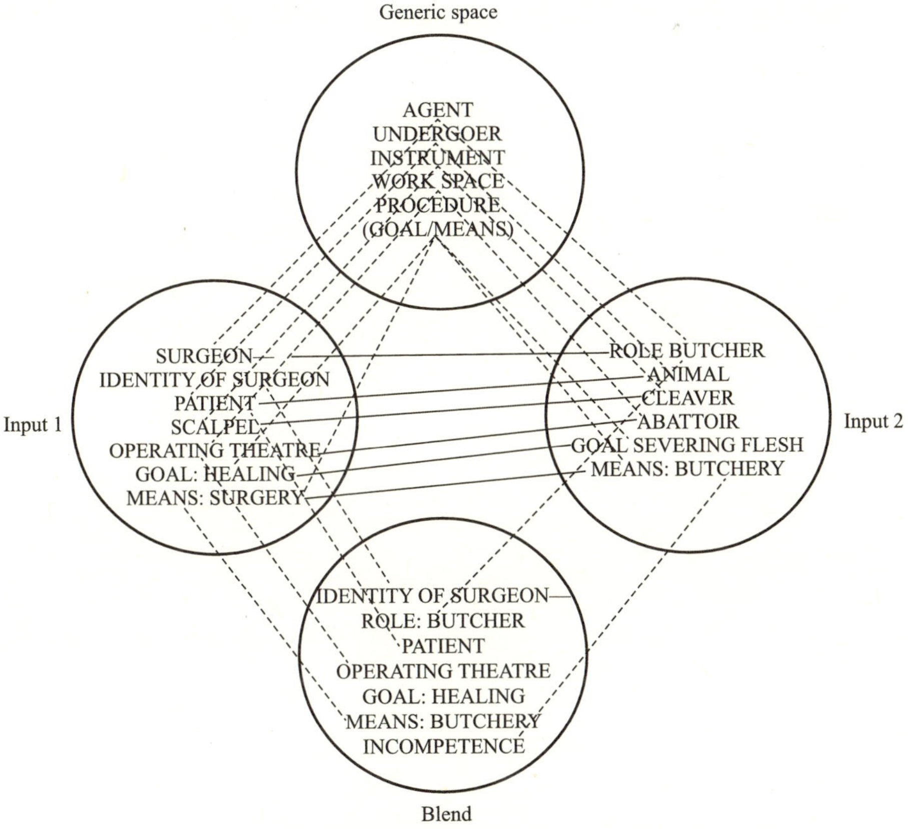

Fig. 10-31 SURGEON AS BUTCHER blend

125) In France, Bill Clinton wouldn't have been harmed by his relationship with Monica Lewinsky.

As with the SURGEON AS BUTCHER metaphor, this counterfactual prompts for a complex conceptualization that is more than the sum of its parts. In particular, it involves the conceptual blending of counterparts in order to produce a blend in which Clinton is not politically harmed by his relationship with Lewinsky, an emergent meaning that does not exist in either of the inputs that give rise to it.

The integration network for this expression includes two inputs. One input space contains CLINTON, LEWINSKY and their RELATIONSHIP. This space is structured by the frame AMERICAN POLITICS. In this frame, there is a role for AMERICAN PRESIDENT, together with certain attributes associated with this role such as MORAL VIRTUE, a symbol of which is marital fidelity. In this space, marital infidelity causes political harm. In the second input space, which is structured by the frame FRENCH POLITICS, there is a role for FRENCH PRESIDENT. In this frame, it is an accepted part of French public life that the President sometimes has a MISTRESS. In this space, marital infidelity does not result in political harm. The two inputs are related by virtue of a generic space, which contains the generic roles COUNTRY, HEAD OF STATE, SEXUAL PARTNER and CITIZENS. The generic space establishes cross-space counterparts. The blended space contains BILL CLINTON and MONICA LEWINSKY, as well as the roles FRENCH PRESIDENT and MISTRESS OF FRENCH PRESIDENT, with which Clinton and Lewinsky are respectively associated. Crucially, the frame that structures the blend is FRENCH POLITICS rather than AMERICAN POLITICS. It follows that in the blend, Clinton is not politically harmed by his marital infidelity. However, because the inputs remain connected to the blend, structure in the blend can project back towards the inputs, giving rise to a **disanalogy** between the US and France. The integration network for this blend is represented in Fig. 10-32.

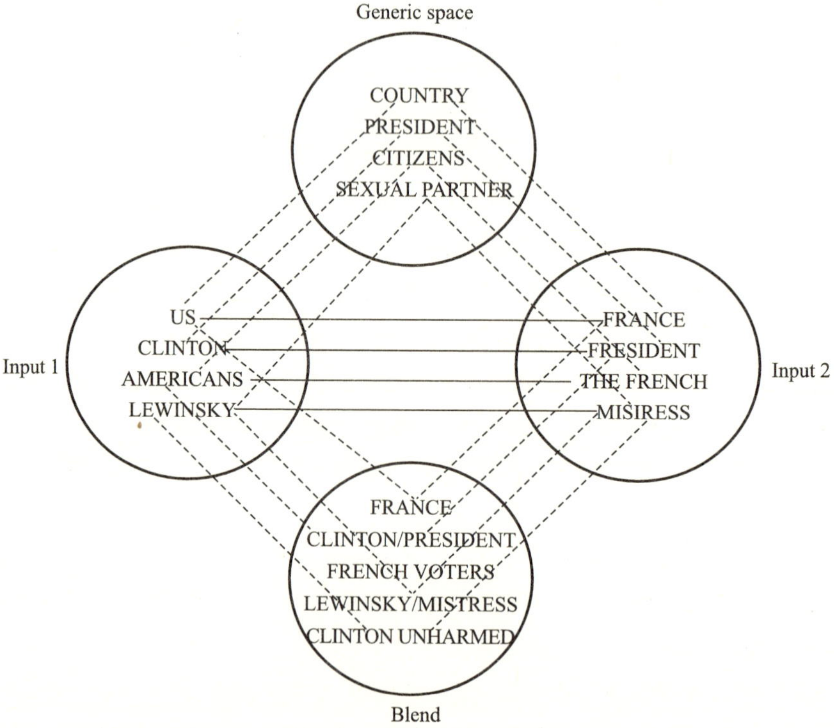

Fig. 10-32 CLINTON AS PRESIDENT OF FRANCE blend

The disanalogy between the United States and France is an important consequence of the counterfactual. The point of the utterance is to emphasize the difference between US and French attitudes, and perhaps moral values, with respect to the behavior of their politicians in their personal lives. In the US, Clinton was censured for his attempts to keep his affair secret. In France, an affair would not have harmed him politically. The disanalogy is achieved by constructing a counterfactual through blending. An important advantage that Blending Theory has over Mental Spaces Theory is that we now have a mechanism that accounts for how structure is recruited and integrated in order to produce emergent structure: novel and highly creative scenarios like counterfactuals.

10.7.3 The nature of blending

As we saw above, metaphorical projection in the SURGEON AS BUTCHER metaphor is better accounted for by a conceptual integration network than by a two-domain mapping. This is because conceptual integration gives rise to a blended space which provides a mechanism that accounts for the emergent structure not found in the input domains. We also saw that counterfactuals, like the CLINTON AS FRENCH PRESIDENT example, are accounted for by an integration network resulting in a blend. Since Fauconnier and Turner first advanced their theory in a seminal 1994 paper, a considerable amount of evidence for conceptual blending has been amassed from a range of non-linguistic phenomena. According to Fauconnier and Turner, blending is a general and ubiquitous operation, central to human cognitive capabilities, and conceptual blending is central not just to language, but to human thought in general. In this subsection we consider in more detail the elements involved in conceptual blending.

10.7.3.1 The elements of conceptual blending

We begin by sketching out the processes that give rise to conceptual blending and proceed in 10.7.3.2 and 10.7.3.3 to explore in detail how these processes apply in both linguistic and non-linguistic phenomena. We saw above that an integration network consists of at least four spaces: a generic space, two inputs and a blended space. We also saw that the generic space establishes **counterpart connectors** between input spaces, which are represented as the bold lines in integration network diagrams. These connections are established by **matching**, the conceptual operation responsible for identifying cross-space counterparts in the input spaces. Connectors between matched elements are then established, which, as we saw in the previous subsection, is a form of conceptual projection. Connectors can be established between matched elements on the basis of identity or role (as we saw in the CLINTON AS FRENCH PRESIDENT example), or based on metaphor (as we saw in the SURGEON AS BUTCHER example).

The input spaces give rise to **selective projection**. In other words, not all the structure from the inputs is projected to the blend, but only the matched information, which is required for purposes of local understanding. For example, in the CLINTON AS FRENCH PRESIDENT example, the fact that the role FRENCH PRESIDENT has a value in reality (currently Francois Hollande) is not projected to the blend. Neither is the fact that Clinton speaks English rather than French, nor the fact that he is unlikely to have considered becoming president of France, nor the fact that he is ineligible, and so on. In other words, much of the structure in the inputs is irrelevant to, or even inconsistent with, the emergent meaning under construction. This type of information is therefore not projected into the blend. Selective projection is one reason why different language users, or even the same language user on different occasions, can produce different blends from the same inputs. In other words, the process of selective projection is not deterministic but flexible. As an example, we consider a scenario in which a child picks up a replica sword in a military museum. In response to the expression of alarm on the face of the parent the curator remarks, "Don't worry, the sword is safe", to which the parent rejoins, "Not from him it isn't". In this exchange, the curator intended that the sword would not cause the child harm. In this intended interpretation, the structure being projected relates to the potential harm that swords can cause, especially when handled by the inexperienced. However, the parent rejects this blend and proposes a new one in which it is the sword, rather than the child, that is at risk from potential harm. This blend arises because the parent projects his personal knowledge of the child, and the child's ability to inflict damage on anything they come into contact with. This example illustrates how it is possible to obtain different blends from the same, or very similar, input spaces by virtue of differential selective projection.

In Blending Theory, there are three component processes that give rise to emergent structure: (1) composition; (2) completion; and (3) elaboration. The first involves the **composition** of elements from separate inputs. In the CLINTON AS FRENCH PRESIDENT example, composition brings together the value BILL CLINTON with the role FRENCH PRESIDENT in the blend, resulting in CLINTON AS FRENCH PRESIDENT. Similarly, the SURGEON AS BUTCHER blend composes the elements projected from the SURGEON input with those projected from the BUTCHER input. The second process, **completion**, involves schema induction. As we saw in the previous chapter, schema induction involves the unconscious and effortless recruitment of background frames. These complete the composition. For example, in the CLINTON AS FRENCH PRESIDENT example, the process of completion introduces the frames for FRENCH POLITICS and FRENCH MORAL ATTITUDES. Without the structure provided by these frames, we would lose the central inference emerging from the blend, which is that his affair with Lewinsky would not harm Clinton in France. This process of schema induction is called "completion" because structure is recruited to "fill out" or complete the information projected from the inputs in order to derive the blend. Finally, **elaboration** is the on-line processing that produces the structure unique to the blend. This process is sometimes called **running the blend**.

The processes that we have discussed in this subsection represent the **constitutive processes** of Blending Theory. These processes together comprise conceptual integration and the conceptual blending that arises from integration.

10.7.3.2 Further linguistic examples

In this part, we consider some further examples of blending presented by Fauconnier and Turner, and look at how the processes described in the previous subsection might apply.

• *Boat race*

Consider the example 126) from a news report in *Latitude 38*, a sailing magazine (Fauconnier and Turner, 2002: 64).

126) As we went to press, Rich Wilson and Bill Biewenga were barely maintaining a 4.5 day lead over the ghost of the clipper *Northern Light*.

This example relates to a 1993 news story in which a modern catamaran

Great American II, sailed by Wilson and Biewenga, set out on a route from San Francisco to Boston. A record for this route had been set in 1853 by the clipper *Northern Light*, which had made the journey in 76 days and 8 hours. This record still held in 1993.

The utterance in 126) sets up an integration network in which there are two input spaces: one relating to the journey of the modern catamaran in 1993 and the other relating to the original journey undertaken by *Northern Light* in 1853. The generic space contains schematic information relating to BOATS and JOURNEYS, which motivates matching operations and thus cross-space connections between the two inputs. In the blend, we have two boats: CATAMARAN and NORTHERN LIGHT. Moreover, in the blend the two boats were engaged in a RACE, in which the CATAMARAN is barely maintaining a lead over NORTHERN LIGHT. As Fauconnier and Turner observe, no one is actually "fooled" by the blend: we do not interpret the sentence to mean that there are actually two boats from two different periods in history engaged in a real side-by-side race. Despite this, we achieve valuable inferences as a result of setting up the conceptual blend. Indeed, it is only by virtue of blending that we can compare the progress of the catamaran against that of its "rival" *Northern Light,* which set the original record over a century earlier. This blend is illustrated in Fig. 10-33.

In achieving this blend, the first process to occur is selective projection from the inputs to the blend. Not all the information in the input spaces is projected. For example, information is not projected relating to weather conditions, whether the boats have cargo or not, the nature of the clipper's crew, what the crew ate for supper and so on. Instead, information is projected that is sufficient to accomplish the inference. For example, we only project the 1993 time frame. Secondly, the structure that is selectively projected into the blend is composed and completed. The schema induction that occurs at the completion stage adds the RACE frame to the blend and thus provides further structure: in a race there are two or more COMPETITORS and the first to complete the course is the WINNER. Next, upon running the blend, the additional structure emerges that has arisen as a result of composition and completion. In Fig. 10-33, this emergent structure is appended to the blend in the box beneath the blended space. Once this has occurred, we can think of the two boats as competitors in a race and compare their relative progress. Finally, as a result of backward projection the blend modifies the input spaces. For

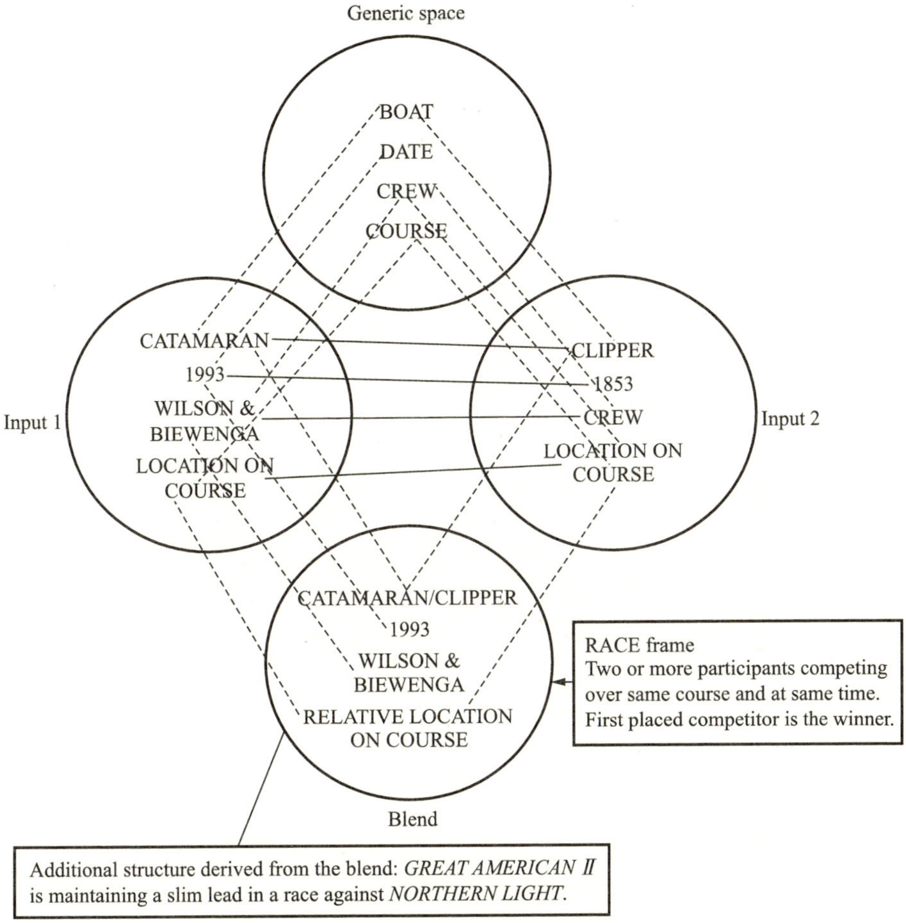

Fig. 10-33 BOAT RACE blend

example, by "living in the blend", the crew of the catamaran, their support team and others who are monitoring their progress can experience a range of emotions attendant upon participating in or watching a race, even though the "race" is an imaginative feat.

• *Formal blends*

Formal blends involve projection of specific lexical forms to the blended space and rely, partly, upon formal (lexical or grammatical) structure for their meaning.

One of the examples of formal blending is **compounding**, the process of blending two (or more) free morphemes to give rise to a new word. Recall from Chapter 4 that new words come into language on a remarkably regular basis. By providing an account of compounding, Blending Theory also offers an insight into this aspect of language change. The formal blend we consider here is the expression *landyacht*. According to Turner and Fauconnier (1995), this novel noun-noun compound relates to a large and expensive luxury car. It consists of two input spaces relating to the forms *land* and *yacht*, and the conventional range of meanings associated with these lexical items. However, projection to the blend is selective. Only a subset of the meanings associated with *land* and *yacht* are projected into the blend, together with the forms (the expressions *land* and *yacht*) themselves. In other words, Fauconnier and Turner suggest that linguistic forms as well as their associated lexical concepts can be projected into the blended space. When a lexical item is projected into the blend, this is known as **word projection**. As a result of composition, the forms as well as their projected meanings are integrated, giving rise to a new form *landyacht* with a distinct meaning: a large expensive luxury car. Fig. 10-34 illustrates the derivation of this compound, a process that could equally explain the compound PET FISH.

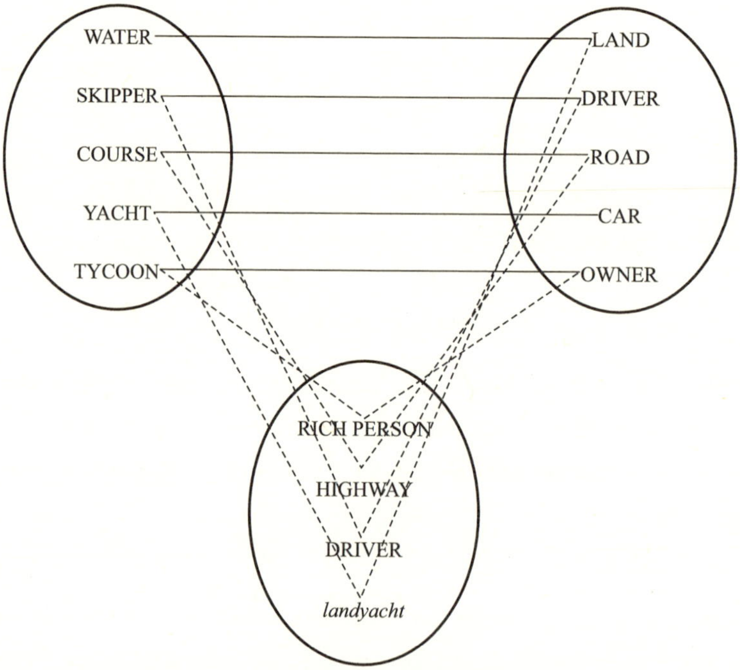

Fig. 10-34 *Landyacht*

10.7.3.3 Non-linguistic examples

The examples we have considered so far have illustrated how Blending

Theory accounts for the on-line meaning construction arising from linguistic prompts, and have also illustrated how this approach can explain certain aspects of the meaning arising from formal linguistic units like grammatical constructions or compounds. However, although blending is a conceptual operation that can be invoked by language and that can also affect linguistic forms themselves, the blending operation itself, like the other cognitive processes that underlie cognitive semantics, is thought to be independent of language. In order to illustrate this, we consider an example from the literature that illustrates conceptual blending at work in non-linguistic aspects of human thought and behavior.

• *Computer desktop*

When we interact with modern computers we do so via a computer "desktop". That is, we have icons on our computer screens that represent folders, files, a wastepaper basket and so on. By selecting a particular icon from the computer "desktop" we are able to tell the computer what we want it to do. The computer "desktop" is a sophisticated blend which integrates structure from the domain of OFFICES and the WORKPLACE, including FILES, FOLDERS and WASTEPAPER BASKET. By providing an interface that translates the complex algorithmic operations that run the computer into simple commands, the blend allows us to understand and interact with our computer. However, the blend also features a range of novel characteristics that are unique to the blend. For instance, in "real" offices we do not normally keep the wastepaper basket on our desktop. Moreover, as pointed out by Fauconnier and Turner (e.g. 2002), in the version of the desktop blend that applies to the Macintosh computer system, the "trashcan", as well as facilitating file deletion, is also the means of ejecting the CD: in order to eject the disk, the user must drag the disk icon on the screen into the "trashcan". This directly contradicts knowledge from the domain of offices and workplaces where we are unlikely to place important disks in the bin in order to retrieve them.

Of course, the computer "desktop" is facilitated by language in the sense that we rely upon linguistic expressions like desktop, file and folder to talk about our interaction with computers. Nevertheless, the blend is achieved by integrating conceptual structure from the domains of OFFICES and COMPUTER OPERATIONS, and relies upon iconic rather than linguistic representations, such as an image of a file or a folder, in order to prompt for these conceptual domains.

10.7.4 Contrasting Blending Theory with Conceptual Metaphor Theory

When Blending Theory was first formulated, its proponents argued that it represented an alternative framework to Conceptual Metaphor Theory. However, there are good reasons to think that Blending Theory and Conceptual Metaphor Theory are complementary rather than competing theories. In this subsection, we compare and contrast Blending Theory and Conceptual Metaphor Theory, and argue that as well as providing complementary perspectives, each theory addresses certain phenomena not accounted for by the other theory.

Blending Theory is distinct from Conceptual Metaphor Theory in a number of ways.

• *Not all blends are metaphorical*

First of all, it is important to emphasize that not all blends are metaphorical. Although a large subset of conceptual metaphors are blends, with counterparts established in the "source" and "target", there is a small but important subset of highly conventionalized conceptual metaphors that are not blends. These are the **primary metaphors**. Primary metaphors conventionally associate concepts that are equally "basic", in the sense that they are both directly experienced and perceived. The following are some examples of primary metaphors together with example sentences.

127) SIMILARITY IS NEARNESS

That color is quite close to the one on our dining-room wall.

128) IMPORTANCE IS SIZE

We've got a big week coming up at work.

129) QUANTITY IS VERTICAL ELEVATION

The price of shares has gone up.

130) CAUSES ARE FORCES

Vanity drove me to have the operation.

131) CHANGE IS MOTION

Things have shifted a little since you were last here.

132) DESIRE IS HUNGER

We're hungry for a victory.

An important achievement of Conceptual Metaphor Theory is that it identifies metaphoric mappings that are directly grounded in experience. Mappings of this kind, which are thought to be among the most foundational aspects of conceptual structure, are not blends, and are not therefore addressed by Blending Theory. In this respect, Conceptual Metaphor Theory retains an important role in the analysis of figurative thought and language.

- *Blending does not involve unidirectional mappings*

Unlike Conceptual Metaphor Theory, Blending Theory involves selective projection of structure from inputs to the blended space rather than unidirectional cross-domain mappings. In addition, structure from the blend can be projected back to the input spaces. Thus the two theories employ different architecture in order to model similar phenomena.

- *Spaces versus domains*

Conceptual metaphors feature mappings (and domains) stored in long-term memory. These mappings hold between domains which are highly stable knowledge structures. In contrast, Conceptual Blending Theory makes use of mental spaces. As we saw in the previous chapter, mental spaces are dynamic and temporary conceptual "packets" constructed "on-line" during discourse. Despite this, blends can become conventionalized, in which case the blend becomes established as a relatively stable knowledge structure in the conceptual system.

- *The many-space model*

In their first Blending Theory paper, Fauconnier and Turner (1994) referred to conceptual integration or blending as the **many-space model**. This points to an obvious difference between Blending Theory and Conceptual Metaphor Theory: while Conceptual Metaphor Theory is a two-domain model, Blending Theory employs a minimum of four spaces.

- *Dynamic versus conventional*

One consequence of the foregoing comparisons is that while Blending Theory emphasizes the dynamic and mutable aspects of blending and its role in meaning construction, Conceptual Metaphor Theory emphasizes the idea that there is a "metaphor system" in which conceptual metaphors interact in order to provide relatively stable structure and organization to the human conceptual system. This reflects the different emphases of the two traditions: metaphor theorists have been concerned with mapping the conventional patterns entrenched in conceptual structure, while blending theorists have been more concerned with investigating the contribution of conceptual integration to ongoing meaning construction. As we have seen, this does not entail that blending cannot give rise to conventionalized representations.

- *Difference in methodological emphasis*

As a consequence of the previous contrast, while conceptual metaphor theorists have sought generalizations across a broad range of metaphoric expressions, conceptual blending theorists, while developing general principles based on specific examples, typically focus on the nature and particulars of those specific examples. This is because Blending Theory places emphasis upon a process of meaning construction rather than a system of knowledge.

- *Emergent structure*

A particularly important difference between the two theories is that, while Blending Theory provides an account of emergent structure, Conceptual Metaphor Theory does not. This follows from the fact that Conceptual Metaphor Theory relies upon a two-domain model.

10.8 Grammaticalization

Where do derivational affixes like *-ful* and *-less* come from? Many affixes like these have come from full words (free morphemes) and gradually changed into affixes (bound morphemes). For example, in *careful*, *beautiful*, or *wonderful*, the suffix *-ful* originates from the adjective *full*, which was first used in compounds such as *mouthful*, and *spoonful*. As a suffix, the form *-ful* has gradually acquired the more generalized and abstract meaning of "possessing some value to a very high degree". The affix *-ful* is the opposite of *-less*, which goes back to Old English *leas* meaning "without". Compare *careful/careless*, *hopeful/hopeless* and *merciful/merciless*. The English verb *must* was a full content verb in Old English meaning "be able" and evolved into a modal auxiliary in Modern English.

The process whereby an independent word is shifted to the status of a grammatical element is called *grammaticalization*. Or grammaticalization is the process where lexical or content words acquire grammatical function. Usually, in grammaticalization, words from major grammatical categories, such as nouns, verbs and adjectives become minor grammatical categories such as prepositions, adverbs and auxiliaries, which in turn may be further grammaticalized into affixes. Full words, with their own lexical content, thus become form words; and this categorial change tends to be accompanied by a reduction in phonological form and a "bleaching" of meaning. Therefore, grammaticalization is not only a syntactic change, but also a global change influencing the morphology, phonology and semantics. Grammaticalization is unidirectional in that this type of change is from the lexical to the grammatical (from the open class to the closed class), and not vice versa.

A famous example in English is the transition of the lexical verb "go" into an auxiliary used to express the future tense. Compare the following examples (Ungerer and Schmid, 1996: 255):

133) a. Susan*'s going* to London next month.
 b. She*'s going* to London to work at our office.
 c. She*'s going* to work at our office.
 d. You*'re going* to like her.
 e. You*'re gonna* like her.
 f. You *gonna* like her. (non-standard)

In these examples, the development starts out from the use of the word "go" as a verb of motion with a directional adverbial. This applies to 133)a and 133)b although 133)b has an adverbial of purpose. 133)c indicates the turning point. The directional adverbial is omitted, and now the meaning focuses on the subject's intention which is to be realized in the future. 133)d takes us one step further because the subject here is no longer an agent, but rather the experiencer of an attitude (the affection towards Susan). The meaning of "going to" is no longer intentional, but a kind of prediction based on the present situation. 133)e and 133)f do not change the semantic meaning, but record the phonological changes which accompany the transition of "going to" into a grammatical form "gonna". However, the fusion of "going" and "to" into "gonna" is conditioned. While the fusion is permitted when the form "(be) going to" is associated with a purely future meaning, it is not permitted when the form is associated with a motion meaning. This is illustrated by the acceptability of *gonna* with a purely future meaning as in 134)a, but not with a motion meaning as in 134)b.

134) a. I'm gonna be a doctor when I grow up.
(= I'm going to be a doctor when I grow up.)
b. *I'm gonna the library.
(= I'm going to the library.)

Grammaticalization brings about typical changes in meanings and the distribution of forms. One of these is that, when a lexical form becomes a grammatical morpheme, the original form may remain as an autonomous element and undergo the same changes as other lexical items. As a result, the lexical and the grammatical forms coexist. This divergence has happened with the Old English adjective "ān" (one, a certain), which was grammaticalized as the indefinite article "a(n)", but continued to exist in its original lexical form as "one" (as well as in the affixed forms "any" "once" "alone" "lone" and "only").

Another characteristic of grammaticalized forms is that the constraints on their grammatical uses tend to reflect their lexical histories. For example, the uses of the English auxiliary "will" include not only predictive future-tense meanings (e.g. "It will rain tomorrow"), but also willingness (e.g. "I will help you with the violin"), and intention (e.g. "I'll put them in the post today"); both of the latter were common meanings of the verb "willan" in Old English. The development of a future-tense meaning occurred by way of encroachment on the earlier meanings, which left them as possible current uses.

Another typical outcome of grammaticalization is the development of different historical levels of nearly equivalent forms. As new ways of expressing functions appear, the older ones are often not discarded, but remain as alternatives. An obvious instance is the English past-tense system, in which the older technique involving a vowel change (e.g. "drive/drove") exists side by side with the newer technique of suffixation (e.g. "cook/cooked").

The study of grammaticalization has recently come back into prominence. This revival of interest is attributable not only to the intrinsic value of grammaticalization for the study of the histories of individual languages, but to the profound questions which are raised by the terms of the study itself: What is grammar? What causes the change of language?

The language we use to express the world is based on our cognitive conceptual structures and the worldly experience from which they come from. Cognitive linguistics provides many new angles for our insight into language. Its significant position in linguistics is evident. It seems to give us hope that some unsolved problems in language studies may be solved in cognitive linguistics.

10.9 Summary

In this chapter we have reviewed the approach known as cognitive semantics. We have seen that a distinctive feature of the approach is its attempt to form an experientialist basis for meaning. Cognitive semanticists propose that the common human experience of maturing and interacting in society motivates basic conceptual structures which make understanding and language possible. In Mark Johnson's (1987) approach, these conceptual structures include pre-linguistic **image schemas**. These image schemas form more abstract cognitive models by processes of **metaphor** and **metonymy**. We saw in Fauconnier's theory of **mental models** a mechanism for explaining how participants in a discourse maintain referential links, set up referential domains and regulate knowledge sharing between them. **Conceptual Blending Theory** (Fauconnier and Turner, 2002; Coulson, 2000) seeks to account for a speaker's abilities to integrate conceptual structures in dynamic and novel ways. In our exploration of categorization we outlined the classical theory of categorization, which assumes necessary and sufficient conditions, and identified the problems inherent in this approach. We then looked in some detail at **prototype theory**, the model of categorization which holds that many categories have prototype structure rather than definitional structure. We also looked at Lakoff's theory of **idealized cognitive models** (ICMs) which is closely related to the prototype theory. The main claim that has emerged from the research of ICMs was that typicality effects are surface phenomenon, arising from underlying ICMs of various kinds. Another topic we explored in this chapter is iconicity, a challenge to the arbitrary view of language, which claims that the structure of language reflects in some way the structure of experience, that is, the structure of the world, including the perspective imposed on the world by the speaker. We ended this chapter with a discussion of **grammaticalization**, the process whereby an independent word is shifted to the status of a grammatical element.

In earlier chapters we discussed the claim that semantic representations have to be grounded in some way, if semantic analysis is not just to be simply a form of translation. In formal semantics this is done by establishing denotational links with the external non-linguistic world. In this chapter we have seen that in cognitive semantics a similar grounding is sought but not directly in reality (which in this view is not directly accessible) but in conceptual structures derived from the experience of having human bodies, and all that this implies.

Bibliography

Anderson R C, Reynolds R E, Schallert D L, et al. 1977. Frameworks for Comprehending Discourse. American Educational Research Journal, 14: 367-381.

Aristotle, Alexander. 1996. Poetics. Trans. Malcolm Heath. New York: Penguin Books.

Aristotle, Alexander. 1954. Rhetoric and Poetics. New York: The Modern Library.

Armstrong, Lee S, Gleitman L, et al. 1983. What Some Concepts Might Not Be. Cognition, 13: 263-308.

Austin J L. 1975. How to Do Things With Words. 2nd ed. Oxford: Clarendon Press.

Barcelona A. 2003. On the Plausibility of Claiming a Metonymic Motivation for Conceptual Metaphor // Barcelona A. Metaphor and Metonymy at the Crossroads: A Cognitive Perspective. Berlin: Mouton de Gruyter.

Berlin B, Kay P. 1969. Basic Color Terms: Their Universality and Evolution. Berkeley: University of California Press.

Black M. 1962. Models and Metaphors. Cornell: Cornell University Press.

Blakemore D. 1992. Understanding Utterances: An Introduction to Pragmatics. Oxford: Blackwell.

Bloomfield L. 1933. Language. London: Allen and Unwin.

Boas F. 1966. Introduction to the Handbook of American Indian Languages. Washington, DC: Smithsonian Institution.

Boroditsky L. 2001. Does Language Shape Thought? Mandarin and English Speakers' Conceptions of Time // Cognitive Psychology, 43: 1-22.

Bransford J D, Johnson M K. 1973. Considerations of Some Problems of Comprehension // Chase W G. Visual Information Processing. New York: Academic Press.

Brown P, Levinson S C. 1978. Universals in Language Usage: Politeness Phenomena // Goody E N. Questions and Politeness: Strategies in Social Interaction, 56-310. Cambridge: Cambridge University Press.

Brown P, Levinson S C. 1987. Politeness: Some Universals in Language Usage. Cambridge: Cambridge University Press.

Brown G, Yule G. 1983. Discourse Analysis. Cambridge: Cambridge University Press.

Brugman C, Lakoff G. 1988. Cognitive Topology and Lexical Networks // Small S, Cottrell G, Tannenhaus M. Lexical Ambiguity Resolution. San Mateo, CA: Morgan Kaufman.

Bussmann H. 1996. Routledge Dictionary of Language and Linguistics. London: Routledge.

Bybee J L. 1985. Morphology. Amsterdam: John Benjamins.

Chomsky N. 1965. Aspects of the Theory of Syntax. Cambridge, Mass.: MIT Press.

Chomsky N. 1972. Studies on Semantics in Generative Grammar. The Hague: Mouton.

Chomsky N. 1988. Language and Problems of Knowledge. The Managua Lectures. Cambridge, MA.: MIT Press.

Clark H H. 1978. Inferring What Is Meant // Levelt W J M, Flores d'Arcais G B. Studies in the Perception of Language, 295-332. Chichester: Wiley.

Clark H H. 1977. Bridging // Johnson-Laird P N, Wason P C. Thinking: Readings in Cognitive Science, 411-420. Cambridge: Cambridge University Press.

Cooper W E, Ross J R. 1975. Word order // Grossman R E. Papers From the Parasession on Functionalism. Chicago: Chicago Linguistic Society.

Croft W. 1990. Typology and Universals. Cambridge: Cambridge University Press.

Croft W. 1993. The Role of Domains in the Interpretation of Metaphors and Metonymies. Cognitive Linguistics, 4: 335-370.

Croft W, Cruse D A. 2004. Cognitive Linguistics. Cambridge: Cambridge University Press.

Cruse D A. 1986. Lexical Semantics. Cambridge: Cambridge University Press.

Cullingford R. 1978. Script Application: Computer Understanding of Newspaper Stories. PhD Thesis, Yale University.

Dixon R M W. 1991. A New Approach to English Grammar on Semantic Principles. Oxford: Oxford University Press.

Dowty D R. 1991. Thematic proto-roles and argument selection. Language, 67: 574-619.

Evans V, Melaine G. 2006. Cognitive Linguistics: An Introduction. Edinburgh: Edinburgh University Press.

Fauconnier G. 1985/1994. Mental Spaces. Cambridge: Cambridge University Press.

Fauconnier G. 1997. Mappings in Thought and Language. Cambridge: Cambridge University Press.

Fauconnier G, Turner M. 2002. The Way We Think: Conceptual Blending and the Mind's Hidden Complexities. New York: Basic Books.

Fillmore C. 1982a. Frame semantics // Linguistic Society of Korea. Linguistics in the Morning Calm. Seoul: Hanshin Publishing.

Fillmore C. 1982b. Towards a Descriptive Framework for a Spatial Deixis // Jarvella R, Klem W. Speech, Place, and Action: Studies in Deixis and Related Topics, 31-59. Chichester/New York: John Wiley and Sons.

Frege G. 1980. On Sense and Reference // Geach P, Black M. Translations From the Philosophical Wrings of Gottlob Frege. Oxford: Basil Blackwell.

Gazdar G. 1979. Pragmatics: Implicature, Presupposition, and Logical Form. New York: Academic Press.

Gentner D, Gentner D R. 1982. Flowing Waters or Teeming Crowds: Mental Models of Electricity // Gentner D, Stevens A. Mental Models, 99–129. Hill Hillsdale, NJ: Lawrence Erlbaum.

Gibbs R. 1994. The Poetic of Mind: Figurative Thought, Language and Understanding. Cambridge: Cambridge University Press.

Givon T. 1989. Mind, Code and Context: Essays in Pragmatics. Hillsdale, NJ: Erlbaum.

Givon T. 1990. Syntax: A Functional-typological Introduction, Vol. Ⅱ. Amsterdam: John Benjamins.

Goffman E. 1967. Interaction Ritual: Essays in Face-to-Face Behavior. Garden City, NY: Anchor Books.

Goffman E. 1971. Relations in Public. New York: Basic Books.

Goffman E. 1981. Forms of Talk. Philadelphia: University of Pennsylvania Press.

Goossens L. 1990. Metonymy: The Interaction of Metaphor and Metonymy in Expressions for Linguistic Action. Cognitive Linguistics, 1 (3): 323-340.

Grady J. 1999. A Typology of Motivation for Conceptual Metaphor: Correlation vs. Resemblance // Gibbs R W, Steen G. Metaphor in Cognitive Linguistics. Amsterdam: John Benjamin.

Grady J, Oakley T, Coulson S. 1999. Blending and Metaphor // Gibbs R W, Steen G. Metaphor in Cognitive Linguistics, 101-124. Amsterdam: John Benjamins.

Grice H P. 1975. Logic and Conversation // Cole P, Morgan J. Syntax and Semantics, Vol. 3: Speech Acts, 43-58. New York: Academic Press.

Grice H P. 1978. Further Notes on Logic and Conversation // Cole P. Syntax and Semantics, Vol. 9: Pragmatics, 113-128. New York: Academic Press.

Haiman J. 1985a. Natural Syntax. Cambridge: Cambridge University Press.

Haiman J. 1985b. Iconicity in Syntax. Amsterdam: John Benjamins.

Halliday M A K. 1985/1994. An Introduction to Functional Grammar. London: Edward Arnold.

Halliday M A K, Hasan R. 1976. Cohesion in English. London: Longman.

Hardman M J. 1986. Data-source Marking in the Jaqi Languages // Chafe W, Nichols J. Evidentiality: The Linguistic Coding of Epistemology, 113-136. Norwood, NJ: Ablex.

Hayward R J. 1990. Notes on the Zayse Language // Hayward R J. Omotic Linguistics. London: School of Oriental and African Studies.

Heider E. 1972. Universals in Color Naming and Memory. Journal of Experiential Psychology, 93: 10-20.

Herkovits A. 1986. Language and Spatial Cognition. Cambridge: Cambridge University Press.

Horn L R. 1984. Towards a New Taxonomy for Pragmatic Inference: Q- and R-based

Implicature // Schiffrin D. Meaning, Form and Use in Context, 11-42. Washington, DC: Georgetown University Press.

Horn L R. 1989. A Natural History of Negation. Chicago: University of Chicago Press.

Horn L R. 1996. Presupposition and Implicature // Lappin S. The Handbook of Contemporary Semantic Theory, 299-320. Oxford: Blackwell.

Hurford J R, Heasley B. 1983. Semantics: A Coursebook. New York: Cambridge University Press.

Jackendoff R. 1972. Semantic Interpretation in Generative Grammar. Cambridge, MA: MIT Press.

Jackendoff R. 1975. On Belief Contexts. Linguistic Inquiry, 6 (1): 53-93.

Jackendoff R. 1990. Semantic Structures. Cambridge, MA: MIT Press.

Jakobson R. 1965. Quest for the Essence of Language. Cambridge: Cambridge University Press.

Jaszczolt K. 2004. Semantics and Pragmatics: Meaning in Language and Discourse. Beijing: Peking University Press.

Jespersen O. 1949. A Modern English Grammar on Historical Principles, Vol. Ⅶ. London: George Allen Unwin.

Johnson M. 1987. The Body in the Mind: The Bodily Basis of Meaning, Imagination and Reason. Chicago: University of Chicago Press.

Katz J J, Fodor J A. 1963. The Structure of a Semantic Theory. Language, 39: 170-210. (Reprinted in Rosenberg J F, Travis C. 1971. Readings in the Philosophy of Language, 472-514. New Jersey: Prentice Hall, Inc.)

Katz J J, Postal P M. 1964. An Integrated Theory of Linguistic Descriptions. Cambridge, MA: MIT Press.

Katz J J. 1972. Semantic Theory. New York: Harper and Row.

Kearney A R, Kaplan S. 1997. Toward a Methodology for the Measurement of Knowledge Structures of Ordinary People: The Conceptual Content Cognitive Map. Environment and Behavior, 29: 579-617.

Kempson R M. 1977. Semantic Theory. Cambridge: Cambridge University Press.

Keshavmurti. 1991. Space and Time. New Delhi: Sterling Publishers.

Kess J F, Hoppe R A. 1985. Bias, Individual Preferences and "Shared Knowledge" in Ambiguity. Journal of Pragmatics, 9: 21-39.

Kittay E. 1987. Metaphor, Its Cognitive Force and Linguistic Structure. Oxford: Clarendon Press.

Kövecses Z. 1986. Metaphors of Anger, Pride, and Love: A Lexical Approach to the Structure of Concepts. Amsterdam/Philadelphia: John Benjamins Publishing Company.

Kövecses Z. 1989. Emotion Concepts. New York: Springer-Verlag.

Kövecses Z, Radden G. 1998. Metonymy: Developing a Cognitive Linguistic View. Cognitive Linguistics, 9: 37-77.

Kövecses Z. 2002. Metaphor: A Practical Introduction. New York: Oxford University Press.

Labov W. 1973. The Boundaries of Words and Their Meaning // Bailey C N, Shuy R W. New Ways of Analyzing Variation in English, 340-373. Washington D.C.: Georgetown University Press.

Lakoff G, Johnson M. 1980. Metaphors We Live by. Chicago: University of Chicago Press.

Lakoff G. 1987a. Women, Fire and Dangerous Things: What Categories Reveal About the Mind. Chicago: University of Chicago Press.

Lakoff G. 1987b. Cognitive Models and Prototype Theory // Neisser U. Concepts and Conceptual Development: Ecological and Intellectual Factors in Categorization, 391-421. Cambridge: Cambridge University Press.

Lakoff G. 1988. Cognitive Semantics //Eco U, Santambrogio M, Violi P. Meaning and Mental Representations. Bloomington and Indianapolis: Indiana University Press.

Lakoff G. 1993. The Contemporary Theory of Metaphor // Ortony A. Metaphor and Thought. Cambridge: Cambridge University Press.

Lakoff G, Johnson M. 1999. Philosophy in the Flesh — The Embodied Mind and Its Challenge to Western Thought. New York: Basic Books.

Lakoff G, Kövecses Z. 1987. The cognitive model of anger inherent in American English // Holland D, Naomi Q. Cultural Models in Language and Thought. Cambridge: Cambridge University Press.

Lakoff G, Turner M. 1989. More than Cool Reason: A Field Guide to Poetic Metaphor. Chicago: University of Chicago Press.

Langacker R W. 1987. Foundations of Cognitive Grammar, Vol. I. Stanford, CA: Stanford University Press.

Langacker R W. 1993. Reference-point Constructions. Cognitive Linguistics, 4: 1-38.

Leech G. 1983a. Semantics. Harmondsworth: Penguin Books.

Leech G. 1983b. Principles of Pragmatics. London: Longman.

Levinson C. 1983. Pragmatics. Cambridge: Cambridge University Press.

Lyons J. 1977. Semantics, Vol. 2. Cambridge: Cambridge University Press.

Matthews P H. 1991. Morphology. Cambridge: Cambridge University Press.

Matthews P H. 1997. Oxford Concise Dictionary of Linguistics. Oxford: Oxford University Press.

Ogden C K, Richard I A. 1923. The Meaning of Meaning. London: Routledge & Kegan Paul.

Ortony A. 1993. Metaphor and Thought. 2nd ed. Cambridge: Cambridge University Press.

Palmer F R. 1976. Semantics. Cambridge: Cambridge University Press.

Palmer F R. 1986. Mood and Modality. Cambridge: Cambridge University Press.

Panther K, Radden G. 1999. Metonymy in Language and Thought. Amsterdam: John Benjamins Publishing Company.

Panther K, Thornburg L. 2003. Metonymy and Pragmatic Inferencing. Amsterdam: John Benjamins.

Peirce C S. 1940. The Philosophy of Peirce: Selected Writings. London: Routledge & Kegan Paul, Ltd.

Peirsman Y, Geeraerts D. 2006. Metonymy as a Prototypical Category. Cognitive Linguistics, 17 (3): 269-314.

Pinker S. 1994. The Language Instinct. Harmondsworth: Penguin.

Poutsma H. 1928. A Grammar of Late Modern English. Groningen: Noordhoff.

Radden G, Kövecses Z. 1999. Towards a Theory of Metonymy // Panther K, Radden G. Metonymy in Language and Thought. Amsterdam: John Benjamins.

Radden G. 2003. How Metonymic Are Metaphors? // Barcelona A. Metaphor and Metonymy at the Crossroads. Berlin: Mouton de Gruyter.

Reddy M. 1979. The Conduit: A Case of Frame Conflict in Our Language About Language. London: Oxford University Press.

Ricoeur P. 1977. The Rule of Metaphor. London: Routedge and Kegan Paul.

Rosch E. 1975. Cognitive Representations of Semantic Categories. Journal of Experimental Psychology: General, 104: 192-233.

Rosch E, Mervis C. 1975. Family Resemblance: Studies in the Internal Structure of Categories. Cognitive Psychology, 7: 573-605.

Rosch E. 1976. Basic Objects in Natural Categories. Cognitive Psychology, 8: 382-439.

Saeed J. 1997. Semantics. Oxford: Blackwell.

Saeed J. 2009. Semantics. Oxford: Wiley-Blackwell.

Sapir-Whorf E. 1921. Language: An Introduction to the Study of Speech. New York: Harcourt Brace.

Sapir E. 1949. Language: An Introduction to the Study of Speech. New York: Harcourt Brace.

Saussure F. 1974. Course in General Linguistics. Glasgow: Fontana/Collins.

Schank R C, Abelson R P. 1977. Scripts, Plans, Goals and Understanding. Hillsdale, NJ: Lawrence Erlbaum.

Schank R, Kass A. 1988. Knowledge Representation in People and Machines // Eco U, Santambrogio M, Violi P. Meaning and Mental Representations, 181-200. Bloomington and Indianapolis: Indiana University Press.

Searle J R. 1969. Speech Acts. Cambridge: Cambridge University Press.

Searle J R. 1975. Indirect Speech Acts // Cole P, Morgan J. Syntax and Semantics, Vol. 3: Speech Acts, 59-82. New York: Academic Press.

Searle J R. 1979. Expression and Meaning: Studies in the Theory of Speech Act. Cambridge:

Cambridge University Press.

Smith C S. 1991. The Parameter of Aspect. Dordrecht: Kluwer.

Sperber D, Wilson D. 1995. Relevance: Communication and Cognition. 2nd ed. Oxford: Blackwell.

Sweetser E. 1990. From Etymology to Pragmatics: Metaphorical and Cultural Aspects of Semantic Structure. Cambridge: Cambridge University Press.

Talmy L. 1975. Semantics and Syntax of Motion // Kimball J P. Syntax and Semantics, Vol. 4: 181-238. London: Academic Press.

Talmy L. 1983. How language structures space // Pick H, Acredolo L. Spatial Orientation: Theory, Research, and Application, 225-282. New York: Plenum Press.

Talmy L. 1985. Lexicalization Patterns: Semantic Structure in Lexical Forms // Shopen T. Language Typology and Syntactic Description, Vol. 3: 57-149. Cambridge: Cambridge University Press.

Talmy L. 1985. Force Dynamics in Language and Thought // Eilfort W, Kroeber P, Peterson K. Papers From the Parasession on Causatives and Agentivity. Chicago: Linguistics Society.

Talmy L. 2000. Toward a Cognitive Semantics, Vol. Ⅱ: Typology and Process in Concept Structuring. Cambridge, MA: MIT Press.

Taylor J R. 2001. Linguistic Categorization: Prototypes in Linguistic Theory. Beijing: Foreign Language Teaching and Research Press.

Taylor J R. 2003. Linguistic Categorization. 3rd ed. Oxford: Oxford University Press.

Thomas J. 1995. Meaning in Interaction: An Introduction to Pragmatics. London: Longman.

Thompson D. 2003. Concise Oxford Dictionary (English-Chinese Version). Beijing: Foreign Language Teaching and Research Press.

Turner M, Fauconnier G. 1995. Conceptual Integration and Formal Expression. Metaphor and Symbolic Activity, 10: 183-203.

Ungerer F, Schmid H J. 2001. An Introduction to Cognitive Linguistics. Beijing: Foreign Language Teaching and Research Press.

Vendler Z. 1967. Linguistics in Philosophy. Ithaca, NY: Cornell University Press.

Whitney W D. 1867. Language and the Study of Language. London and New York: Charles Scribner & Sons // Silverstein M. 1971: Whitney on Language, 7-110. Cambridge, MA: MIT Press.

Whorf B L. 1956. Language, Thought and Reality. Cambridge, Mass.: MIT Press & New York: Wiley.

Wilson D, Carston R. 2006. Metaphor, Relevance and the “Emergent Property” Issue. Mind and Language, 21(3):404-33.

Wilson D, Sperber D. 2004. Relevance Theory // Horn L R, Ward G. The Handbook of Pragmatics, 607-632. Oxford: Blackwell.

Yu N. 1998. The Contemporary Theory of Metaphor: A Perspective From Chinese. Amsterdam/ Philadelphia: John Benjamins Publishing Company.

Yule G. 1996. Pragmatics. Oxford: Oxford University Press.

Zifp G. 1935. The Psychobiology of Language. Boston: Houghton & Mifflin.

陈家旭.2007.英汉隐喻认知对比研究.上海:学林出版社.

戴瑞亮.2005.英语词典汉译中存在的问题.上海翻译(S1):50-52,96.

戴瑞亮,刘典忠,孙承荣.2006.英语理论语法概论.东营:中国石油大学出版社.

戴瑞亮.2009.语义研究中的原型范畴理论.石油大学学报(6):95-100.

戴瑞亮.2010.谈语义研究中成分分析的局限性.社科纵横(1):100-101,41.

戴瑞亮.2010.语言符号任意性和象似性探析.社科纵横(5):169-170.

戴瑞亮.2010.论认知语言学与体验哲学的辩证一体.作家(8):153-154.

戴瑞亮.2011.象似性与诗歌翻译.社科纵横(7):173-176.

戴瑞亮,张建科,安昌光.2011.新编英语语言学教程.东营:中国石油大学出版社.

戴瑞亮.2012.索绪尔语言理论探源.湖南社会科学(6):185-188.

戴瑞亮.2012.翻译中语序的归化和异化.中国石油大学学报(4):100-104.

戴瑞亮,马溶梓.2015.英汉思维差异对比与翻译.社科纵横(9):147-149.

戴炜栋,何兆熊.2002.新编简明英语语言学教程.上海:上海外语教育出版社.

胡壮麟.2006.认知隐喻学.3版.北京:北京大学出版社.

蓝纯.2003.从认知角度看汉语和英语的空间隐喻.北京:外语教学与研究出版社.

李雪.2011.英汉移动动词词汇化模式的对比研究.北京:外语教学与研究出版社.

刘润清,文旭.2006.新编语言学教程.北京:外语教学与研究出版社.

罗伯特•路威.1986.文明与野蛮.北京:三联书店.

马清华.2000.文化语义学.南昌:江西人民出版社.

秦洪武.2001.语言结构的顺序象似性.外语研究(1):39-42.

沈家煊.1993.句法的象似性问题.外语教学与研究(1):2-8,80.

沈家煊.1999.不对称和标记论.南昌:江西教育出版社.

王寅.2007.认知语言学.上海:上海外语教育出版社.

文旭.2001.词序的拟象性探索.外语学刊(3):90-96,112.

许国璋.1988.语言符号的任意性问题.外语教学与研究(3):2-10,79.

严辰松.1997.语言临摹性概说.国外语言学(3):21-25.

杨琳.1996.汉语词汇与华夏文化.北京:语文出版社.

杨信彰.2005.语言学概论.北京:高等教育出版社.

张辉,卢卫中.2010.认知转喻.上海:上海外语教育出版社.

赵艳芳.2001.认知语言学概论.上海:上海外语教育出版社.

中国社会科学院语言研究所词典编辑室.2002.现代汉语词典(汉英双语).北京:外语教学与研究出版社.